SNCF/FRENCH NATIONAL RAILWAYS

LOCOMOTIVES & MULTIPLE UNITS

D1639000

The complete guide to all Locomotives and
Multiple Units of the SNCF

Brian Garvin, Peter Fox & Chris Appleby

Thanks for all your
help!

PLATFORM
5

Brian Garvin.

Published by Platform 5 Publishing Ltd., Lynthorpe House, 86 Charlotte Road,Sheffield S1 4TL, England.

Printed by Waddington & Sons (Printers) Ltd., Fielden Square, Rochdale Road, Todmorden.

ISBN 0 906579 62 7

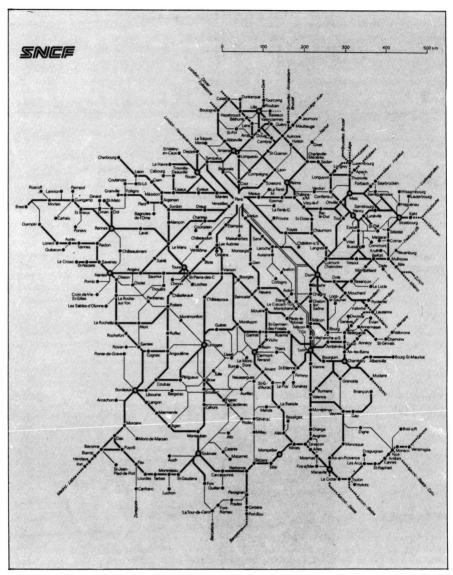

Map courtesy SNCF

DIAGRAMMATIC MAP OF THE SNCF

CONTENTS

INTRODUCTION

This book contains full details of all locomotives and multiple units of the Société Nationale des Chemins de Fer Français hereafter referred to as the SNCF. Details of the stock of certain minor railways are also included.

ROVER TICKETS

The France Vacances Railrover ticket is available for the visitor to France. This gives the freedom of the SNCF for any 9 days in one calendar month and costs £94 (£55) 2nd class and £137.00 (£76) 1st class. For 16 days in any calendar month the cost is £120 (£68) 2nd class and £175 (£96) 1st class. Prices in parentheses are foe children aged 4–11. In addition to the freedom of the SNCF, the ticket also includes a two day Paris Metro rover plus one days travel on the Chemins de Fer de la Provence.

CLASS DIMENSIONS

Principal dimensions are given for each class in metric units. Standard abbreviations used in this book are:

km/h   kilometres per hour
kN   kilonewtons
kW   kilowatts

VEHICLE TYPE CODES FOR MULTIPLE UNITS AND HAULED STOCK

These are given in the French system with the British codes in parentheses.

(1) CONTINENTAL SYSTEM:

T   Turbotrain driving motor.
TGV   TGV driving motor.
TGVZ TGV vehicle with one power bogie.
X   Diesel railcar or multiple unit driving motor.
Z   Electric multiple unit driving motor.
R   indicates a trailer vehicle. (French=remorque).
A   1st Class
B   2nd Class
D   Luggage, i.e., vehicle with luggage space and guard's compartment
r   Catering vehicle.
P   Post, i.e., vehicle with compartment(s) for mail (and guard)
x   indicates a driving trailer.

Examples:

XBD   Second class d.m.u. driving motor with luggage/guard's compartment.
ZRABx Composite e.m.u. driving trailer.

Note—The continental system does not differentiate between open and compartment stock or indicate toilet facilities.

(2) BRITISH SYSTEM:

Coaching Stock codes are as used in Multiple Unit Pocket Book and Coaching Stock Pocket Book, e.g., F=first, S=second, C=composite, B=brake, O=open, K=side corridor with lavatory, so=semi-open. D=driving, M=motor, T=trailer, R=rectifier vehicle.

The number of seats, lavatory compartments and washrooms are shown as nF nS nL nW, e.g., 80S 2L 2W has 80 second class seats, two lavatory compartments and two washrooms.

BUILDERS

The following builder codes are used in this publication:

ANF   Ateliers Construction du Nord de la France, Blanc Misseron.
Alsthom   Société Générale de Constructions Electriques et Mechaniques Alsthom.
Baldwin   Baldwin Locomotive Works, Philadelphia, PA, USA.
Billard   Anciens Établissements Billard & Cie., Tours.

Brissonneau & Lotz SA des Établissements Brissonneau & Lotz, Aytré.
Brown Boveri Brown Boveri & Cie.
CAFL Compagnie des Ateliers et Forges de la Loire, St. Chamond.
CEM Compagnie Electro-Mechanique, Le Havre.
CFD Compagnie des Chemins de Fer Départementaux.
CGC Compagnie Générale de Constructions Batignolles, Paris, Chatillon & Nantes.
CIMT Compagnie Industrielle de Matériel de Transport, Marly les Valenciennes.
Carde & Cie Çarde & Compagnie, Bordeaux.
Carel & Fouché Établissements Carel & Fouché SA, Le Mans.
De Dietrich De Dietrich & Cie., Reichshoffen.
De Dion Société des Automobiles De Dion, Puteaux, Paris.
Decauville Société Nouvelle Decauville-Aîné, Corbeil.
Études Société d'Études pour l'Electrification des Chemins de Fer.
Fauvet Giral Établissements Fauvet-Giral, Sursnes, Arras & Lille.
Fives-Lille Compagnie de Fives-Lille pour Constructions Méchaniques et Entreprises, Fives, Lille.
Francorail-MTE Consortium of various french builders.
Jeumont Forges et Ateliers de Constructions Électriques de Jeumont.
MTE Société de Matériel de Traction Électrique.
Moyse Établissements Gaston Moyse, La Courneuve.
Oerlikon Société Oerlikon, Switzerland.
Renault Regie Nationale des Usines Renault, Billancourt.
SACM Société Alsacienne des Constructions Méchaniques.
SEMT Société des Études des de Machines Thermiques, Chantiers de l'Atlantique, St. Denis.
SLM Schweizerische Lokomotiv- und Maschinenfabrik, Winterthur, Switzerland.
Saurer Saurer, Arbon, Switzerland.
Schneider Société des Forges et Acieries du Creusot, Usines Schneider, Le Creusot.
Siemens Siemens AG, Berlin, Nürnberg & Erlangen, West Germany.
Soulé Soulé Fer et Froide, Bagnères de Bigorre.
Sprague–Thomson Société Parisienne de Matériel Roulant, Paris.
Séchéron SA des Ateliers de Séchéron, Genève, Switzerland.

ACKNOWLEDGEMENTS

We would like to thank all who have helped with the preparation of this book, especially Messrs. E. Dunkling and M.A. Jacob, other photographers, members of the LCGB, various officials and staff of the SNCF also the Groupe d'Étude des Chemins de Fer de la Provence.

In addition to much research by the authors, the following references have been consulted:

Les Engins Moteurs Français (SNCF) (Stenvall), Matériel Moteur de la SNCF, Jane's World Railways, World Electric Locomotives (K. Harris) (Janes).

Magazines:

La Vie du Rail, LCGB Bulletin, Rail Magazine, Voies Ferrées, French Railway Techniques, Echoes du Rail, Le Train du Sud.

SNCF–GENERAL

SNCF was formed in 1937 when several private companies were nationalised. These formed the basis of the SNCF "Réseaux" or systems/networks. They were:

1. Est (East)–former CF de l'Est.
2. Nord (North)–former CF du Nord.
3. Ouest (West)–former CF d'État.
4. Sud Ouest (South West)–former PO-Midi.
5. Sud Est (South East)–former CF PLM.

These areas have remained stable for many years but changes are now taking place. From 01/01/85 réseaux 1 and 2 were combined into a new region "Nord-Est" and soon numbers 3 and 4 will be combined into a new region but no name has yet been announced. However most SNCF staff continue to refer to Réseau Nord and Réseau Est as if they were still seperate.

NUMBERING SYSTEM

The SNCF numbering system for steam locomotives was based on axle grouping so that a 4–6–2 became a 231 etc. Class letters then followed the axle details and then came the running number. eg 231 E 22. For tank locomotives an additional T followed the axle arrangement eg 141 TC 8.

No electric locomotives were renumbered on the formation of SNCF. Most locos came from the PO-Midi system with just a few others from the État and PLM. Those delivered to SNCF between 1938–50 continued the PO-Midi series. However from 1950 a new system was introduced bringing the locomotives somewhat into line with the steam system, but here the axle arrangement was shown by letters so that a Bo–Bo became a BB.

Diesel locomotives were originally given a steam type number with an additional D in the number after the axle arrangement e.g. 040 DA 1 but in 1960 the whole fleet was renumbered into the present system.

SNCF traction is numbered in several different ways. eg BB 4750, CC 6505, A1AA1A 68001, T 2001, X 2101, Y 8101, Z 6101.

In this book locomotive numbers are listed without their prefix, but letter prefixes are used for multiple units or shunting tractors. (NB: not all locomotives carry their prefixes).

Electric locomotives are numbered as follows:

1– 9999	DC locomotives.
10000–19999	AC locomotives.
20000–29999	Dual voltage locomotives.
30000–39999	Triple voltage locomotives.
40000–49999	Quadruple voltage locomotives.

Examples: BB 8500, DC locomotive with BB axle arrangement; BB 17000, AC locomotive with BB axle arrangement; BB 25500 dual voltage locomotive of same type. (8500+17000=25500).

Diesel locomotives are numbered as follows:

50000–51999	Diesel locomoteurs (No longer in stock).
61000–79999	Diesel locomotives.

Shunting locos ("locotracteurs") are prefixed Y and numbered between 2201–9999.

Multiple units:

"T" denotes a turbotrain, power car numbers ranging between 1001 and 2082.
"X" denotes a d.m.u., power car numbers ranging between 2101 and 4999.
"Z" denotes an e.m.u., power car numbers ranging between 3711 and 9636.

Trains à Grande Vitesse:

TGV power cars are numbered as 2 or 3-voltage locomotives but they also carry a set number, e.g. TGV power cars 23001/2 are set 01 and can be referred to as TGV 01.

Note: Diesel and electric units owned or subsidised by local authorities or other "third parties" have their numbers prefixed by "9". eg XP 94750 is a d.m.u. belonging to the Post Office and similar to SNCF X 4750 class.

There can be some confusion with the present numbering system. 7301 can be a BB electric locomotive, an e.m.u., or a tractor. SNCF have recognised this problem and a new numbering system has been devised to eliminate duplicate numbers. In future locomotives will be numbered up to 499 in a series and 500 upwards will be an m.u. of some description. eg. 11001–499 would be ac electric locomotives, 11500–999 would be ac e.m.u.s. It is not at present intended to renumber any existing stock.

MOTIVE POWER ORGANISATION

The main depots are listed on the inside front cover together with their former Réseau number. Generally speaking the depots have large allocations but many locomotives and units stable at other places. A list of known stabling points follows with details of how many locos/multiple units might be found there on a typical Sunday. Where there are more than 10 a breakdown into types is given. (E = electric locomotive, D = diesel locomotive, T = tractors, DM = d.m.u.s, EM = e.m.u.s). The list is in old Reseau order.

Former Reseau 1–Est (East).

Belfort	21 (4E,8D,9DM)	Mulhouse Nord	15 (5E,4D,6T)
Blainville	35	Nancy	39 (16E,14D,7DM,2T)
Conflans Jarny	32 (13E,13D,6DM)	Noisy-le-Sec	15 (2E,12D,1T)
Epinal	15 (5D,10DM)	Reims	26 (7E,12D,1T,6DM)
Hausbergen	38 (14E,22D,1T,1DM)	Sarreinsming	15
Longwy	38 (14E,22D,1T,1DM)	Vaires	27 (19E,8D)
Mulhouse Ville	31 (14E,8D,8DM,1T)	Woippy	14 (7E,6D,1T)

Other locations: Chaumont, Lauterbourg (7), Lumes, Neufchateau.

Former Reseau 2–Nord (North).

Amiens	47 (6E,6D,1T,34DM)	Lilles Fives	60 (27E,17D,16DM)
Aulnoye	22 (16E,6D)	Lille La Deliverance	
Bobigny	35 (2E,12D)	Mitry Claye	30 (30EM)
Boulogne Ville	20 (9D,3T,8DM)	Persan Beaumont	24 (20EM,4EL)
Calais Ville	17 (7D,2T,8DM)	Pontoise	17 (5E,1T,11EM)
Creil Petit Therain	22 (9E,1D)	Somain	32 (18E,11D,3T)
Creil Ville	11 (3E,6EM,2DM)	Tergnier	30 (18E,12D)
Douai	14 (5E,5D,1T,3DM)	Valenciennes	14 (7E,6D,1T)
Dunkerque Gr. Synthe	19 (3E,16D)		

Former Reseau 3–Ouest (West).

Angers	15 (3E,3D,2T,7DM)	Le Mans Triage	31 (7E,18D,4EM,2T)
Argentan	12 (4D,1T,7DM)	Mantes La Jolie	20 (10E,3D,2T,5DM)
Brest	16 (6D,1T,9DM)	St. Cloud	15 (15EM)
La Rochelle Ville	12 (10D,2DM)	Trappes	27 (17E,9D,1T)
Le Havre	20 (11E,8D,1T)	Versailles	12 (12EM)

Other locations: Auray (8), Batignolles (6), Chartres (6), Cherbourg (6), Dieppe (4), Mezidon (9), Brieoc (8), Saintes (6), Thouars (5), Quimper (8).

Former Reseau 4–Sud Ouest (South West).

Bourges	12 (3D,6T,DM)	Montluçon	10 (D,7DM)
Bretigny	29 (5E,5D,4T,15EM)	Pau	10 (4E,2T,4EM)
Brive	14 (3E,8D,2T,1DM)	Perigueax	12 (7D,5DM)
Étampes	16 (3T,13EM)	Poitiers	10 (3E,6D,1T)
Massy Paliseau	30 (30EM)	Vierzon	40 (23E,11D,3DM,3T)

Other locations: Angouleme (7), Aurillac (9), Bayonne (6), Capdenac (8), Chateauroux (9), Juvisy (9), Rodez (6).

Reseau 5 - Sud Est (South East).

Amberieu	36 (30E,5D,1T)	Mirimas	75 (36E,30D,2T,7DM)
Besançon	16 (3E,4D,4T,5DM)	Modane	18 (15E,2D,1T)
Cerbère	20 (16E,2D,2T)	Narbonne	42 (28E,12D,2T)
Chasse Triage	12 (6E,6D)	Nice St.Rochelle	24 (10E,10D,4T)
Clermont Ferrand	36 (25D,3T,8DM)	Portes	17 (10E,4D,3T)
Dijon Ville	19 (4E,1D,2EM,12DM)	Paris Lyon (Charlois)	34 (31E,2D,1T)

Dôle	15 (10E,5D)	St.Etienne	36 (6E,20D,3T,7DM)
Grenoble	40 (10E,10D,2T,12DM,6EM)	St.Germain des Fosses	12 (9D,1DM)
Laroche Migennes	21 (11E,10D)	St.Jean de Maurienne	11 (11E)
Marseille St.Charles	49 (49E)	Sibelin Triage	15 (10E,5D)
Melun	16 (2E,2D,12EM)	Veynes	14 (8D,3T,3DM)

Other locations: Annemasse (5), Aix Les Bains (7), Bellegarde (9), Bourg (3), Cannes La Bocca (6), Culoz (8), Dijon Gevrey (7), Lyon Perrache (6), Montargis (7), Moret Les Sablons (6), Neussargues (6), Perpignan (7), Roanne (8), Valenton (9).

WORKSHOPS

The SNCF has no really large locomotive works, but has kept open many pre-nationalisation workshops. These have recently been reorganised and each deals with specific classes for major overhauls.

Workshop	Types overhauled
Béziers	BB 300, CC 1100, BB 4200, BB 4700, BB 8100, BB 8500, BB 9400, Z 100.
Bischeim (Strasbourg)	TGV 23000, TGV 33000.
Bordeaux	X 2100, X 2200, X 2720, X 2800 + trailers, T 2000.
Épernay	BB 12000, BB 16500.
Hellemmes (Lille)	BB 15000, BB 16000, BB 17000, BB 20200, BB 25100, BB 25150, BB 25200, CC 40100.
La Folie (Paris)	Z 6000, Z 6100, Z 6300, Z 6400.
Le Mans	X 4300, X 4500, X 4630, X 4750, X 4900, T 1000, T 1500.
Nevers	BB 63400, BB 63500, BB 66000, BB 66400, BB 66600, BB 66700, BB 67000, BB 67200, BB 67300, Y 2400, Y 5100, Y 7100, Y 7400, Y 8000.
Oullins (Lyon)	CC 6500, BB 7200, BB 9200, BB 9300, CC 21000, BB 22200, BB 25500, Z 600, Z 7100, Z 7300, Z 7500, Z 9500, Z 9600.
Quatre Mares (SOT)	BB 63000, BB 67400, A1AA1A 68000, A1AA1A 68500, CC 72000.
Vitry (Paris)	Z 5100, Z 5300, Z 5600, Z 8100, Z 8800.

BB 325 class Nos. BB 349 & BB 341 on a southbound freight at Juvisy   [E. Dunkling

SNCF STANDARD GAUGE VEHICLES
ELECTRIC LOCOMOTIVES

Special Note: Many SNCF locos have monomotor bogies which can be regeared by the driver. Anarrow on the bogie will be found pointing to the letter "M" or "V" denoting "marchandises" or "voyageurs" (freight/passenger) and this indicator is one of the items a driver must check when preparing a locomotive. In this publication, where two sets of figures are shown for max. speed, tractive effort, power etc., the first refers to the low gear ratio ("petite vitesse") and the second to the high gear ratio ("grande vitesse").

BB 300 CLASS   Bo–Bo

A pre-nationalisation design. Ordered by the PO-Midi but actually delivered to SNCF in 1938/9 as E 241–64 becoming BB 301 etc. in 1950. E 258 never became BB 318 as it was a war loss in 1944. The class was a development of the Midi E 4700 class. Today all have been downgraded to shunting duties and the maximum speed lowered to 75 km/h. The class will be found on station pilot and e.c.s. duties in their respective areas.

Built: 1938–39.
Builders: Siemens/Alsthom.
Continuous Rating: 1240 kW.
Maximum Tractive Effort: kN.
Driving Wheel Dia.: 1350 mm.

System: 1500 V dc.

Weight: 80 tonnes.
Length over Buffers: 12930 mm.
Max. Speed: 75 km/h.

301	PSO	308	PSO	312	VSG	316	PSO	321	PSO
302	CBY	309	CBY	313	LYM	317	LYM	322	PSO
304	PSO	310	PSO	314	PSO	319	PSO	323	VSG
305	PSO	311	PSO	315	PSO	320	LYM	324	VSG
307	VSG								

BB 325 CLASS   Bo–Bo

This class is a further development of the Midi E 4700, delivered to SNCF as 0325–55 and becoming BB 325 etc in 1950. They were similar in appearance to BB 301 when built but were rebuilt without end doors in 1967–70. Now being downgraded to "MV (manoeuvres)" use (†), i.e. shunting, e.c.s. and trip working. Those not converted are all based at Tours St.Pierre and still reach the Paris area on freights.

Built: 1946–48.
Builder-Mech. Parts: Alsthom/Schneider-Jeumont.
Builder-Elec. Parts: Alsthom/Jeumont/Siemens.
Continuous Rating: 1240 kW.
Maximum Tractive Effort: kN.
Driving Wheel Dia.: 1350 mm.

System: 1500 V dc.

Weight: 80 tonnes.
Length over Buffers: 12930 mm.
Max. Speed: 105 (75 m) km/h.

326	TSP	333	TSP	341	TSP	346	TSP	351	† LYM
327	† VSG	334	† LYM	342	† LYM	347	† DIJ	352	TSP
328	† LYM	335	† LYM	343	† LYM	348	† DIJ	353	† VSG
330	TSP	336	† VSG	344	† LYM	349	† VSG	354	† VSG
331	† LYM	337	† LYM	345	TSP	350	† LYM	355	† VSG
332	TSP	340	† LYM						

BB 900 CLASS   Bo–Bo

Built as BB 101–35 for the État railway they became 901–35 in 1950. This class is also developed from the Midi E 4700 and had end doors when built. Doors were removed during rebuilding in 1960–67.

Built: 1936–37.
Builder: Alsthom.
Continuous Rating: 1200 kW.
Maximum Tractive Effort: kN.
Driving Wheel Dia.: 1400 mm.

System: 1500 V dc.

Weight: 79 tonnes.
Length over Buffers: 12870 mm.
Max. Speed: 105 km/h.

908	LIM	915	LIM	926	LIM	928	LIM	929	LIM
909	LIM	924	LIM						

CC 1100 class No. CC 1109 on a freight at Tours St. Pierre des Corps on 14/04/83.
[Brian Garvin

BB 4100 class Nos. BB 4178 & BB 4174 on a southbound freight at St. Chely d'Apcher on 03/09/82. Both these locos are now withdrawn.
[G.J. Wiseman

CC 1100 CLASS C–C

This class was ordered by the PO–Midi with the first two being delivered in December 1937 as E 1001/2. Put into stock in 1938 they do not appear to have entered traffic until 1943. The remainder of the class was delivered in 1943–48 as E 1003–12. The whole class was renumbered in 1950 to CC 1101–12. They were built for heavy shunting duties, a task they still perform today. Some are now radio fitted and it is intended that they can be remotely controlled. Those at Villeneuve St.George can often be found on shed on a Monday morning but at other times they are scattered around the extensive yards.

Built: 1937–48.
Builder-Mech. Parts: CGC.
Builder-Elec. Parts: Oerlikon.
Continuous Rating: 400 kW.
Maximum Tractive Effort: 183 kN.
Driving Wheel Dia.: 1400 mm.

System: 1500 V dc.

Weight: 91 tonnes.
Length over Buffers: 17910 mm.
Max. Speed: 25 km/h.

1101	VSG	1104	VSG	1107	VSG	1109	TSP	1111	TSP
1102	TSP	1105	TOU	1108	LYM	1110	VSG	1112	TOU
1103	TOU	1106	TOU						

BB 4100 CLASS Bo–Bo

The next three classes all originated on the Midi Railway and owe their ancestory to the electric locomotives built for the Newport–Shildon line of the North Eastern Railway (England). Locomotives numbered BB 4152 onwards were rebuilt from BB 4600s but the history is very complex as many of the former BB 4600s were themselves rebuilt from BB 4100s! 4152–93 were rebuilt in 1976–80 exchanging wheels and traction motors with BB 4200s the latter then becoming BB 4730 class. Although allocated to Avignon the main operating base is Béziers for freight work on the line to Neussargues. 4119 and 4123 have been retained for snowplough work on the La Tour de Carol line, 4119 normally being based at Foix and 4123 at La Tour de Carol.

Built: 1928–32.
Builder: Carel & Fouché.
Continuous Rating: 1160 kW.
Maximum Tractive Effort: kN.
Driving Wheel Dia.: 1400 mm.

System: 1500 V dc.

Weight: 78 tonnes.
Length over Buffers: 12870 mm.
Max. Speed: 75 km/h.

4110	TOU	4116	AVI	4123	TOU	4154	AVI	4179	AVI
4114	AVI	4119	TOU	4152	AVI	4156	AVI	4193	AVI

BB 4200 CLASS Bo–Bo

This is another class wih a complex history. The class was built for the Midi railway, with 67 locos originally numbered E 4201–50, and E 4701–17. Four BB 4200s became BB 4718–21 in 1954 followed by ten BB 4700s becoming BB 4251–60 between 1973–5. BB 4227/35 were written off in 03/70 when they ran away on the Canfranc line demolishing the Estanguet bridge. (Line closed since this incident). This left 65 locos (54 BB 4200, 11 BB 4700). Then 37 BB 4200 and all BB 4700 wre rebuilt to BB 4730 class in 1975–80 receiving wheels and traction motors from BB 4600s, most of the latter becoming BB 4152 onwards. Thus 17 BB 4200 were left which did not have parts from BB 4600 and these were downgraded to "MV" use in 1980–83.

Built: 1933–35.
Builder-Mech. Parts: Carel & Fouché.
Builder-Elec. Parts: Alsthom.
Continuous Rating: 1160 kW.
Maximum Tractive Effort: kN.
Driving Wheel Dia.: 1400 mm.

System: 1500 V dc.

Weight: 75 tonnes.
Length over Buffers: 12870 mm.
Max. Speed: 75 km/h.

Multiple working within class and with BB 4700.

4206	PSO	4221	TOU	4228	TOU	4239	PSO	4245	PSO
4208	TOU	4224	PSO	4231	TSP	4240	TSP	4246	TSP
4209	TOU	4226	TOU	4234	PSO	4242	TOU	4249	TOU
4211	PSO								

BB 4700 class No. BB 4765 on Tours St. Pierre des Corps Hump. [Brian Garvin

Former "Maurienne line" CC 6500 class No. CC 6540 in green livery departs from Bourg en Bresse with the fridays only Strasbourg–Nice Corail train. [G.J. Wiseman

BB 4700 CLASS   Bo–Bo

This is another former Midi Railway type. All were rebuilt from BB 4200/4700 with parts from BB 4600 in 1975–80. Found as station pilots and also as hump shunters.

Built: 1933–35.
Builders: Alsthom.
Continuous Rating: 1160 kW.
Maximum Tractive Effort: kN.
Driving Wheel Dia.: 1400 mm.

System: 1500 V dc.
Weight: 75 tonnes.
Length over Buffers: 12870 mm.
Max. Speed: 90 km/h.

4730 (4204)	TAR		4747 (4220)	PSO		4763 (4255)	TSP
4731 (4702)	TSP		4749 (4205)	LAB		4764 (4219)	PSO
4732 (4216)	LIM		4750 (4225)	LAB		4765 (4248)	PSO
4733 (4218)	BOR		4752 (4256)	TSP		4766 (4241)	LAB
4734 (4201)	BOR		4753 (4260)	TSP		4767 (4250)	LAB
4735 (4213)	BOR		4754 (4254)	PSO		4768 (4237)	PSO
4736 (4202)	TAR		4755 (4238)	PSO		4769 (4701)	LIM
4737 (4222)	TAR		4756 (4251)	LAB		4770 (4714)	LIM
4738 (4252)	TAR		4757 (4253)	PSO		4771 (4709)	LIM
4739 (4215)	LIM		4758 (4214)	LAB		4772 (4716)	LIM
4740 (4207)	LIM		4759 (4210)	PSO		4773 (4712)	LAB
4741 (4703)	TSP		4760 (4243)	PSO		4774 (4715)	LAB
4743 (4242)	TSP		4761 (4233)	TSP		4775 (4717)	LAB
4745 (4212)	LAB		4762 (4223)	LAB		4777 (4719)	PSO

CC 6500 CLASS   C–C

This class, together with the similar dual-voltage locos of class CC 21000 are the most powerful on the SNCF. There are three sub series: 6501–38, 6539–59 and 6560–74. with different body side grills. The second batch is of particular interest as these locos were originally fitted out for working off third-rail supply on the Chambéry–Modane "Maurienne" route. They were all converted to standard some years ago but may still exist in their original light green livery. They will all receive the standard red and grey livery which was designed to blend with TEE and Grand Confort liveries. The class is fitted with monomotor bogies with two gear ratios.

Built: 1969–75.
Builders: Alsthom/MTE.
Continuous Rating: 5900 kW.
Maximum Tractive Effort: 288/131 kN.
Driving Wheel Dia.: 1140 mm.

System: 1500 V dc.
Weight: 116 (120†) tonnes.
Length over Buffers: 20190 mm.
Max. Speed: 100 /220 km/h.

Rheostatic brake, electro-pneumatic braking, press button emergency brake, flange lubricators, driver-guard, Radio fitted for train-signal box communication.

6501	LYM		6521	PSO	SAINTES
6502	PSO	IVRY-SUR-SEINE	6522	PSO	LIMOGES
6503	PSO		6523	PSO	BRIVE
6504	PSO	VITRY-SUR-SEINE	6524	PSO	TOULOUSE
6505	PSO	SAINTE-FOY-LA-GRANDE	6525	PSO	CHÂTEAUROUX
6506	PSO		6526	PSO	CHOISY-LE-ROI
6507	PSO		6527	PSO	AMBOISE
6508	PSO	MONTAUBAN	6528	PSO	
6509	PSO	AGEN	6529	PSO	ISSOUDUN
6510	PSO	CARCASSONNE	6530	PSO	CAHORS
6511	PSO		6531	PSO	SAINT-PIERRE-DES-CORPS
6512	PSO	NARBONNE	6532	PSO	
6513	PSO	COGNAC	6533	PSO	BEAUTIRAN
6514	PSO	POITIERS	6534	PSO	BÉZIERS
6515	PSO	BLOIS	6535	PSO	SAINT-CHAMOND
6516	PSO	CHÂTELLERAULT	6536	PSO	ANNECY
6517	PSO	ARCACHON	6537	PSO	SALON-DE-PROVENCE
6518	PSO	ORLÉANS	6538	PSO	
6519	PSO	ANGOULÊME	6539	PSO	
6520	PSO	RUFFEC	6540	LYM	

6541 LYM		6558 LYM		
6542 LYM		6559 LYM		
6543 LYM		6560 LYM	OULLINS	
6544 LYM		6561 LYM		
6545 LYM		6562 LYM		
6546 LYM		6563 LYM	LAVAL	
6547 LYM		6564 LYM	BEAUNE	
6548 LYM		6565 LYM		
6549 LYM		6566 LYM	MAUBERGE	
6550 LYM		6567 LYM	BREST	
6551 LYM		6568 LYM		
6552 LYM		6569 LYM	LA MULATIÈRE	
6553 LYM		6570 LYM	ARMENTIÈRES	
6554 LYM		6571 LYM	JEUMONT	
6555 LYM		6572 LYM	RÉSISTANCE-FER	
6556 LYM		6573 PSO		
6557 LYM		6574 PSO	DOLE	

CC 7000/7100 CLASSES   Co–Co

The outline of these locomotives will be familiar to visitors to The Netherlands and Spain where examples exist as class 1300 and class 276 respectively. The two prototypes 7001/2 were the first big Co–Co locomotives on the SNCF that were designed for express passenger use, previous ones being 2D2s. The class has moved around somewhat over the years but is now seeing out its days based at Avignon but still operating over a large area from the Pyrenees to Paris. The advent of TGVs has reduced their workload but they still turn up in Paris on overnight trains from the south and have fill in turns on e.c.s. trips at Paris Lyon. This class is now being withdrawn but 7107 will be preserved as it is joint holder of the 331 km/h speed record attained in 1955. It is already a favourite locomotive for attending special events such as open days etc.

Built: 1949*/1952–55.   **System:** 1500 V dc.
Builder-Mech. Parts: Alsthom/Fives-Lille.
Builder-Elec. Parts: Alsthom/MTE.
Continuous Rating: 3490 (2770*, 3240†) kW. **Weight:** 107 (104*, 106†) tonnes
Maximum Tractive Effort: 260 kN.   **Length over Buffers:** 18920 (18830*) mm.
Driving Wheel Dia.: 1250 mm.   **Max. Speed:** 150 km/h.

7001 *	AVI	7111	AVI	7122	AVI	7135	AVI	7145 †	AVI
7002 *	AVI	7112	AVI	7123	AVI	7136	AVI	7146 †	AVI
7101	AVI	7113	AVI	7124	AVI	7137	AVI	7149 †	AVI
7102	AVI	7115	AVI	7125	AVI	7138	AVI	7151 †	AVI
7103	AVI	7116	AVI	7126	AVI	7139	AVI	7152 †	AVI
7105	AVI	7117	AVI	7128	AVI	7140	AVI	7153 †	AVI
7106	AVI	7118	AVI	7130	AVI	7141	AVI	7154 †	AVI
7107	AVI	7119	AVI	7131	AVI	7142	AVI	7155 †	AVI
7109	AVI	7120	AVI	7132	AVI	7143	AVI	7157 †	AVI
7110	AVI	7121	AVI	7134	AVI	7144 †	AVI	7158 †	AVI

BB 7200 CLASS   B–B

This mixed traffic class is part of a large family of locomotives, BB 7200 is the dc version, BB 15000 the ac version and BB 22200 the dual-voltage version. (7200 + 15000 = 22200). Unlike most monomotor-bogied locomotives class 7200 has fixed gearing for freight or passenger use, certain locos being limited to 100 km/h with the remainder having the higher rating of 160 km/h. The last batch also features modern microprocessor controls and other refinements.

Built: 1976–85.   **System:** 1500 V dc.
Builders: Alsthom/MTE.
Continuous Rating: 4360 kW.   **Weight:** 84 tonnes.
Maximum Tractive Effort: 288 (3xx*†) kN. **Length over Buffers:** 17480 mm.
Driving Wheel Dia.: 1250 mm.   **Max. Speed:** 160 (100*†) km/h.

Rheostatic brakes. Electro-pneumatic brakes. Flange lubricators. Driver-guard communication. Radio fitted for train-signal box communication. Press button emergency direct air brake. Many locos are being fitted with Cowcatchers.

c Modified for working the "Catalan Talgo".
† Fitted for multiple working over the Maurienne line.

7201 *	LIM	7250	PSO	7298	VSG	7346 †	CBY	7394	VSG
7202 *	LIM	7251	PSO	7299	VSG	7347 †	CBY	7395	VSG
7203 *	LIM	7252	PSO	7300	VSG	7348 †	CBY	7396	VSG
7204 *	LIM	7253	PSO	7301	VSG	7349 †	CBY	7397	VSG
7205 *	LIM	7254	PSO	7302	VSG	7350 †	CBY	7398	VSG
7206 *	LIM	7255	PSO	7303	VSG	7351 †	CBY	7399	VSG
7207 *	LIM	7256	PSO	7304	VSG	7352 †	CBY	7400	VSG
7208 *	LIM	7257	PSO	7305	VSG	7353 †	CBY	7401	VSG
7210 *	LIM	7258	PSO	7306	VSG	7354 †	CBY	7402	VSG
7211 *	LIM	7259	PSO	7307	VSG	7355 †	CBY	7403	VSG
7212 *	LIM	7260	PSO	7308	VSG	7356 †	CBY	7404	VSG
7213 *	LIM	7261	PSO	7309	VSG	7357 †	CBY	7405	VSG
7214 *	LIM	7262	PSO	7310	VSG	7358 †	CBY	7406	VSG
7215 *	LIM	7263	PSO	7311	VSG	7359 †	CBY	7407	VSG
7216 *	LIM	7264	VSG	7312	VSG	7360 †	CBY	7408	VSG
7217 *	LIM	7265	VSG	7313	VSG	7361 †	CBY	7409	VSG
7218 *	LIM	7266	VSG	7314	VSG	7362 †	CBY	7410	VSG
7219 *	LIM	7267	VSG	7315	VSG	7363 †	CBY	7411 †	CBY
7220 *	LIM	7268	VSG	7316	VSG	7364 †	CBY	7412 †	CBY
7221 *	LIM	7269	VSG	7317	VSG	7365 †	CBY	7413 †	CBY
7222 *	LIM	7270	VSG	7318	VSG	7366 †	CBY	7414 †	CBY
7223 *	LIM	7271	VSG	7319	VSG	7367 †	CBY	7415 †	CBY
7224 *	LIM	7272	VSG	7320	VSG	7368 †	CBY	7416 †	CBY
7225 *	LIM	7273	VSG	7321	VSG	7369 †	CBY	7417 †	CBY
7226 *	LIM	7274	VSG	7322	VSG	7370 †	CBY	7418 †	CBY
7227 *	LIM	7275	VSG	7323	VSG	7371 †	CBY	7419 †	CBY
7228 *	LIM	7276	VSG	7324	VSG	7372 †	CBY	7420 †	CBY
7229 *	LIM	7277	VSG	7325	VSG	7373 †	CBY	7421 †	CBY
7230 *	LIM	7278	VSG	7326	VSG	7374 †	CBY	7422 †	CBY
7231 *	LIM	7279	VSG	7327	VSG	7375 †	CBY	7423 †	CBY
7232 *	LIM	7280	VSG	7328	VSG	7376 †	CBY	7424 †	CBY
7233 *	LIM	7281 c	VSG	7329	VSG	7377 †	CBY	7425 †	CBY
7234 *	LIM	7282 c	VSG	7330	VSG	7378 †	CBY	7426 †	CBY
7235 *	LIM	7283 c	VSG	7331	VSG	7379 †	CBY	7427 †	CBY
7236	PSO	7284 c	VSG	7332	VSG	7380 †	CBY	7428 †	CBY
7237	PSO	7285 c	VSG	7333	VSG	7381	VSG	7429 †	CBY
7238	PSO	7286 c	VSG	7334	VSG	7382	VSG	7430 †	CBY
7239	PSO	7287 c	VSG	7335	VSG	7383	VSG	7431 †	CBY
7240	PSO	7288 c	VSG	7336	VSG	7384	VSG	7432 †	CBY
7241	PSO	7289 c	VSG	7337	VSG	7385	VSG	7433 †	CBY
7242	PSO	7290 c	VSG	7338	VSG	7386	VSG	7434 †	CBY
7243	PSO	7291 c	VSG	7339	VSG	7387	VSG	7435 †	CBY
7244	PSO	7292 c	VSG	7340	VSG	7388	VSG	7436 †	CBY
7245	PSO	7293 c	VSG	7341	VSG	7389	VSG	7437 †	CBY
7246	PSO	7294 c	VSG	7342	VSG	7390	VSG	7438 †	CBY
7247	PSO	7295 c	VSG	7343 †	CBY	7391	VSG	7439 †	CBY
7248	PSO	7296 c	VSG	7344 †	CBY	7392	VSG	7440 †	CBY
7249	PSO	7297 c	VSG	7345 †	CBY	7393	VSG		

Names:

7203	SAINT-FLOUR	7240	SAINT-ETIENNE
7221	SAINT-ARMAND-MONTRAND	7241	VILLEURBANNE
7223	LA SOUTERRAINE	7242	VIENNE
7236	CHAMBÉRY	7243	VILLENEUVE-SAINT-GEORGES
7237	PIERRELATTE	7244	VERNOU-LA CELLE-SUR-SEINE
7238	THONON-LES-BAINS	7256	VALENTON
7239	SAINT-PIERRE-D'ALBIGNY	7411	LAMURE-SUR-AZERQUES

CC 7100 class No. CC 7107 on Avignon Depot on 31/03/86. [E. Dunkling

BB 8100 class No. BB 8150 with a freight at Lyon Perrache Station on 30/03/86. [E. Dunkling

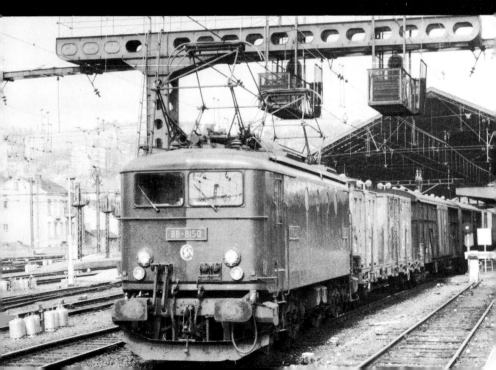

BB 8000 CLASS   Bo–Bo

A post war development of BB 300 and exported to other countries. The Netherlands Railway has some as class 1100). Although only based at two depots the class sees general use on freight trains all over the Sud Est area and examples often turn up at Paris Lyon station on e.c.s duties.

Built: 1947–55   **System:** 1500 V dc.
Builder-Mech. Parts: Alsthom/Schneider-Jeumont/CGC.
Builder-Elec. Parts: Alsthom/Siemens/Jeumont/Oerlikon.
Continuous Rating: 2100 kW.   **Weight:** 92 tonnes.
Maximum Tractive Effort: 152 kN.   **Length over Buffers:** 12930 mm.
Driving Wheel Dia.: 1400 mm.   **Max. Speed:** 105 km/h.

Multiple working fitted.Radio fitted for train-signal box communication. Various locos also fitted with rail lubricators.

8001	AVI	8135	DIJ	8170	AVI	8204	DIJ	8238	DIJ
8101	AVI	8136	DIJ	8171	DIJ	8205	AVI	8239	DIJ
8102	AVI	8137	DIJ	8172	DIJ	8206	DIJ	8240	AVI
8103	AVI	8138	DIJ	8173	DIJ	8207	DIJ	8241	DIJ
8104	AVI	8139	AVI	8174	DIJ	8208	DIJ	8242	AVI
8105	AVI	8140	AVI	8175	DIJ	8209	DIJ	8243	DIJ
8106	AVI	8141	AVI	8176	DIJ	8210	DIJ	8244	DIJ
8107	AVI	8142	DIJ	8177	AVI	8211	DIJ	8245	DIJ
8108	AVI	8143	DIJ	8178	DIJ	8212	DIJ	8246	DIJ
8109	AVI	8144	AVI	8179	AVI	8213	DIJ	8247	AVI
8110	AVI	8145	DIJ	8180	DIJ	8214	DIJ	8248	AVI
8111	AVI	8146	AVI	8181	AVI	8215	DIJ	8249	DIJ
8112	AVI	8147	AVI	8182	AVI	8216	DIJ	8250	DIJ
8113	AVI	8148	DIJ	8183	AVI	8217	DIJ	8251	AVI
8114	DIJ	8149	AVI	8184	AVI	8218	DIJ	8252	AVI
8115	AVI	8150	AVI	8185	DIJ	8219	AVI	8253	DIJ
8116	AVI	8151	AVI	8186	DIJ	8220	DIJ	8254	DIJ
8117	AVI	8152	AVI	8187	DIJ	8221	AVI	8255	AVI
8118	AVI	8153	DIJ	8188	DIJ	8222	AVI	8256	DIJ
8119	AVI	8154	AVI	8189	AVI	8223	AVI	8257	DIJ
8120	AVI	8155	DIJ	8190	DIJ	8224	DIJ	8258	AVI
8121	AVI	8156	DIJ	8191	DIJ	8225	DIJ	8259	AVI
8122	DIJ	8157	DIJ	8192	DIJ	8226	DIJ	8260	AVI
8123	AVI	8158	AVI	8193	DIJ	8227	DIJ	8261	DIJ
8124	AVI	8159	DIJ	8194	AVI	8228	AVI	8262	AVI
8125	DIJ	8160	DIJ	8195	DIJ	8229	DIJ	8263	DIJ
8126	AVI	8161	AVI	8196	DIJ	8230	AVI	8264	DIJ
8127	DIJ	8162	AVI	8197	DIJ	8231	DIJ	8265	DIJ
8128	AVI	8163	AVI	8198	DIJ	8232	DIJ	8266	AVI
8129	AVI	8164	DIJ	8199	DIJ	8233	DIJ	8267	DIJ
8130	DIJ	8165	AVI	8200	AVI	8234	AVI	8268	DIJ
8131	DIJ	8166	AVI	8201	DIJ	8235	DIJ	8269	AVI
8132	DIJ	8167	DIJ	8202	DIJ	8236	DIJ	8270	DIJ
8133	DIJ	8168	DIJ	8203	DIJ	8237	DIJ	8271	DIJ
8134	DIJ	8169	AVI						

BB 8500 CLASS   B–B

A mixed traffic loco being a dc version of BB 17000. Monomotor bogies with two gear ratios. Being such a large class there are detail variations between batches. They are found on mixed duties all over the dc network. They also work push-pull trains from Paris Lyon and Paris Montparnasse and Toulouse based locos can be found on the "Stelyrail" service between Lyon and St. Etienne!

Built: 1964–74   **System:** 1500 V dc.
Builder: Alsthom.
Continuous Rating: 2610 (2940*†) kW.**Weight:** 78 (79*, 80†) tonnes.
Maximum Tractive Effort: 323 /197 kN.**Length over Buffers:** 14700 (14940*, 15570†) mm.
Driving Wheel Dia.: 1100 mm.   **Max. Speed:** 90/140 km/h.

BB 8500 class No. BB 8561 with a push & pull double-decker suburban train at Villeneuve-St. Georges on 23/02/85. [E. Dunkling

2D2 9100 class No. 2D2 9134 on the turntable at Lyon Mouche Depot on 30/03/86. [E. Dunkling

Multiple working fitted. Rheostatic brake. Press button emergency direct air brake. Some oddexamples with rail lubricators. Radio fitted for train-signal box communication.

8501		LAB	8531		LAB	8560	*	VSG	8589	†	MON	8618	†	TOU
8502		LAB	8532		LAB	8561	*	VSG	8590	†	MON	8619	†	TOU
8503		LAB	8533		LAB	8562	*	TOU	8591	†	MON	8620	†	TOU
8504		LAB	8534		LAB	8563	*	VSG	8592	†	MON	8621	†	TOU
8505		LAB	8535		LAB	8564	*	VSG	8593	†	MON	8622	†	TOU
8506		LAB	8536		LAB	8565	*	VSG	8594	†	MON	8623	†	TOU
8507		LAB	8537	*	LAB	8566	*	VSG	8595	†	MON	8624	†	TOU
8508		LAB	8538	*	LAB	8567	*	VSG	8596	†	MON	8625	†	TOU
8509		LAB	8539	*	LAB	8568	*	TOU	8597	†	MON	8626	†	TOU
8510		LAB	8540	*	LAB	8569	*	TOU	8598	†	MON	8627	†	TOU
8511		LAB	8541	*	LAB	8570	*	TOU	8599	†	TOU	8628	†	TOU
8512		LAB	8542	*	LAB	8571	*	TOU	8600	†	TOU	8629	†	TOU
8513		LAB	8543	*	LAB	8572	*	TOU	8601	†	TOU	8630	†	TOU
8514		LAB	8544	*	LAB	8573	*	TOU	8602	†	TOU	8631	†	TOU
8515		LAB	8545	*	VSG	8574	*	TOU	8603	†	TOU	8632	†	TOU
8516		LAB	8546	*	MON	8575	*	TOU	8604	†	TOU	8633	†	TOU
8517		LAB	8547	*	MON	8576	*	TOU	8605	†	TOU	8634	†	TOU
8518		LAB	8548	*	MON	8577	*	TOU	8606	†	TOU	8635	†	TOU
8519		LAB	8549	*	LAB	8578	*	TOU	8607	†	TOU	8636	†	TOU
8520		LAB	8550	*	VSG	8579	*	TOU	8608	†	TOU	8637	†	TOU
8521		LAB	8551	*	LAB	8580	*	TOU	8609	†	TOU	8638	†	TOU
8522		LAB	8552	*	MON	8581	*	MON	8610	†	TOU	8639	†	TOU
8523		LAB	8553	*	MON	8582	*	TOU	8611	†	TOU	8640	†	TOU
8524		LAB	8554	*	MON	8583	*	TOU	8612	†	TOU	8641	†	TOU
8525		LAB	8555	*	VSG	8584	*	TOU	8613	†	TOU	8642	†	TOU
8526		LAB	8556	*	MON	8585	*	MON	8614	†	TOU	8643	†	MON
8527		LAB	8557	*	MON	8586	*	TOU	8615	†	TOU	8644	†	TOU
8528		LAB	8558	*	MON	8587	*	TOU	8616	†	TOU	8645	†	MON
8529		LAB	8559	*	MON	8588	†	MON	8617	†	TOU	8646	†	MON
8530		LAB												

Names:

8600 FLEURY-LES-AUBRAIS
8602 FOIX
8603 LANNEMEZAN

8604 CERDAGNE
8605 SAINT-GAUDENS

2D2 9100 CLASS   2Do2

Now in the process of being withdrawn but examples may last into 1987. 9135 certainly will as it is to be preserved in working order. This design is another post-war one updating a pre-war one. Although based at Avignon the class can be found working between Paris and Marseille.

Built: 1950–51
Builder-Mech. Parts: Fives-Lille.
Builder-Elec. Parts: CEM.
Continuous Rating: 3690 kW.
Maximum Tractive Effort: 226 kN.
Driving Wheel Dia.: 1750 mm.
Pony Wheel Dia.: 1000 mm.

System: 1500 V dc.

Weight: 144 tonnes.
Length over Buffers: 18080 mm.

Max. Speed: 140 km/h.

9102	LYM	9121	LYM	9132	LYM	9134	LYM	9135	LYM
9117	LYM	9130	LYM						

BB 9200 CLASS   Bo–Bo

This class was the first of the SNCF standard types of the late 1950s. The same styling is also found on BB 9300, 9400, 16000, 25100, 25150, 25200. Class BB 9200 was originally scattered over the dc network south of Paris but now they are concentrated at Bordeaux and Paris Sud Ouest.

BB 9200 class No. BB 9216 with a clerestory roofed postal vehicle at Les Aubrais on 14/04/83
[E. Dunkling

A pair of BB 9400 class locos working in multiple Nos. BB 9499 and BB 9514 on an e.c.s. at Bannasac-La Canourge (ligne des Causses) to form an overnight relief on 03/09/82. BB 9499 is in the new grey and brown livery, whereas BB 9514 is in the old green and white.
[G.J. Wiseman

Built: 1957–64
System: 1500 V dc.
Builders: Schneider-Jeumont/CEM.
Continuous Rating: 3850 kW.
Weight: 82 (80*) tonnes.
Maximum Tractive Effort: 260 kN (160* kN).
Length over Buffers: 16200 mm.
Driving Wheel Dia.: 1250 mm.
Max. Speed: 160 (250*) km/h.

p Modified for push-pull operation with Corail stock.
Early in 1986 9243/52/5/6/8 were in store at Paris Sud Ouest with others in store at Vierzon.

9201	BOR	9220	BOR	9238	BOR	9257	PSO	9275	PSO
9202	BOR	9221	BOR	9239	PSO	9258	PSO	9276	PSO
9203	BOR	9222	BOR	9240	PSO	9259	PSO	9277	PSO
9204	BOR	9223	BOR	9241	PSO	9260	PSO	9278	PSO
9205	BOR	9224	BOR	9242	PSO	9261	PSO	9279	PSO
9206	BOR	9225	BOR	9243	PSO	9262	PSO	9280 p	PSO
9207	BOR	9226	BOR	9244	PSO	9263	PSO	9281 p	PSO
9208	BOR	9227	BOR	9245	PSO	9264	PSO	9282 p	PSO
9209	BOR	9228	BOR	9246	PSO	9265	PSO	9283	PSO
9210	BOR	9229	BOR	9247	PSO	9266	PSO	9284	PSO
9211	BOR	9230	BOR	9248	PSO	9267	PSO	9285	PSO
9212	BOR	9231	BOR	9250	PSO	9268	PSO	9286	PSO
9213	BOR	9232	BOR	9251	PSO	9269	PSO	9287	PSO
9214	AVI	9233	BOR	9252	PSO	9270	PSO	9288 p	PSO
9215	BOR	9234	BOR	9253	PSO	9271	PSO	9289	PSO
9216	BOR	9235	BOR	9254	PSO	9272	PSO	9290	PSO
9217	BOR	9236	BOR	9255	PSO	9273	PSO	9291 p*	PSO
9218	BOR	9237	BOR	9256	PSO	9274	PSO	9292 p*	PSO
9219	BOR								

Names:

9248 LA-TESTE-DE-BUCH   9280 ARPAJON

BB 9300 CLASS   Bo–Bo

An updated version of BB 9200. All are now grouped at Toulouse but see widespread use on the Paris–Sud Ouest main lines and the Toulouse–Marseille route.

Built: 1967–69
System: 1500 V dc.
Builders: Schneider-Jeumont, MTE, CEM.
Continuous Rating: 3850 kW.
Weight: 84 tonnes.
Maximum Tractive Effort: 260 kN.
Length over Buffers: 16200 mm.
Driving Wheel Dia.: 1250 mm.
Max. Speed: 160 km/h.

Rheostatic brakes. Driver-guard communication.

9301	TOU	9309	TOU	9317	TOU	9325	TOU	9333	TOU
9302	TOU	9310	TOU	9318	TOU	9326	TOU	9334	TOU
9303	TOU	9311	TOU	9319	TOU	9327	TOU	9335	TOU
9304	TOU	9312	TOU	9320	TOU	9328	TOU	9336	TOU
9305	TOU	9313	TOU	9321	TOU	9329	TOU	9337	TOU
9306	TOU	9314	TOU	9322	TOU	9330	TOU	9338	TOU
9307	TOU	9315	TOU	9323	TOU	9331	TOU	9339	TOU
9308	TOU	9316	TOU	9324	TOU	9332	TOU	9340	TOU

Name:

9329 CASTRES

BB 9400 CLASS   B–B

Although classed as a mixed traffic locomotive their main duties are on freight trains, often in multiple. The low weight of the locomotive however has proved to be a problem and is the main reason why the class has had mixed success. It is no suprise to learn that some 30 locomotives are stored surplus during the present recession. Some examples have been seen recently working e.c.s. trains at Paris Lyon. Their main use on passenger trains is on the difficult Béziers–Neussargues route.

BB 12000 class No. BB 12027 at Mohon depot on 22/02/85 [E. Dunkling.

BB 13000 class No. BB 13018 leaves Longuyon for Longwy with a Paris–Luxembourg express on 23/08/86. At Longwy, a CFL 3600 class (similar to SNCF BB 12000) will take over. [G.J. Wiseman

Built: 1967–69
Builder-Mech. Parts: Fives/MTE.
Builder-Elec. Parts: CEM/MTE.
Continuous Rating: 2210 kW.
Maximum Tractive Effort: 270 kN.
Driving Wheel Dia.: 1020 mm.

System: 1500 V dc.

Weight: 60 tonnes.
Length over Buffers: 14400 mm.
Max. Speed: 130 km/h.

Multiple working and push & pull fitted. Six channel radio fitted. Many also have rail lubricators. 9532–35 also press button emergency brake and rail lubricators.

9401	BOR	9427	BOR	9453	BOR	9482	LYM	9509	AVI
9402	BOR	9428	BOR	9454	BOR	9483	LYM	9510	AVI
9403	BOR	9429	BOR	9455	BOR	9484	LYM	9511	AVI
9404	BOR	9430	BOR	9456	BOR	9485	LYM	9512	AVI
9405	AVI	9431	BOR	9457	BOR	9486	LYM	9513	AVI
9406	BOR	9432	AVI	9458	BOR	9487	LYM	9514	AVI
9407	BOR	9433	BOR	9459	AVI	9488	LYM	9515	AVI
9408	BOR	9434	BOR	9460	AVI	9489	LYM	9516	AVI
9409	BOR	9435	BOR	9461	AVI	9490	LYM	9517	AVI
9410	BOR	9436	BOR	9462	AVI	9491	LYM	9518	AVI
9411	BOR	9437	BOR	9463	AVI	9492	AVI	9519	AVI
9412	BOR	9438	BOR	9464	LYM	9493	AVI	9520	AVI
9413	BOR	9439	BOR	9465	LYM	9494	AVI	9521	AVI
9414	BOR	9440	BOR	9466	LYM	9495	AVI	9522	AVI
9415	BOR	9441	BOR	9467	LYM	9496	AVI	9523	AVI
9416	BOR	9442	BOR	9468	LYM	9497	AVI	9524	AVI
9417	BOR	9443	BOR	9470	LYM	9498	AVI	9525	AVI
9418	BOR	9444	BOR	9471	LYM	9499	AVI	9526	AVI
9419	BOR	9445	BOR	9473	LYM	9500	AVI	9527	AVI
9420	AVI	9446	BOR	9474	LYM	9502	AVI	9528	AVI
9421	BOR	9447	BOR	9476	LYM	9503	AVI	9529	AVI
9422	BOR	9448	BOR	9477	LYM	9504	AVI	9530	AVI
9423	BOR	9449	BOR	9478	LYM	9505	AVI	9532	AVI
9424	BOR	9450	BOR	9479	LYM	9506	AVI	9533	AVI
9425	BOR	9451	BOR	9480	LYM	9507	AVI	9534	AVI
9426	BOR	9452	BOR	9481	LYM	9508	AVI	9535	AVI

BB 10000 CLASS   B–B

The SNCF numbers its experimental locomotives at the beginning of a series so that the experimental ac locos are in the 10000 series. These two particular locomotives are modified BB 15000s. 10003 is fitted with synchronous motors whilst 10004 is fitted with asynchronous motors. Both locomotives spend long periods in workshops between tests and may well be fitted out for completely different tests whilst this book is being prepared. For dimensions see BB 15000 class.

10003 (15007)   STR   10004 (15055)   STR

BB 12000 CLASS   Bo–Bo

Called "Monocabines" or even "flat irons" this class was built for the newly electrified Valenciennes–Thionville line and was the first 25 kV dc type to go into series production. Considered to be a mixed traffic locomotive they rarely appear on passenger work being concentrated now on freight trains along the route from Basel to Dunkerque and also along the newly electrified Amiens–Rouen route. They also reach Paris via Amiens and via Chalons-sur-Marne. Examples may still be around in the year 2000.

Built: 1954–61.
Builder-Mech. Parts: Siemens.
Builders-Elec. Parts: MTE/Alsthom.
Continuous Rating: 2470 kW.
Maximum Tractive Effort: 353 kN.
Driving Wheel Dia.: 1250 mm.

System: 25 kV dc.

Weight: 82–86 tonnes.
Length over Buffers: 15200 mm.
Max. Speed: 120 km/h.

12002	LEN	12005	MOH	12008	THI	12011	MOH	12014	MOH
12003	MOH	12006	LEN	12009	MOH	12012	LEN	12015	LEN
12004	MOH	12007	MOH	12010	MOH	12013	MOH	12016	MOH

12017	MOH	12043	LEN	12069	MOH	12096	MOH	12123	MOH
12018	MOH	12044	LEN	12070	MOH	12097	MOH	12124	MOH
12019	LEN	12045	MOH	12071	MOH	12098	MOH	12125	MOH
12020	MOH	12046	MOH	12072	MOH	12099	MOH	12126	LEN
12021	THI	12047	MOH	12073	LEN	12100	THI	12127	LEN
12022	LEN	12048	LEN	12074	MOH	12101	LEN	12128	LEN
12023	LEN	12049	MOH	12075	MOH	12103	THI	12129	LEN
12024	LEN	12050	MOH	12076	LEN	12104	LEN	12130	LEN
12025	MOH	12051	MOH	12077	MOH	12105	LEN	12131	LEN
12026	LEN	12052	MOH	12078	THI	12106	THI	12132	MOH
12027	LEN	12053	LEN	12079	MOH	12107	THI	12133	LEN
12028	LEN	12054	MOH	12080	MOH	12108	LEN	12134	THI
12029	MOH	12055	MOH	12081	LEN	12109	THI	12135	LEN
12030	MOH	12056	LEN	12082	MOH	12110	THI	12136	THI
12031	LEN	12057	LEN	12083	MOH	12111	THI	12137	LEN
12032	LEN	12058	MOH	12084	LEN	12112	LEN	12138	LEN
12033	MOH	12059	MOH	12085	LEN	12113	MOH	12139	LEN
12034	MOH	12060	MOH	12086	LEN	12114	MOH	12140	THI
12035	LEN	12061	MOH	12087	MOH	12115	MOH	12141	THI
12036	MOH	12062	MOH	12088	MOH	12116	MOH	12142	LEN
12037	MOH	12063	MOH	12089	MOH	12117	MOH	12143	LEN
12038	MOH	12064	MOH	12090	LEN	12118	MOH	12144	THI
12039	LEN	12065	LEN	12091	MOH	12119	MOH	12145	THI
12040	MOH	12066	MOH	12092	MOH	12120	LEN	12146	LEN
12041	MOH	12067	MOH	12094	MOH	12121	MOH	12147	THI
12042	MOH	12068	MOH	12095	LEN	12122	THI	12148	LEN

BB 13000 CLASS   Bo–Bo

A mixed traffic locomotive of similar appearance to BB 12000 but with technical differences. Changing fortunes with freight traffic could lead to an early withdrawal but meanwhile the survivors still get around from their base at Strasbourg and can often be seen in the Paris area at Vaires or La Villette.

Built: 1954–57.

System: 25 kV dc.

Builder-Mech. Parts: MTE/Fives-Lille/SLM.
Builder-Elec. Parts: Jeumont/Oerlikon/Brown Boveri/Sécheron.
Continuous Rating: 2130 (2000*) kW.　　　**Weight:** 84 tonnes.
Maximum Tractive Effort: 255 kN.　　　**Length over Buffers:** 15200 mm.
Driving Wheel Dia.: 1250 mm.　　　**Max. Speed:** 120 (105*) km/h.

13001*	STR	13009*	STR	13024	STR	13034	STR	13045	STR
13002*	STR	13011*	STR	13026	STR	13037	STR	13046	STR
13003*	STR	13017	STR	13027	STR	13038	STR	13047	STR
13004*	STR	13019	STR	13028	STR	13039	STR	13050	STR
13005*	STR	13020	STR	13029	STR	13041	STR	13051	STR
13006*	STR	13021	STR	13031	STR	13043	STR	13052	STR
13007*	STR	13022	STR	13032	STR	13044	STR	13053	STR
13008*	STR	13023	STR	13033	STR				

CC 14100 CLASS   Co–Co

A heavy freight locomotive that is now on the way out. Its slow speed and heavy pulling power was useful 30 years ago when steam was replaced. Today however wagon speeds have increased as have the speeds of most trains so no more overhauls are being done and the locomotives will be withdrawn as they reach overhaul time or need major repairs. All are expected to be gone by 1990.

Built: 1954–58.

System: 25 kV dc.

Builder-Mech. Parts: Alsthom/Fives.
Builder-Elec. Parts: Alsthom/CEM.
Continuous Rating: 2600 kW.　　　**Weight:** 127 tonnes.
Maximum Tractive Effort: 422 kN.　　　**Length over Buffers:** 18890 mm.
Driving Wheel Dia.: 1100 mm.　　　**Max. Speed:** 60 km/h.

14101	THI	14129	THI	14151	THI	14169	THI	14187	THI
14102	THI	14131	THI	14152	THI	14172	THI	14188	THI
14104	THI	14133	THI	14153	THI	14173	THI	14189	THI
14109	MOH	14135	THI	14154	THI	14174	THI	14191	THI
14113	MOH	14136	THI	14155	THI	14176	THI	14192	THI
14116	MOH	14137	THI	14156	MOH	14180	THI	14195	THI
14123	THI	14138	THI	14161	MOH	14181	THI	14196	THI
14124	MOH	14140	THI	14162	MOH	14182	THI	14200	THI
14125	MOH	14146	THI	14166	MOH	14183	THI	14201	THI
14126	THI	14147	THI	14167	MOH	14184	THI	14202	THI
14128	THI	14148	THI						

BB 15000 CLASS   B–B

The first of the 1970 generation of locomotives. All are based at Strasbourg and work between Paris Est and Metz/Luxembourg/Basel together with odd workings from Basle to Lille. 15007 became prototype 7003 later becoming 10003. 15055 became prototype 10004. They may at some time in the future revert to their original identities.

Built: 1971-78.
Builders: Alsthom/MTE.
Continuous Rating: 4620 kW.
Maximum Tractive Effort: 294 kN.
Driving Wheel Dia.: 1250 mm.

System: 25 kV ac.

Weight: 87-90 tonnes.
Length over Buffers: 17480 mm.
Max. Speed: 160 km/h.

Rheostatic brake. Press button emergency direct air brake.

15001	STR	GRETZ-AMAINVILLIERS	15034	STR	SÈTE
15002	STR	LONGWY	15035	STR	NOGENT-SUR-MARNE
15003	STR	SARREGUEMINES	15036	STR	LE PERREUX-SUR-MARNE
15004	STR	SEDAN	15037	STR	LA FERTÉ-SOUS-JOUARRE
15005	STR	SAINT-LOUIS	15038	STR	
15006	STR	METZ	15039	STR	ROSNY-SOUS-BOIS
15008	STR	NANCY	15040	STR	
15009	STR	REIMS	15041	STR	
15010	STR	STRASBOURG	15042	STR	
15012	STR	CHÂLONS-SUR-MARNE	15043	STR	MAIZIÈRES-LÈS-METZ
15013	STR	LONGUYON	15044	STR	
15014	STR	THIONVILLE	15045	STR	
15015	STR	BIARRITZ	15046	STR	
15016	STR	CHARLEVILLE-MEZIERS	15047	STR	
15017	STR	SAINT-AVOLD	15048	STR	
15018	STR		15049	STR	
15019	STR	MONTIGNY-LÈS-METZ	15050	STR	VITRY-LE-FRANÇOIS
15020	STR	PAU	15051	STR	AULNOYES-AYMERIES
15021	STR	CHÂTEAU-THIERRY	15052	STR	CAMBRAI
15022	STR	PANTIN	15053	STR	TROUVILLE
15023	STR	MEAUX	15054	STR	
15024	STR	LUNÉVILLE	15056	STR	VANNES
15025	STR		15057	STR	
15026	STR	ÉPERNAY	15058	STR	ÉPINAL
15027	STR	CREUTZWALD	15059	STR	TOURCOING
15028	STR	VILLIERS-LE-BEL	15060	STR	CREIL
15029	STR	AURILLAC	15061	STR	SARREBOURG
15030	STR	FORBACH	15062	STR	MONTMÉDY
15031	STR	MOYEUVRE-GRANDE	15063	STR	VERDUN
15032	STR	CHAMBLY	15064	STR	SAVERNE
15033	STR	GAGNY	15065	STR	VAIRES-SUR-MARNE

BB 16000 CLASS   Bo–Bo

This is an ac version of BB 9200. At one time split between La Chapelle and Strasbourg the delivery of new BB 15000 allowed all BB 16000 to be concentrated at La Chapelle. After many years of working the principal expresses from Paris Nord 10 locomotives now see use on trains from Paris St.Lazare to Le Havre for which duties they were fitted with Corail type

Two views of locos of the BB 16500 class. BB 16700 shown above has modified end design and an automatic coupling at one end. It is seen at Metz depot on 21/02/86. j [E. Dunkling

BB 16701, a standard member of the class is shown on a push & pull suburban train at Paris Gare de l'Est on in the snow on 22/02/86.   [E. Dunkling

push-pull equipment. 16028 spent some time converted to dual-voltage prototype BB 20005 from which classes 25100, 25200 were developed.

Built: 1958–63.   **System:** 25 kV ac.
Builder: MTE.
One Hour Rating: 4130 kW.   **Weight:** 88 tonnes.
Maximum Tractive Effort: 309 kN.   **Length over Buffers:** 16200 mm.
Driving Wheel Dia.: 1250 mm.   **Max. Speed:** 160 km/h.

p Push & pull fitted.

16001	PLC	16013	PLC	16026	PLC	16039p	PLC	16051	PLC
16002	PLC	16014	PLC	16027	PLC	16040	PLC	16052	PLC
16003p	PLC	16015	PLC	16028	PLC	16041	PLC	16053p	PLC
16004	PLC	16016	PLC	16029	PLC	16042	PLC	16054	PLC
16005	PLC	16017	PLC	16030	PLC	16043	PLC	16055	PLC
16006p	PLC	16018p	PLC	16031	PLC	16044p	PLC	16056	PLC
16007p	PLC	16019	PLC	16032p	PLC	16045	PLC	16057	PLC
16008p	PLC	16020	PLC	16033	PLC	16046	PLC	16058	PLC
16009	PLC	16021	PLC	16034	PLC	16047p	PLC	16059	PLC
16010	PLC	16022	PLC	16035	PLC	16048	PLC	16060	PLC
16011	PLC	16023	PLC	16036	PLC	16049	PLC	16061	PLC
16012	PLC	16024	PLC	16037	PLC	16050	PLC	16062	PLC

Names:

16001 NEUILLY-SUR-MARNE   16008 DRANCY
16007 MANTES-LA-JOLIE   16062 DOL-DE-BRETAGNE

BB 16500 CLASS   B–B

The monomotor bogie originated with this class and with it the idea of providing alternative gear ratios to create true mixed traffic locomotives. With such a large class there are bound to be detail variations but worthy of mention is 16700 which has been fitted with an automatic coupling at one end together with modified cab front end panels. The 294 locomotives are split between only two depots. The Lens examples appear on a variety of duties in the old Reseau Nord area whilst those at La Villette appear anywhere from Paris to Basel. Besides working the push-pull suburban services out of Paris Est they also work similar duties on the "Metrolor" services between Nancy and Thionville . La Villette shed at weekends often has about 30 of them in one long line alongside the main line!

Built: 1958-64.   **System:** 25 kV ac.
Builder: Alsthom.
One Hour Rating: 2580 kW.   **Weight:** 71–74 (81*) tonnes.
Maximum Tractive Effort: 324/192 kN.   **Length over Buffers:** 14400 (15270*) mm.
Driving Wheel Dia.: 1100 mm.   **Max. Speed:** 90/140 km/h.

Multiple working and push & pull fitted.
16540 spent some time running as BB 20004, the prototype for the BB 25500 series.

16501	LEN	16519	LEN	16537	LEN	16555	PLV	16573	PLV
16502	LEN	16520	LEN	16538	LEN	16556	PLV	16574	PLV
16503	LEN	16521	LEN	16539	LEN	16557	PLV	16575	PLV
16504	LEN	16522	LEN	16540	LEN	16558	PLV	16576	PLV
16505	LEN	16523	LEN	16541	LEN	16559	PLV	16577	PLV
16506	LEN	16524	LEN	16542	LEN	16560	PLV	16578	PLV
16507	LEN	16525	LEN	16543	LEN	16561	PLV	16579	PLV
16508	LEN	16526	LEN	16544	LEN	16562	PLV	16580	PLV
16509	LEN	16527	LEN	16545	LEN	16563	PLV	16581	PLV
16510	LEN	16528	LEN	16546	LEN	16564	PLV	16582	PLV
16511	LEN	16529	LEN	16547	LEN	16565	PLV	16583	PLV
16512	LEN	16530	LEN	16548	LEN	16566	PLV	16584	PLV
16513	LEN	16531	LEN	16549	LEN	16567	PLV	16585	PLV
16514	LEN	16532	LEN	16550	LEN	16568	PLV	16586	PLV
16515	LEN	16533	LEN	16551	PLV	16569	PLV	16587	PLV
16516	LEN	16534	LEN	16552	PLV	16570	PLV	16588	PLV
16517	LEN	16535	LEN	16553	PLV	16571	PLV	16589	PLV
16518	LEN	16536	LEN	16554	PLV	16572	PLV	16590	PLV

16591	PLV	16632	PLV	16673	PLV	16714	PLV	16755	LEN
16592	PLV	16633	PLV	16674	PLV	16715	PLV	16756	LEN
16593	PLV	16634	PLV	16675	PLV	16716	PLV	16757	LEN
16594	PLV	16635	PLV	16676	PLV	16717	PLV	16758	LEN
16595	PLV	16636	PLV	16677	PLV	16718	PLV	16759	LEN
16596	PLV	16637	PLV	16678	PLV	16719	PLV	16760	LEN
16597	PLV	16638	PLV	16679	PLV	16720	PLV	16761	LEN
16598	PLV	16639	PLV	16680	PLV	16721	PLV	16762	LEN
16599	PLV	16640	PLV	16681	PLV	16722	PLV	16763	LEN
16600	PLV	16641	PLV	16682	PLV	16723	PLV	16764	LEN
16601	PLV	16642	PLV	16683	PLV	16724	PLV	16765	LEN
16602	PLV	16643	PLV	16684	PLV	16725	LEN	16766	LEN
16603	PLV	16644	PLV	16685	PLV	16726	LEN	16767	LEN
16604	PLV	16645	PLV	16686	PLV	16727	LEN	16768	LEN
16605	PLV	16646	PLV	16687	PLV	16728	LEN	16769	LEN
16606	PLV	16647	PLV	16688	PLV	16729	LEN	16770	LEN
16607	PLV	16648	PLV	16689	PLV	16730	LEN	16771	LEN
16608	PLV	16649	PLV	16690	PLV	16731	LEN	16772	LEN
16609	PLV	16650	PLV	16691	PLV	16732	LEN	16773	LEN
16610	PLV	16651	PLV	16692	PLV	16733	LEN	16774	LEN
16611	PLV	16652	PLV	16693	PLV	16734	LEN	16775	LEN
16612	PLV	16653	PLV	16694	PLV	16735	LEN	16776	LEN
16613	PLV	16654	PLV	16695	PLV	16736	LEN	16777	LEN
16614	PLV	16655	PLV	16696	PLV	16737	LEN	16778	LEN
16615	PLV	16656	PLV	16697	PLV	16738	LEN	16779	LEN
16616	PLV	16657	PLV	16698	PLV	16739	LEN	16780	LEN
16617	PLV	16658	PLV	16699	PLV	16740	LEN	16781	LEN
16618	PLV	16659	PLV	16700*	PLV	16741	LEN	16782	LEN
16619	PLV	16660	PLV	16701	PLV	16742	LEN	16783	LEN
16620	PLV	16661	PLV	16702	PLV	16743	LEN	16784	LEN
16621	PLV	16662	PLV	16703	PLV	16744	LEN	16785	LEN
16622	PLV	16663	PLV	16704	PLV	16745	LEN	16786	LEN
16623	PLV	16664	PLV	16705	PLV	16746	LEN	16787	LEN
16624	PLV	16665	PLV	16706	PLV	16747	LEN	16788	LEN
16625	PLV	16666	PLV	16707	PLV	16748	LEN	16789	LEN
16626	PLV	16667	PLV	16708	PLV	16749	LEN	16790	LEN
16627	PLV	16668	PLV	16709	PLV	16750	LEN	16791	LEN
16628	PLV	16669	PLV	16710	PLV	16751	LEN	16792	LEN
16629	PLV	16670	PLV	16711	PLV	16752	LEN	16793	LEN
16630	PLV	16671	PLV	16712	PLV	16753	LEN	16794	LEN
16631	PLV	16672	PLV	16713	PLV	16754	LEN		

BB 17000 CLASS　　　　　　　　　　　　　　　　　B–B

Similar in outline to BB 16500. Their main use is on suburban trains in the greater Paris area with fill in turns between Paris St. Lazare and Le Havre, Paris Nord and Lille, and Amiens and Rouen.

Built: 1965-68.
Builder: Alsthom.
One Hour Rating: 2940 kW.
Maximum Tractive Effort: 323/197 kN.
Driving Wheel Dia.: 1100 mm.

System: 25 kV ac.

Weight: 78 tonnes.
Length over Buffers: 14940 mm.
Max. Speed: 90/140 km/h.

Multiple working and push & pull fitted.

17001	ACH	17022	ACH	17043	ACH	17064	PLC	17085	PLC
17002	ACH	17023	ACH	17044	ACH	17065	PLC	17086	PLC
17003	ACH	17024	ACH	17045	ACH	17066	PLC	17087	PLC
17004	ACH	17025	ACH	17046	ACH	17067	PLC	17088	PLC
17005	ACH	17026	ACH	17047	ACH	17068	PLC	17089	PLC
17006	ACH	17027	ACH	17048	ACH	17069	PLC	17090	PLC
17007	ACH	17028	ACH	17049	ACH	17070	PLC	17091	PLC
17008	ACH	17029	ACH	17050	ACH	17071	PLC	17092	PLC
17009	ACH	17030	ACH	17051	ACH	17072	PLC	17093	PLC
17010	ACH	17031	ACH	17052	ACH	17073	PLC	17094	PLC
17011	ACH	17032	ACH	17053	ACH	17074	PLC	17095	PLC
17012	ACH	17033	ACH	17054	ACH	17075	PLC	17096	PLC
17013	ACH	17034	ACH	17055	ACH	17076	PLC	17097	PLC
17014	ACH	17035	ACH	17056	PLC	17077	PLC	17098	PLC
17015	ACH	17036	ACH	17057	PLC	17078	PLC	17099	PLC
17016	ACH	17037	ACH	17058	PLC	17079	PLC	17100	PLC
17017	ACH	17038	ACH	17059	PLC	17080	PLC	17101	PLC
17018	ACH	17039	ACH	17060	PLC	17081	PLC	17102	PLC
17019	ACH	17040	ACH	17061	PLC	17082	PLC	17103	PLC
17020	ACH	17041	ACH	17062	PLC	17083	PLC	17104	PLC
17021	ACH	17042	ACH	17063	PLC	17084	PLC	17105	PLC

Name: 17051 CORMEILLES-EN-PARISIS

BB 20011 CLASS   B–B

Originally ordered as BB 22379/80 these two locomotives were never delivered as such but their body shells used to become the synchronous dual voltage prototypes for class BB 26000. Livery is a striking white, blue and yellow.

Built: 1976–86.
Builders: Alsthom/MTE.
One Hour Rating: kW.
Maximum Tractive Effort: kN.
Driving Wheel Dia.: 1250 mm.

Systems: 1500 V dc/25 kV ac.

Total Weight: tonnes.
Length over Buffers: 17480 mm.
Max. Speed: 200 km/h.

20011	STR	20012	STR	

BB 20200 CLASS   B-B

This small class which is a dual-voltage version of the BB 17000 class is allocated to Strasbourg for working into the West German and Swiss systems which use 15 kV ac. They rarely astray from these duties.

Built: 1970.
Builder: Alsthom.
One Hour Rating: 1660/2940 kW.
Maximum Tractive Effort: 324/197 kN.
Driving Wheel Dia.: 1100 mm.

Systems: 25 kV ac 50 Hz/15 kV ac 16⅔ Hz.

Total Weight: 80 tonnes.
Length over Buffers: 14940 mm.
Max. Speed: 90/140 km/h.

20201	STR	20204	STR	20207	STR	20210	STR	20212	STR
20202	STR	20205	STR	20208	STR	20211	STR	20213	STR
20203	STR	20206	STR	20209	STR						

CC 21000 CLASS   C–C

These are dual-voltage CC 6500s. The introduction of TGVs to Switzerland has reduced their daytime use but they still appear on overnight workings. 21001/2 have seen use on test trains on the TGV route and are fitted with cab signalling for that line. 20001–2 have bodysides as for CC 6501–8 whilst 20003/4 are like CC 6560–74.

Built: 1969/1974*.
Builders: Alsthom/MTE.
One Hour Rating: 5900 kW.
Maximum Tractive Effort: 288/131 kN.
Driving Wheel Dia.: 1140 mm.

Systems: 1500 V dc/25 kV ac.

Total Weight: 124 (128*) tonnes.
Length over Buffers: 20190 mm.
Max. Speed: 100/200 km/h.

CC 21000 class No. CC 21001 at Charolais Depot, Paris on 23/02/85.   [E. Dunkling

BB 22200 class No. BB 22301 VILLENEUVE D'ASCQ waits to leave Lille with the 13.20 to Paris Nord.   [Brian Garvin

Fitted with snowploughs, electro-pneumatic brakes, press button emergency brake,flange lubricators, driver-guard communication, radio fitted for train-signal box communication, emergency rheostatic brake. 21001/2 also cab signalling. 21003 went on loan to the USA in 1976 where it ran as Amtrak X 996.

| 21001 | DIJ | 21002 | DIJ | 21003 | DIJ | 21004 | DIJ | |

BB 22200 CLASS   B–B

This dual-voltage version of BB 7200/15000 started off working in the Marseille area but can be found virtually over the whole electrified network on through trains from or over routes with different voltages. They even turn up at Amiens to work the VSOE! 22278 has for some years worked on dc only between Paris and Bordeaux as a test locomotive for high speed running on 1500 V dc. As such it was a prototype for 22351–70. It has been run into the ground and may now have to be given a thorough overhaul. 22351–70 are at Rennes for high speed services on the Paris–Rennes/Nantes routes. 22379/80 have not existed as such being delivered as experimental locos 20011/2. No more are expected to be built as the future lies with synchronous motors and the BB 26000 class.

Built: 1976–1986.
Builders: Alsthom/MTE.
One Hour Rating: 4360 kW.
Maximum Tractive Effort: 294 kN.
Driving Wheel Dia.: 1250 mm.

Systems: 1500 V dc/25 kV ac.

Total Weight: 89 tonnes.
Length over Buffers: 17480 mm.
Max. Speed: 160 (200*) km/h.

Rheostatic brake. Cowcatcher, Electro-pneumatic brakes. Press button emergency direct air brake. Flange lubricators. Driver-guard communication. Many also radio fitted for train-signal box communication.

22201	DIJ	22216	DIJ	22231	DIJ	22246	MAR	22261	MAR
22202	DIJ	22217	DIJ	22232	DIJ	22247	MAR	22262	MAR
22203	DIJ	22218	DIJ	22233	DIJ	22248	MAR	22263	MAR
22204	DIJ	22219	DIJ	22234	DIJ	22249	MAR	22264	MAR
22205	DIJ	22220	DIJ	22235	MAR	22250	MAR	22265	MAR
22206	DIJ	22221	DIJ	22236	DIJ	22251	MAR	22266	MAR
22207	DIJ	22222	DIJ	22237	DIJ	22252	MAR	22267	MAR
22208	DIJ	22223	DIJ	22238	DIJ	22253	MAR	22268	MAR
22209	DIJ	22224	DIJ	22239	DIJ	22254	MAR	22269	MAR
22210	DIJ	22225	DIJ	22240	DIJ	22255	MAR	22270	MAR
22211	DIJ	22226	DIJ	22241	DIJ	22256	MAR	22271	MAR
22212	DIJ	22227	DIJ	22242	DIJ	22257	MAR	22272	MAR
22213	DIJ	22228	DIJ	22243	DIJ	22258	MAR	22273	MAR
22214	DIJ	22229	DIJ	22244	DIJ	22259	MAR	22274	MAR
22215	DIJ	22230	DIJ	22245	MAR	22260	MAR	22275	MAR

Names:

22202 OYONNAX
22218 FOURMIES
22219 ALBERTVILLE

22235 AUBERGE
22239 LONS LE SAUNIER
22242 MULHOUSE

22276	MAR	DIJON	22292	DIJ	
22277	DIJ	IS-SUR-TILLE	22293	DIJ	
22278*	DIJ		22294	DIJ	
22280	MAR	HAZEBROUCK	22295	DIJ	
22281	MAR		22296	DIJ	
22282	MAR		22297	DIJ	
22283	MAR		22298	DIJ	
22284	MAR	GEVRY-CHAMBÉRY	22299	DIJ	
22285	MAR	CHANTILLY	22300	DIJ	CHALON-SUR-SAÔNE
22286	DIJ	BÉTHUNE	22301	DIJ	VILLENEUVE-D'ASCQ
22287	DIJ	ST-JEAN-DE-MAURIENNE	22302	DIJ	RIVE-DE-GIER
22288	DIJ	LOUHANS	22303	DIJ	CROIX
22289	DIJ		22304	DIJ	LANGEAC
22290	DIJ		22305	DIJ	ST-RAMBERT-D'ALBON
22291	DIJ	LA FERTÉ-ALAIS	22306	DIJ	

22307	DIJ	LE TEIL		22356*	REN	LORIENT
22308	DIJ	GISORS		22357*	REN	
22309	DIJ			22358*	REN	
22310	DIJ			22359*	REN	
22311	DIJ	PIERREFITTE		22360*	REN	
22312	MAR	ANTIBES JUAN-LES-PINS		22361*	REN	
22313	MAR	DIGNE-LES-BAINS		22362*	REN	
22314	MAR	TAIN-L'HERMITAGE		22363*	REN	
22315	MAR	MIRAMAS		22364*	REN	
22316	MAR	LOMME		22365*	REN	
22317	MAR	LA-TOUR-DU-PIN		22366*	REN	MALAKOFF
22318	MAR	CARPENTRAS		22367*	REN	
22319	MAR	SORGUES-SUR-OUVÈZE		22368*	REN	
22320	MAR	ISTRES		22369*	REN	
22321	MAR	BELLEVILLE-SUR-SAÔNE		22370*	REN	
22322	MAR	BOLLÈNE		22371*	REN	LADOIX-SERRIGNY
22323	MAR	CAGNES-SUR-MER		22372*	REN	MAURIAC
22324	MAR	LANNION		22373*	REN	AULNAY-SOUS-BOIS
22325	MAR	CHAMPIGNY-SUR-MARNE		22374*	REN	NOYON
22326	MAR			22375	DIJ	MÉRICOURT
22327	MAR			22376	DIJ	DOUAI
22328	MAR			22377	DIJ	ROUBAIX
22329	MAR	QUIMPER		22378	DIJ	LE QUESNOY
22330	MAR			22381	DIJ	LE BOURGET
22331	MAR			22382	DIJ	CLERMONT DE L'OISE
22332	MAR			22383	DIJ	
22333	MAR			22384	DIJ	SAINT-ANDRÉ LÈS LILLE
22334	MAR			22385	DIJ	LONGUEAU
22335	MAR			22386	DIJ	
22336	MAR			22387	DIJ	
22337	MAR			22388	DIJ	
22338	MAR			22389	DIJ	
22339	MAR			22390	DIJ	
22340	MAR			22391	DIJ	
22341	MAR			22392	DIJ	
22342	MAR			22393	DIJ	
22343	MAR			22394	DIJ	
22344	MAR			22395	DIJ	
22345	MAR			22396	DIJ	
22346	MAR	AUBAGNE		22397	DIJ	
22347	MAR			22398	DIJ	
22348	MAR			22399	DIJ	
22349	MAR			22400	DIJ	
22350	MAR			22401	DIJ	
22351*	REN	VALOGNES		22402	DIJ	
22352*	REN	SABLÉ-SUR-SARTHE		22403	DIJ	
22353*	REN	PLAISIR		22404	DIJ	
22354*	REN	ANCENIS		22405		
22355*	REN					

BB 25100 CLASS   Bo–Bo

An early dual-voltage locomotive based at Chalindrey for working the Dijon–Metz route from which they rarely stray. However recently their passenger duties on this route have been taken over by Dijon based BB 22200.

Built: 1964–1965.
Builder: MTE.
One Hour Rating: 3400 (1500 V)/4130 (25 kV) kW.
Maximum Tractive Effort: 367 kN.
Driving Wheel Dia.: 1250 mm.

Systems: 1500 V dc/25 kV ac.
Total Weight: 85 tonnes.
Length over Buffers: 16200 mm.
Max. Speed: 130 km/h.

25101	CLY	25106	CLY	25111	CLY	25116	CLY	25121	CLY
25102	CLY	25107	CLY	25112	CLY	25117	CLY	25122	CLY
25103	CLY	25108	CLY	25113	CLY	25118	CLY	25123	CLY
25104	CLY	25109	CLY	25114	CLY	25119	CLY	25124	CLY
25105	CLY	25110	CLY	25115	CLY	25120	CLY	25125	CLY

BB 25150 CLASS   Bo–Bo

Similar to BB 25100 from which it was developed. The class is split between Chalindrey and Chambéry and the allocation of 25168/9 varies as to which depot has the greater demand for locomotives, Chambéry usually needing more locomotives during the winter sports period. Chambéry locomotives are mainly used on the Bellegarde–Evian les Bains and Aix les Bains–St.Gervais routes plus through workings and fill-in turns in this area.

Built: 1967–69/1974*/1976–77†.
Builder: MTE.
Continuous Rating: 3400 (1500 V)/4130 (25 kV) kW.
Maximum Tractive Effort: 367 kN.
Driving Wheel Dia.: 1250 mm.

Systems: 1500 V dc/25 kV ac.
Weight: 85 (89*†) tonnes.
Length over Buffers: 16200 (16680*,16730†) m
Max. Speed: 130 km/h.

Rheostatic brake. Press button emergency brakes. Radio fitted for train-signal box communication. Many are also fitted with flange lubricators, rail lubricators and snowploughs.

25151	CLY	25160	CLY	25169	CLY	25178†	CBY	25187†	CBY
25152	CLY	25161	CLY	25170	CLY	25179†	CBY	25188†	CBY
25153	CLY	25162	CLY	25171*	CBY	25180†	CBY	25189†	CBY
25154	CLY	25163	CLY	25172*	CBY	25181†	CBY	25190†	CBY
25155	CLY	25164	CLY	25173*	CBY	25182†	CBY	25191†	CBY
25156	CLY	25165	CLY	25174*	CBY	25183†	CBY	25192†	CBY
25157	CLY	25166	CLY	25175*	CBY	25184†	CBY	25193†	CBY
25158	CLY	25167	CLY	25176†	CBY	25185†	CBY	25194†	CBY
25159	CLY	25168	CLY	25177†	CBY	25186†	CBY	25195†	CBY

Name:25175 LE CREUSOT

BB 25200 CLASS   Bo–Bo

A faster version of the preceding two classes, being a dual voltage version of BB 9200 and BB 16000. For many years all have been used on services between Paris and Le Mans/Rennes. However delivery of BB 22351–70 to Rennes has meant the loss of most of their high speed work and their operating area has spread to include duties on the Paris–Le Havre route. In 1987 at least 10 will be transferred to Chambéry and converted for push-pull operation for use on Grenoble–Lyon trains.

Built: 1965–67/1974*.
Builder: MTE.
Continuous Rating: 3400 (1500 V)/4130 (25 kV) kW.
Maximum Tractive Effort: 304 kN.
Driving Wheel Dia.: 1250 mm.

Systems: 1500 V dc/25 kV ac.
Weight: 85 (89*) tonnes.
Length over Buffers: 16200 (16680*) mm.
Max. Speed: 160 km/h.

25201	MON	25212	MON	25222	REN	25232	REN	25242	MON
25202	MON	25213	MON	25223	REN	25233	REN	25243	MON
25203	MON	25214	MON	25224	REN	25234	REN	25244	MON
25204	MON	25215	MON	25225	REN	25235	REN	25245	MON
25205	MON	25216	MON	25226	REN	25236	MON	25246	MON
25206	MON	25217	MON	25227	REN	25237	MON	25247*	MON
25207	MON	25218	MON	25228	REN	25238	MON	25248*	MON
25208	MON	25219	MON	25229	REN	25239	MON	25249*	MON
25209	MON	25220	REN	25230	REN	25240	MON	25250*	MON
25210	MON	25221	REN	25231	REN	25241	MON	25251*	MON
25211	MON								

Names:

25201 LE MANS
25247 COMBOURG

25250 VITRÉ
25251 VERSAILLES

BB 25500 CLASS   B–B

A dual voltage version of BB 8500 and BB 17000 and built in three batches with detail variations in styling and cabs. Mostly used in pairs on freight trains especially those that work around or through Paris. The Marseille locomotives will be found on push-pull trains in the area whilst those at Tours St.Pierre are recent arrivals for working the newly electrified line towards Nantes.

Built: 1964–76.
Builder: Alsthom.
Continuous Rating: 2610/2940 kW.
Maximum Tractive Effort: 330/197 kN.
Driving Wheel Dia.: 1100 mm.

Systems: 1500 V dc/25 kV ac.

Weight: 81 (79*,77§,80†) tonnes.
Length over Buffers: 15570 (14940*§, 14700†) m
Max. Speed: 90/140 km/h.

Rheostatic brake. Multiple working and push & pull fitted. Dijon locos snowplough fitted. Many also have rail lubricators.

25501* LAB	25540* LAB	25579§ ACH	25618 MON	25657 ACH
25502* LAB	25541* TSP	25580§ ACH	25619 MON	25658 DIJ
25503* DIJ	25542* TSP	25581§ ACH	25620 MAR	25659 ACH
25504* LAB	25543* TSP	25582§ ACH	25621 MAR	25660 ACH
25505* LAB	25544* TSP	25583§ ACH	25622 MAR	25661 ACH
25506* LAB	25545† TSP	25584§ ACH	25623 MAR	25662 ACH
25507* LAB	25546† TSP	25585§ ACH	25624 MAR	25663 ACH
25508* LAB	25547† TSP	25586§ ACH	25625 MAR	25664 ACH
25509* LAB	25548† TSP	25587§ ACH	25626 MAR	25665 DIJ
25510* LAB	25549† TSP	25588 ACH	25627 MAR	25666 MAR
25511* LAB	25550† TSP	25589 ACH	25628 MAR	25667 MAR
25512* LAB	25551† TSP	25590 ACH	25629 MAR	25668 MAR
25513* LAB	25552† TSP	25591 ACH	25630 MAR	25669 ACH
25514* LAB	25553† TSP	25592 ACH	25631 DIJ	25670 ACH
25515* LAB	25554† TSP	25593 ACH	25632 DIJ	25671 DIJ
25516* LAB	25555† TSP	25594 ACH	25633 MAR	25672 DIJ
25517* LAB	25556§ ACH	25595 ACH	25634 DIJ	25673 DIJ
25518* LAB	25557§ ACH	25596 ACH	25635 MAR	25674 DIJ
25519* LAB	25558§ ACH	25597 ACH	25636 DIJ	25675 DIJ
25520* LAB	25559§ ACH	25598 ACH	25637 MAR	25676 DIJ
25521* LAB	25560§ ACH	25599 ACH	25638 MAR	25677 DIJ
25522* LAB	25561§ ACH	25600 ACH	25639 MAR	25678 DIJ
25523* ACH	25562§ ACH	25601 ACH	25640 MAR	25679 DIJ
25524* ACH	25563§ ACH	25602 ACH	25641 MAR	25680 DIJ
25525* ACH	25564§ ACH	25603 ACH	25642 MAR	25681 DIJ
25526* ACH	25565§ ACH	25604 ACH	25643 MAR	25682 DIJ
25527* ACH	25566§ ACH	25605 ACH	25644 MAR	25683 DIJ
25528* ACH	25567§ ACH	25606 ACH	25645 MAR	25684 DIJ
25529* ACH	25568§ ACH	25607 ACH	25646 MAR	25685 DIJ
25530* ACH	25569§ ACH	25608 ACH	25647 MAR	25686 DIJ
25531* ACH	25570§ ACH	25609 ACH	25648 MAR	25687 DIJ
25532* LAB	25571§ ACH	25610 ACH	25649 ACH	25688 DIJ
25533* LAB	25572§ ACH	25611 ACH	25650 ACH	25689 DIJ
25534* LAB	25573§ ACH	25612 MON	25651 MAR	25690 DIJ
25535* LAB	25574§ ACH	25613 MON	25652 MAR	25691 DIJ
25536* LAB	25575§ ACH	25614 MON	25653 DIJ	25692 DIJ
25537* LAB	25576§ ACH	25615 MON	25654 DIJ	25693 DIJ
25538* LAB	25577§ ACH	25616 MON	25655 DIJ	25694 DIJ
25539* LAB	25578§ ACH	25617 MON	25656 ACH	

BB 26000 CLASS   B–B

On order. These new dual voltage locomotives will feature synchronous motors and are already known as "Sybics" (*Synchronous-bicourant*). BB 20011/2 are the prototypes. The operating base for these locomotives has yet to be announced, but some are expected to appear on services out of Paris Nord to replace BB 16000 on top line duties. Technical data not yet available.
Systems: 1500 V dc/25 kV ac.

26001	26010	26019	26028	26037
26002	26011	26020	26029	26038
26003	26012	26021	26030	26039
26004	26013	26022	26031	26040
26005	26014	26023	26032	26041
26006	26015	26024	26033	26042
26007	26016	26025	26034	26043
26008	26017	26026	26035	26044
26009	26018	26027	26036	

CC 40100 CLASS   C–C

A small class for working under 4 different voltages. There is now no need for the 1500 V dc and 15 kV ac capabilities as for many years now they have worked only between Paris and Brussels/Liège. They share these duties with Belgian Railways classes 1500 & 1800. At one time it was intended CC 40100 would work through to Amsterdam and KÖln on trains from Paris Nord. They were finished off in stainless steel to match the TEE stock used on these services. 40106 was a virtual write-off after an accident near Brussels circa 1970. It was reconstructed (almost new) when SNCB class 1800 was being built as an extra loco after this batch and re-entered service in 1974.

Built: 1964/1969–1970.
Systems: 1500 V dc/3000 V dc/25 kV ac 50 Hz/15 kV ac 16⅔ Hz.
Builder: Alsthom.
Continuous Rating: 5410 (4480*) kW.   **Weight**: 109 tonnes.
Maximum Tractive Effort: 198/142 kN.   **Length over Buffers**: 22030 mm.
Driving Wheel Dia.: 1100 mm.   **Max. Speed**: 160 km/h.

40101* PLC	PERPIGNAN	
40102* PLC	MENTON	
40103* PLC	BRIOUDE	
40104* PLC	SAINT-JEAN-DE-LUZ	
40105 PLC	HYÈRES	

40106 PLC	COMPIÈGNE	
40107 PLC	BAYONNE	
40108 PLC	HENDAYE	
40109 PLC	CANNES	
40110 PLC	NICE	

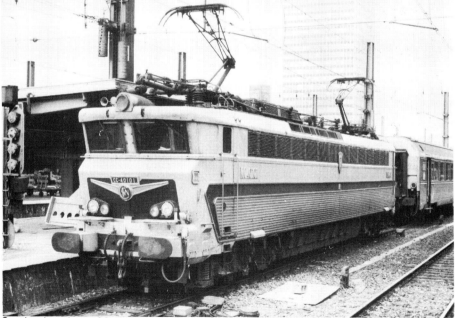

Quadruple voltage CC 40100 class No. CC 40101 PERPIGNAN at Brussels Midi on 20/04/84.
[E. Dunkling

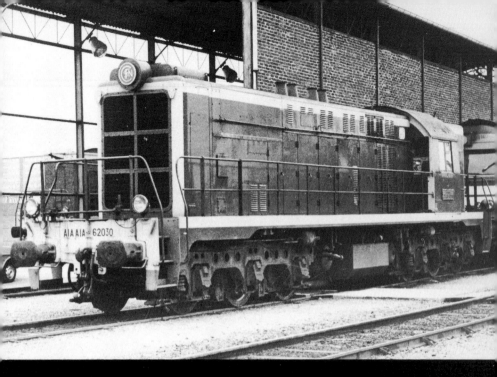

A1AA1A 62000 class No. A1A A1A 62030 at Bobigny on 10/04/83. [E. Dunkling

BB 63500 class No. BB 63692 in the new yellow livery at Venissieux depot on 30/03/86.
[E Dunkling

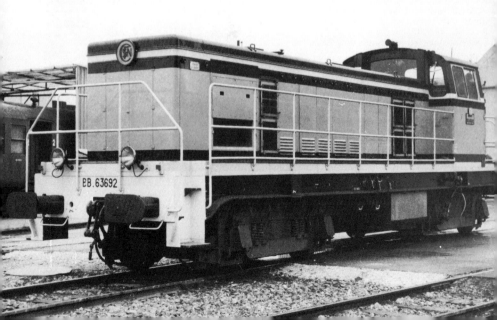

DIESEL LOCOMOTIVES

A1AA1A 62000 CLASS   A1A–A1A

These are typical American hood units of the immediate post war period and continue to be known as "Baldwins" after the USA constructor. They have spent most of their life along the Eastern corridor on heavy shunting duties in large yards between Dunkerque and Mulhouse with a few in the Paris area at Le Bourget. The class is no longer receiving overhauls and as locomotives come up for main overhaul they will be withdrawn. Two have already been preserved.

Built: 1946–47.
Builder: Baldwin.
Engine: Baldwin 606NA of 560 kW.
Transmission: Electric.
Train Heating: None.
Maximum Tractive Effort: 143 kN.
Driving Wheel Dia.: 1100 mm.
Weight in Full Working Order: 110 tonnes.
Length over Buffers: 17700 mm.
Max. Speed: 96 km/h.

62001	LEN	62022	STR	62044	THI	62064	THI	62081	THI
62002	LEN	62025	THI	62046	PLP	62065	STR	62082	LEN
62003	PLP	62026	LEN	62048	LEN	62067	THI	62083	THI
62005	LEN	62027	STR	62049	LEN	62068	STR	62084	THI
62006	STR	62028	LEN	62050	LEN	62069	STR	62088	THI
62007	LEN	62029	LEN	62051	LEN	62070	LEN	62089	STR
62010	THI	62030	PLP	62055	THI	62071	THI	62090	STR
62011	LEN	62032	THI	62056	THI	62072	THI	62091	THI
62012	LEN	62033	PLP	62057	STR	62073	STR	62092	STR
62014	STR	62038	PLP	62058	THI	62074	THI	62094	LEN
62015	LEN	62040	LEN	62059	THI	62076	THI	62095	THI
62016	LEN	62041	STR	62060	LEN	62078	LEN	62098	THI
62018	THI	62042	LEN	62061	LEN	62079	STR	62099	THI
62019	THI	62043	THI	62062	THI	62080	STR		

BB 63000 CLASS   Bo–Bo

BB 63000, 63400, 63500 are all virtually identical and form a large family of over 800 locomotives. These low powered locomotives are found on station pilot duties, freight trips and general shunting duties and appear all over France. Those assigned to big yards invariably have radios fitted whilst some also have BSI automatic couplings. This type of locomotive will also be found in Spain (class 307), Portugal (class 1200), Luxembourg (class 850/900) and Yugoslavia (class 642/643).

Built: 1953–64.
Builder: Brissonneau & Lotz.
Engine: Sulzer 6LDA22B of 440 kW (Sulzer 6LDA22C of 440 kW*, Sulzer 6LDA22C of 535 kW†, Sulzer 6LDA22D of 535 kW§, Sulzer 6LDA22E of 550 kW●).
Transmission: Electric.
Train Heating: None.
Maximum Tractive Effort: 167 kN.
Driving Wheel Dia.: 1050 mm.
Weight in Full Working Order: 64–69 tonnes.
Length over Buffers: 14680 mm.
Max. Speed: 80 km/h.

63001	VSG	63012	TSP	63023	MAR	63034	VSG	63045	MAR
63002	VSG	63013	TSP	63024	VSG	63035	TSP	63046	MAR
63003	TSP	63014	NEV	63025	VSG	63036	TSP	63047	MAR
63004	TSP	63015	VSG	63026	VSG	63037	PSO	63048	MAR
63005	TSP	63016	MAR	63027	VSG	63038	TSP	63049	MAR
63006	TSP	63017	MAR	63028	VSG	63039	MAR	63050	MAR
63007	TSP	63018	MAR	63029	VSG	63040	NEV	63051	MAR
63008	TSP	63019	MAR	63030	VSG	63041	MAR	63052	MAR
63009	TSP	63020	MAR	63031	VSG	63042	MAR	63053	VSG
63010	TSP	63021	MAR	63032	VSG	63043	MAR	63054	VSG
63011	TSP	63022	NEV	63033	NEV	63044	MAR	63055	VSG

63056 VSG	63095* CBY	63134§ PLV	63173§ LEN	63212● PLV
63057 VSG	63096* DIJ	63135§ PLV	63174§ LEN	63213● LEN
63058 VSG	63097* DIJ	63136§ PLV	63175§ LEN	63214● PLP
63059 VSG	63098* DIJ	63137§ LEN	63176§ LEN	63215● LEN
63060 PSO	63099* DIJ	63138§ LEN	63177§ PLV	63216● CLY
63061 PSO	63100* DIJ	63139§ CLY	63178§ LEN	63217● CLY
63062 NEV	63101* TSP	63140§ LEN	63179§ LEN	63218● LEN
63063 NEV	63102* DIJ	63141§ LEN	63180§ PLV	63219● LEN
63064 NEV	63103* CBY	63142§ LEN	63181§ PLV	63220● LEN
63065 MAR	63104* DIJ	63143§ LEN	63182§ LEN	63221● CLY
63066 MAR	63105* TSP	63144§ LAB	63183§ LEN	63222● LEN
63067 NEV	63106* TSP	63145§ LEN	63184§ LEN	63223● LEN
63068 VSG	63107* TSP	63146§ LEN	63185§ LEN	63224● LEN
63069 MAR	63108* PSO	63147§ LAB	63186§ LEN	63225● CLY
63070 MAR	63109† CLY	63148§ VSG	63187§ LEN	63226● DIJ
63071 MAR	63110† PLV	63149§ LEN	63188§ LEN	63227● DIJ
63072 NEV	63111† CBY	63150§ LEN	63189§ PLV	63228● DIJ
63073* DIJ	63112† LEN	63151§ LAB	63190§ PLV	63229● CLY
63074* CBY	63113† PLV	63152§ LAB	63191§ PLV	63230● LEN
63075* CBY	63114† PLV	63153§ LEN	63192§ LEN	63231● DIJ
63076* CBY	63115† PLV	63154§ LEN	63193§ DIJ	63232● DIJ
63077* CBY	63116† LEN	63155§ LEN	63194§ LEN	63233● DIJ
63078* CBY	63117† CBY	63156§ LAB	63195§ PLV	63234● LEN
63079* CBY	63118† CBY	63157§ LAB	63196● CLY	63235● PLP
63080* CBY	63119† PLV	63158§ LAB	63197● LEN	63236● DIJ
63081* CBY	63120† CLY	63159§ PLV	63198● LEN	63237● DIJ
63082* PSO	63121† LEN	63160§ PLV	63199● LEN	63238● CLY
63083* PSO	63122† LEN	63161§ PLV	63200● DIJ	63239● LEN
63084* CBY	63123† LEN	63162§ LEN	63201● PLV	63240● CLY
63085* DIJ	63124† CLY	63163§ LEN	63202● CLY	63241● LEN
63086* DIJ	63125† CBY	63164§ PLV	63203● LEN	63242● LEN
63087* PSO	63126† LEN	63165§ PLV	63204● LEN	63243● LEN
63088* CBY	63127† CBY	63166§ PLV	63205● DIJ	63244● LAB
63089* CBY	63128† LEN	63167§ LEN	63206● PLV	63245● LAB
63090* CBY	63129§ CLY	63168§ LEN	63207● LEN	63246● LEN
63091* CBY	63130§ VSG	63169§ LEN	63208● LEN	63247● LEN
63092* DIJ	63131§ PLV	63170§ PLV	63209● LEN	63248● LEN
63093* PSO	63132§ LEN	63171§ PLV	63210● DIJ	63249● LAB
63094* DIJ	63133§ LEN	63172§ LEN	63211● CLY	63250● LAB

BB 63400 CLASS   Bo–Bo

These locomotoives were financed under the Eurofima arrangements and are similar to BB 63500. For many years all were based at Nantes but the spread of electrification and changing requirements has meant some transferring to other areas. Mostly used as yard pilots.

Built: 1959–60.
Builder: Brissonneau & Lotz.
Engine: MGO V12SH of 605 kW.
Transmission: Electric.
Train Heating: None.
Maximum Tractive Effort: 167 kN.
Driving Wheel Dia.: 1050 mm.
Weight in Full Working Order: 68 tonnes.
Length over Buffers: 14680 mm.
Max. Speed: 80 km/h.

63401 NAN	63406 NAN	63411 ACH	63416 NAN	63420 NAN
63402 SOT	63407 NAN	63412 NAN	63417 NAN	63421 NAN
63403 NAN	63408 BOR	63413 NAN	63418 LIM	63422 NAN
63404 SOT	63409 NAN	63414 NAN	63419 NAN	63423 LIM
63405 NAN	63410 NAN	63415 ACH		

BB 63500 CLASS   Bo–Bo

A slightly more powerful version of BB 63000 but with lots of detail variations within the class. The e.t.h. locos at La Plaine are used for tripping passenger trains around the Petit Ceinture from Paris Nord to Paris Lyon. Consideration is being given to a plan to convert 50 locos to slave shunters by removing the cab and other superfluous fittings.

Built: 1956–71.
Builder: Brissonneau & Lotz.
Engine: MGO V12SH of 605 kW.
Transmission: Electric.
Train Heating: None.   **Weight in Full Working Order:** 64–68 tonnes.
Maximum Tractive Effort: 167 kN.   **Length over Buffers:** 14680 mm.
Driving Wheel Dia.: 1050 mm.   **Max. Speed:** 80 km/h.

m—Multiple working fitted.
e—E.t.h. fitted.

63501	NAN	63549	VEN	63597	PLP	63645	ACH	63693	VEN
63502	SOT	63550	TOU	63598	CAN	63646	VEN	63694	VEN
63503	CAN	63551	BOR	63599	REN	63647	REN	63695	MOH
63504	BOR	63552	LIM	63600	BOR	63648	NAN	63696	MET
63505	SOT	63553	PLP	63601	BOR	63649	REN	63697	VEN
63506	NAN	63554	AVI	63602	ACH	63650	CAN	63698	REN
63507	SOT	63555	REN	63603	SOT	63651	MOH	63699	NIM
63508	CAN	63556	SOT	63604	NAN	63652	CAN	63700	MOH
63509	REN	63557	TOU	63605	BOR	63653	SOT	63701	STR
63510	SOT	63558	PLP	63606	PLP	63654	BOR	63702	AVI
63511	SOT	63559	TOU	63607	STR	63655	MET	63703	LON
63512	SOT	63560	TOU	63608	CAN	63656	VEN	63704	LON
63513	AVI	63561	CAN	63609	BOR	63657	NIM	63705	PLP
63514	AVI	63562	REN	63610	VEN	63658	BOR	63706	PLP
63515	VSG	63563	CAN	63611	REN	63659	AVI	63707	PLP
63516	SOT	63564	PLP	63612	SOT	63660	NAN	63708	MOH
63517	CAN	63565	NAN	63613	SOT	63661	MET	63709	PLP
63518	CAN	63566	PLP	63614	SOT	63662	MET	63710	AVI
63519	SOT	63567	PLP	63615	SOT	63663	REN	63711	PLP
63520	ACH	63568	ACH	63616	SOT	63664	NAN	63712	PLP
63521	REN	63569	TOU	63617	STR	63665	MOH	63713	PLP
63522	SOT	63570	ACH	63618	STR	63666	MET	63714	LON
63523	REN	63571	CAN	63619	NIM	63667	REN	63715	NIM
63524	SOT	63572	NAN	63620	NAN	63668	PLP	63716	MOH
63525	SOT	63573	ACH	63621	SOT	63669	SOT	63717	MOH
63526	CAN	63574	PLP	63622	STR	63670	MOH	63718	STR
63527	PLP	63575	MET	63623	SOT	63671	NIM	63719	PLP
63528	BOR	63576	ACH	63624	NIM	63672	BOR	63720	NIM
63529	SOT	63577	TOU	63625	LON	63673	SOT	63721m STR
63530	SOT	63578	BOR	63626	NAN	63674	SOT	63722m STR
63531	PLP	63579	AVI	63627	AVI	63675	REN	63723m STR
63532	PLP	63580	TOU	63628	NAN	63676	PLP	63724m LON
63533	ACH	63581	SOT	63629	NIM	63677	PLP	63725m SOT
63534	NIM	63582	TOU	63630	SOT	63678	NAN	63726m MET
63535	REN	63583	TOU	63631	REN	63679	NIM	63727m STR
63536	BOR	63584	AVI	63632	LIM	63680	MOH	63728m STR
63537	PLP	63585	SOT	63633	BOR	63681	MET	63729m LON
63538	REN	63586	BOR	63634	VEN	63682	ACH	63730m PLP
63539	CAN	63587	BOR	63635	AVI	63683	BOR	63731m MET
63540	TOU	63588	CAN	63636	CAN	63684	BOR	63732m LON
63541	PLP	63589	VEN	63637	NAN	63685	PLP	63733m LON
63542	TOU	63590	ACH	63638	PLP	63686	PLP	63734m LON
63543	AVI	63591	SOT	63639	CAN	63687	ACH	63735m LON
63544	AVI	63592	BOR	63640	VEN	63688	VEN	63736m MET
63545	VEN	63593	BOR	63641	NAN	63689	VEN	63737m LON
63546	PLP	63594	BOR	63642	MOH	63690	MOH	63738m LON
63547	BOR	63595	TOU	63643	ACH	63691	MOH	63739m LON
63548	VEN	63596	CAN	63644	SOT	63692	VEN	63740m LON

63741m MET	63805 VEN	63869m LIM	63933 NAN	63997m PLP
63742m MET	63806 PLP	63870m STR	63934 VEN	63998m PLP
63743m MET	63807 PLP	63871m MET	63935 LON	63999m STR
63744m LON	63808 PLP	63872m MET	63936 LON	64000m PLP
63745m LON	63809 PLP	63873m STR	63937 MET	64001m BOR
63746m MOH	63810 STR	63874m STR	63938 PLP	64002m BOR
63747m MET	63811m MET	63875m STR	63939 REN	64003m SOT
63748m MET	63812m MET	63876m STR	63940 VEN	64004m BOR
63749m MET	63813m AVI	63877m STR	63941 NAN	64005m BOR
63750m MET	63814m AVI	63878m STR	63942 MET	64006m BOR
63751 LIM	63815m MET	63879m STR	63943 PLP	64007m LIM
63752 STR	63816m MET	63880m SOT	63944 BOR	64008m LIM
63753 REN	63817m AVI	63881m STR	63945 PLP	64009m SOT
63754 REN	63818m VEN	63882m MET	63946 VEN	64010m SOT
63755 REN	63819m MET	63883m STR	63947 BOR	64011m LIM
63756 MET	63820m MET	63884m STR	63948 BOR	64012m LIM
63757 REN	63821m VEN	63885m LON	63949 MOH	64013m LIM
63758 REN	63822m SOT	63886 PLP	63950 PLP	64014m SOT
63759 REN	63823m MET	63887 PLP	63951 AVI	64015m SOT
63760 REN	63824m MET	63888 MET	63952 MET	64016m BOR
63761 REN	63825m NIM	63889 MET	63953 PLP	64017m BOR
63762 NAN	63826m PLP	63890 AVI	63954 PLP	64018m BOR
63763 NAN	63827m MOH	63891 PLP	63955 LIM	64019m SOT
63764 NAN	63828m MET	63892 MET	63956 LON	64020m SOT
63765 BOR	63829m SOT	63893 MET	63957 LIM	64021 LON
63766 NAN	63830m NIM	63894 PLP	63958 TOU	64022 SOT
63767 NAN	63831m NIM	63895 AVI	63959 MET	64023 NIM
63768 NAN	63832m NIM	63896e NIM	63960 LON	64024 AVI
63769 NAN	63833m MOH	63897 NAN	63961 NAN	64025 SOT
63770 NAN	63834m MOH	63898 STR	63962 LIM	64026 LIM
63771 MET	63835m MOH	63899 LON	63963 NAN	64027 LIM
63772 LON	63836m LIM	63900 NIM	63964 TOU	64028 LON
63773 PLP	63837m NIM	63901e NIM	63965 TOU	64029 NIM
63774 PLP	63838m NIM	63902e PLP	63966 MOH	64030 PLP
63775 BOR	63839m MOH	63903 SOT	63967 NAN	64031 SOT
63776 LON	63840m MOH	63904 PLP	63968 NAN	64032 LIM
63777 PLP	63841m NIM	63905 ACH	63969 AVI	64033 MET
63778 PLP	63842m SOT	63906e PLP	63970 MET	64034 SOT
63779 VSG	63843m MOH	63907 NAN	63971 VEN	64035 NIM
63780 VEN	63844m MOH	63908 NAN	63972 NIM	64036 MET
63781 MET	63845m MOH	63909 STR	63973 MOH	64037 LIM
63782 BOR	63846m NIM	63910 STR	63974 PLP	64038 AVI
63783 PLP	63847m MOH	63911 STR	63975 VEN	64039 MET
63784 VSG	63848m PLP	63912 STR	63976 NIM	64040 PLP
63785 VEN	63849m MOH	63913 MET	63977 MOH	64041 SOT
63786 LIM	63850m MET	63914 PLP	63978 AVI	64042 SOT
63787 BOR	63851m MET	63915 SOT	63979 VEN	64043 BOR
63788 LIM	63852m MET	63916 AVI	63980 NAN	64044 AVI
63789 VEN	63853m VSG	63917 STR	63981m BOR	64045 MET
63790 VEN	63854m VSG	63918 NIM	63982m BOR	64046 PLP
63791 PLP	63855m VSG	63919 MET	63983m LIM	64047 SOT
63792 ACH	63856m SOT	63920 VEN	63984m LON	64048 REN
63793 CAN	63857m SOT	63921 SOT	63985m BOR	64049 AVI
63794 ACH	63858m MET	63922 VEN	63986m LIM	64050 NIM
63795 VEN	63859m VEN	63923 LON	63987m LIM	64051 MET
63796 LON	63860m STR	63924 LON	63988m LON	64052 REN
63797 PLP	63861m MET	63925 MET	63989m BOR	64053 NIM
63798 ACH	63862m NIM	63926 VEN	63990m LIM	64054 BOR
63799 ACH	63863m MOH	63927 REN	63991m LON	64055 PLP
63800 ACH	63864m AVI	63928 VEN	63992m VEN	64056 LIM
63801 PLP	63865m VEN	63929 LON	63993m LIM	64057 VEN
63802 ACH	63866m LIM	63930 PLP	63994m SOT	64058 ACH
63803 CAN	63867m MET	63931 MET	63995m LON	64059 SOT
63804 PLP	63868m MET	63932 VEN	63996m SOT	64060 MET

Four CC 65000 class diesels arriving at Saintes from Nantes on 12/08/84. In order they are CC 65016/17/02/06.

[G.J. Wiseman

CC 65500 class No. CC 65503 stands spare at Montchanin on 21/04/81.][Brian Garvin

64061	MET	64065	LON	64069	LON	64073	STR	64077	PLP
64062	MET	64066	LON	64070	NIM	64074	STR	64078	STR
64063	PLP	64067	LON	64071	NIM	64075	NIM	64079	PLP
64064	MET	64068	LON	64072	NIM	64076	PLP	64080	PLP

CC 65000 CLASS   Co–Co

The oldest of SNCF main line diesel locomotives has been given a reprieve for a few years by the need to construct TGV-Atlantique. It is fully expected they will find use on works train on this line. Originally fitted with steam boilers for passenger train workings the class has been restricted to freight use on the Nantes–La Rochelle–Bordeaux route for some years now. Many are now spare at Nantes waiting their call to duty on TGV–Atlantique construction trains.

Built: 1956–58.
Builders: Alsthom/CAFL.
Engine: Two SACM MGO V12SR of 660 kW each.
Transmission: Electric.
Train Heating: None.   **Weight in Full Working Order:** 103 tonnes.
Maximum Tractive Effort: 255 kN.   **Length over Buffers:** 19814 mm.
Driving Wheel Dia.: 1050 mm.   **Max. Speed:** 80/130 km/h.

Multiple Working fitted.

65001	NAN	65005	NAN	65009	NAN	65015	NAN	65018	NAN
65002	NAN	65006	NAN	65011	NAN	65016	NAN	65019	NAN
65003	NAN	65007	NAN	65012	NAN	65017	NAN	65020	NAN
65004	NAN	65008	NAN	65013	NAN				

CC 65500 CLASS   Co–Co

The first heavy duty diesel introduced for freight work around the Grande Ceinture route in Paris. They were made redundant by electrification and the introduction of dual-voltage electric locomotives on transfer freights. Saved from the scrapyard by the need to have powerful locomotives for use on construction trains on TGV Sud Est, they have now been given a second reprieve as there is a similar need for locomotives for the construction of TGV-Atlantique. Although no longer being overhauled by main works, the workshop at La Plaine depot is going a fantastic job refurbishing these locomotives. Many have been given a complete repaint and look as good as new. Some have been sold out of service to track repair contractors or loaned to coal mines.

Built: 1955–59.
Builders: CAFL/CEM.
Engine: Sulzer 12LDA of 1470 kW.
Transmission: Electric.
Train Heating: None.   **Weight in Full Working Order:** 123 tonnes.
Maximum Tractive Effort: 359 kN.   **Length over Buffers:** 19420 mm.
Driving Wheel Dia.: 1200 mm.   **Max. Speed:** 75 km/h.

65501	PLP	65511	PLP	65518	PLP	65527	PLP	65532	PLP
65502	PLP	65513	PLP	65519	PLP	65528	PLP	65533	PLP
65503	PLP	65515	PLP	65520	PLP	65529	PLP	65534	PLP
65506	PLP	65516	PLP	65521	PLP	65530	PLP	65535	PLP
65508	PLP	65517	PLP	65524	PLP	65531	PLP		

BB 66000 CLASS   Co–Co

A mixed traffic locomotive once found on passenger trains but with the introduction of electric heating they are rarely found now on this type of work. At one time they worked in multiple either side of a boiler van. BB 66400 have taken over local passenger train work while BB 67300, 67400 work the heavier trains. Some have been rebuilt into BB 66600 and a further rebuilding programme is now underway converting two a year into BB 66700.

Built: 1960–68.
Builders: CAFL/CEM/Alsthom/Fives-Lille/SACM.
Engine: MGO V16BSHR of 1030 kW.
Transmission: Electric.
Train Heating: None. **Weight in Full Working Order:** 66/67 tonnes.
Maximum Tractive Effort: 167 kN. **Length over Buffers:** 14898 mm.
Driving Wheel Dia.: 1100 mm. **Max. Speed:** 120 km/h.

Multiple working fitted. Some have snowploughs and/or rail greasers.

66001	TOU	66057	NEV	66116	LON	66177	SOT	66232	NAN
66002	TOU	66058	STR	66117	VEN	66178	LON	66233	VEN
66003	TOU	66059	NEV	66118	LON	66179	SOT	66234	VEN
66004	TOU	66060	TOU	66119	LAB	66180	SOT	66235	VEN
66005	TOU	66061	AVI	66120	VEN	66181	SOT	66236	VEN
66006	TOU	66062	STR	66121	LAB	66182	SOT	66237	VEN
66007	VEN	66063	STR	66122	LAB	66183	SOT	66238	NAN
66008	LAB	66064	TOU	66123	AVI	66184	LAB	66239	LIM
66009	VEN	66065	AVI	66124	AVI	66185	LAB	66240	LIM
66011	TOU	66066	STR	66125	SOT	66186	SOT	66241	LIM
66012	VEN	66067	STR	66126	LON	66187	LAB	66242	CLY
66013	VEN	66068	AVI	66127	AVI	66188	STR	66243	CLY
66014	TOU	66069	VEN	66128	VEN	66189	VEN	66244	LIM
66015	TOU	66070	TOU	66129	LAB	66190	LIM	66245	LIM
66016	VEN	66071	TOU	66130	LAB	66191	CLY	66246	VEN
66017	VEN	66072	TOU	66131	STR	66192	LON	66247	LAB
66018	TOU	66073	NEV	66133	STR	66193	LIM	66248	LIM
66019	VEN	66074	LON	66134	STR	66194	LIM	66249	LON
66020	TOU	66075	TOU	66135	NEV	66195	CLY	66250	VEN
66021	LAB	66076	NEV	66136	LAB	66196	LON	66251	CLY
66022	TOU	66077	NEV	66137	VEN	66197	VEN	66252	SOT
66023	TOU	66078	LON	66138	SOT	66198	AVI	66253	LIM
66024	TOU	66079	NEV	66139	NEV	66199	CLY	66254	LIM
66025	AVI	66081	STR	66140	SOT	66200	LON	66255	VEN
66026	TOU	66082	LAB	66141	STR	66201	VEN	66256	NAN
66027	TOU	66083	TOU	66142	LON	66202	LIM	66257	LIM
66028	TOU	66084	TOU	66143	NEV	66203	CLY	66258	SOT
66029	AVI	66085	STR	66144	NEV	66204	VEN	66259	VEN
66030	TOU	66086	TOU	66145	AVI	66205	LIM	66260	LIM
66031	TOU	66087	TOU	66147	VEN	66206	AVI	66261	VEN
66032	AVI	66088	SOT	66148	STR	66207	VEN	66262	LAB
66033	TOU	66089	VEN	66149	SOT	66208	NAN	66263	NAN
66034	TOU	66090	STR	66150	VEN	66209	LIM	66264	NAN
66035	TOU	66091	LON	66151	SOT	66210	AVI	66265	VEN
66036	TOU	66092	LIM	66153	SOT	66211	CLY	66266	VEN
66037	AVI	66093	LIM	66154	SOT	66212	LON	66267	LON
66038	VEN	66094	LON	66155	SOT	66213	LIM	66268	VEN
66039	LAB	66095	LON	66156	SOT	66214	VEN	66269	LIM
66040	AVI	66096	LON	66157	SOT	66215	CLY	66270	LON
66041	TOU	66097	LIM	66158	SOT	66216	LON	66271	LON
66042	STR	66099	LON	66159	SOT	66217	CLY	66272	LAB
66043	TOU	66100	LON	66160	LON	66218	LIM	66273	VEN
66044	NEV	66101	LIM	66161	SOT	66219	CLY	66274	LON
66045	STR	66103	SOT	66162	SOT	66220	CLY	66275	LON
66046	STR	66104	SOT	66163	SOT	66221	LIM	66276	LON
66047	TOU	66105	LAB	66164	SOT	66222	AVI	66277	CLY
66048	TOU	66107	LIM	66165	SOT	66223	CLY	66278	CLY
66049	NEV	66108	VEN	66166	SOT	66224	NAN	66279	LIM
66050	STR	66109	SOT	66167	SOT	66225	NAN	66280	LON
66051	TOU	66110	LON	66169	SOT	66226	LIM	66281	LIM
66052	TOU	66111	VEN	66170	SOT	66227	CLY	66282	VEN
66053	NEV	66112	VEN	66171	SOT	66228	CLY	66283	VEN
66054	STR	66113	LON	66173	SOT	66229	NAN	66284	LON
66055	TOU	66114	LON	66175	LON	66230	VEN	66285	NAN
66056	TOU	66115	SOT	66176	SOT	66231	CLY	66286	LIM

66287	LIM	66294	NAN	66301	NAN	66307	LIM	66313	LIM
66288	LON	66295	LIM	66302	LIM	66308	LON	66314	LIM
66289	VEN	66296	LON	66303	AVI	66309	LON	66315	LIM
66290	AVI	66297	AVI	66304	LON	66310	LIM	66316	VEN
66291	AVI	66298	AVI	66305	LON	66311	LIM	66317	LAB
66292	LON	66299	AVI	66306	LIM	66312	NAN	66318	NAN
66293	CLV	66300	LON						

BB 66400 CLASS   Bo–Bo

This class is a development of BB 66000 and incorporates three-phase transmission.

Built: 1968–71.
Builders: CAFL/CEM/Alsthom/Fives-Lille/SACM.
Engine: MGO V16BSHR of 1030 kW.
Transmission: Three-phase electric.
Train Heating: None   **Weight in Full Working Order:** 64 tonnes.
Maximum Tractive Effort: 167 kN.   **Length over Buffers:** 14972 mm.
Driving Wheel Dia.: 1100 mm.   **Max. Speed:** 120 km/h.

e–Fitted with e.t.h., multiple working and push & pull.

66401e	LEN	66423e	CLY	66444e	CLY	66465	NEV	66486e	LEN
66402e	LEN	66424e	CLY	66445e	PLP	66466	NEV	66487e	LEN
66403e	LEN	66425e	CLY	66446e	CLY	66467	NEV	66488e	LEN
66404e	LEN	66426e	CLY	66447e	CLY	66468	NEV	66489e	LEN
66405e	LEN	66427e	CLY	66448e	CLY	66469	NEV	66490e	LEN
66406e	LEN	66428e	NAN	66449e	CLY	66470	NEV	66491e	LEN
66407e	LEN	66429e	PLP	66450e	PLP	66471	NEV	66492e	LEN
66408e	LEN	66430e	NAN	66451	SOT	66472	NEV	66493e	LEN
66409e	LEN	66431e	CLY	66452	SOT	66473	NEV	66494e	LEN
66410e	LEN	66432e	TOU	66453	SOT	66474	NEV	66495e	LEN
66411e	LEN	66433e	LEN	66454	SOT	66475	NEV	66496e	LEN
66412e	CLY	66434e	CLY	66455	SOT	66476e	LEN	66497e	NAN
66413e	CLY	66435e	NAN	66456	SOT	66477e	TOU	66498e	NAN
66414e	CLY	66436e	CLY	66457	SOT	66478e	CLY	66499e	TOU
66415e	CLY	66437e	CLY	66458	SOT	66479e	CLY	66500e	NAN
66416e	CLY	66438e	CLY	66459	SOT	66480e	PLP	66501e	NAN
66417e	PLP	66439e	NAN	66460	SOT	66481e	TOU	66502e	NAN
66418e	NAN	66440e	CLY	66461	SOT	66482e	NAN	66503e	LON
66419e	PLP	66441e	CLY	66462	SOT	66483e	LEN	66504e	LON
66420e	CLY	66442e	CLY	66463	NEV	66484e	LEN	66505e	LON
66421e	CLY	66443	CLY	66464	NEV	66485e	LEN	66506e	LON
66422e	CLY								

BB 66600 CLASS   Bo–Bo

Several BB 66000 were rebuilt with a slightly more powerful engine to form this sub class. The experiment does not appear to have been a success as no more conversion followed. All are based at Nîmes for work on the line to Clermont Ferrand.

Built: 1960–62.
Builders: CAFL/CEM/Alsthom/Fives-Lille.
Engine: SEMT 12PA4 of 1100 kW.
Transmission: Electric.
Train Heating: None.   **Weight in Full Working Order:** 71 tonnes.
Maximum Tractive Effort: 167 kN.   **Length over Buffers:** 14898 mm.
Driving Wheel Dia.: 1100 mm.   **Max. Speed:** 120 km/h.

Multiple working fitted. e–E.t.h. fitted.

66604 (66304) e	NIM	66608 (66308) e	NIM	66614 (66098)	NIM
66605 (66305) e	NIM	66610 (66310) e	NIM	66615 (66102)	NIM
66606 (66306) e	NIM	66611 (66311) e	NIM	66616 (66106) e	NIM
66607 (66307) e	NIM	66612 (66312) e	NIM		

BB 66700 CLASS   Bo–Bo

These are converted BB 66000. The ever increasing weight of wagons has led to the need for more powerful shunting locomotives. These locomotives have been regeared at Nevers works and the weight increased slightly. It is expected further locomotives will be converted at the rate of 2 a year. Some of those allocated to Venissieux operate at yards often far away (e.g. Miramas).

Built: 1985.
Builders: CAFL/CEM/Alsthom/Fives-Lille/SACM.
Engine: MGO V16BSHR of 1030 kW.
Transmission: Electric.
Train Heating: Electric.   **Weight in Full Working Order**: 71 tonnes.
Maximum Tractive Effort: 167 kN.   **Length over Buffers**: 14898 mm.
Driving Wheel Dia.: 1100 mm.   **Max. Speed**: 90 km/h.

66701 (66146)	VEN	66703 (66166)	VEN	66705 (66152)
66702 (66080)	VEN	66704 (66174)	VEN	66706 (66172)

BB 67000 CLASS   B–B

This is the first of the SNCF big diesels that played a part in the elimination of steam workings. These and subsequent series were one of the first to have the exterior styling by Paul Arzens who has since been responsible for most SNCF locomotive body designs. Originally a mixed traffic locomotive with a two gear bogie, they are now regarded as freight only and the bogie geared accordingly. Never fitted with boiler equipment, they used to operate with boiler vans. Many have been rebuilt into BB 67200 or BB 67300 and the missing numbers will be found under those series except 67036 which became e.t.h. prototype 67291.

Built: 1963–68.
Builders: Brissonneau and Lotz/MTE/SEMT.
Engine: SEMT 16PA4 of 1470 kW.
Transmission: Electric.
Train Heating: None.   **Weight in Full Working Order**: 80 tonnes.
Maximum Tractive Effort: 304/202 kN.   **Length over Buffers**: 17090 mm.
Driving Wheel Dia.: 1150 mm.   **Max. Speed**: 90/130 km/h.

Multiple Working fitted (also with 67200, 68000, 68500). Press button emergency brake.

67001	NEV	67023	NEV	67046	CAN	67060	MAR	67074	NEV
67002	NEV	67024	NEV	67047	NEV	67061	NEV	67076	REN
67003	NEV	67025	NEV	67048	CAN	67062	MAR	67077	NEV
67005	NEV	67026	MAR	67049	MAR	67063	MAR	67079	REN
67009	NEV	67027	CAN	67050	MAR	67064	MAR	67080	NEV
67010	NEV	67031	NEV	67051	CAN	67065	MAR	67083	NEV
67012	NEV	67032	CAN	67052	REN	67066	MAR	67084	NEV
67013	NEV	67033	NEV	67053	MAR	67067	MAR	67085	REN
67014	NEV	67035	CAN	67054	REN	67068	NEV	67086	NEV
67015	MAR	67038	CAN	67055	MAR	67069	NEV	67087	NEV
67016	NEV	67041	NEV	67056	MAR	67070	NEV	67088	REN
67017	NEV	67042	NEV	67057	MAR	67071	NEV	67089	NEV
67019	MAR	67043	NEV	67058	MAR	67072	NEV	67090	NEV
67020	NEV	67044	NEV	67059	MAR	67073	REN	67097	NEV
67022	NEV	67045	CAN						

BB 67200 CLASS   B–B

With the introduction of the LGV Sud Est route it was realised that some locomotives would be required that could operate over the line on ballast trains and in emergencies. The line does not have conventional signalling and thus 30 BB 67000 were modified and fitted with cab signalling and radio. All are based at Nevers but have duties that take them close to the LGV route. However some stray away from time to time.

Built: 1980–84.

New liveried BB 66700 class No. BB 66702 stands at Venissieux Depot on 30/03/86. [E. Dunkling

BB 67300 class No. 67330 arrives at St. Germain des Fosses with an express from Lyon on 03/09/82. [G.J. Wiseman

Builders: Brissonneau and Lotz/MTE.
Engine: SEMT 16PA4 of 1470 kW.
Transmission: Electric.
Train Heating: None.   **Weight in Full Working Order**: 80 tonnes.
Maximum Tractive Effort: 304/202 kN.**Length over Buffers**: 17090 mm.
Driving Wheel Dia.: 1150 mm.   **Max. Speed**: 90/130 km/h.

Multiple Working fitted (also with 67000, 68000, 68500). Press button emergency brake. Snowplough fitted. Some have rail greasers.

67201 (67006)	NEV	67211 (67108)	NEV	67221 (67081)	NEV
67202 (67011)	NEV	67212 (67122)	NEV	67222 (67078)	NEV
67203 (67040)	NEV	67213 (67115)	NEV	67223 (67082)	NEV
67204 (67034)	NEV	67214 (67123)	NEV	67224 (67103)	NEV
67205 (67037)	NEV	67215 (67102)	NEV	67225 (67029)	NEV
67206 (67030)	NEV	67216 (67121)	NEV	67226 (67028)	NEV
67207 (67021)	NEV	67217 (67117)	NEV	67227 (67007)	NEV
67208 (67008)	NEV	67218 (67112)	NEV	67228 (67039)	NEV
67209 (67118)	NEV	67219 (67091)	NEV	67229 (67004)	NEV
67210 (67120)	NEV	67220 (67114)	NEV	67230 (67018)	NEV

BB 67300 CLASS   B–B

As mentioned under BB 67000 one of that class was modified to provide e.t.h. and became the prototype for this class. The production series featured other improvements such as three-phase transmission. Later, rather than build more new locomotives , some 67000 were converted and the old numbers of these are shown below. A mixed traffic locomotive with some fitted out for working push-pull trains.

Built: 1967–79.
Builders: Brissonneau and Lotz/MTE.
Engine: SEMT 16PA4 of 1764 kW.
Transmission: Three-phase electric.
Train Heating: Electric   **Weight in Full Working Order**: 80 tonnes.
Maximum Tractive Effort: 304/202 kN.**Length over Buffers**: 17090 mm.
Driving Wheel Dia.: 1150 mm.   **Max. Speed**: 90/140 km/h.

Multiple working fitted within class and with BB 67400. Odd examples have snowploughs and rail geasers. 67330–4/40 once fitted out for working the "Catalan Talgo". 20 locomotives are push and pull fitted.

67301	CBY	67319	TSP	67337	CBY	67355	CBY	67373	CAN
67302	CBY	67320	TSP	67338	CBY	67356	NAN	67374	CAN
67303	TSP	67321	TSP	67339	CBY	67357	CBY	67375	CAN
67304	TSP	67322	TSP	67340	CBY	67358	CBY	67376	CAN
67305	NAN	67323	TSP	67341	NAN	67359	CBY	67377	CAN
67306	NAN	67324	TSP	67342	CBY	67360	CBY	67378	CAN
67307	CBY	67325	CBY	67343	CBY	67361	CBY	67379	CAN
67308	CBY	67326	CBY	67344	NAN	67362	CBY	67380	CAN
67309	TSP	67327	CBY	67345	NAN	67363	CBY	67381	CAN
67310	TSP	67328	CBY	67346	CBY	67364	CBY	67382	CAN
67311	TSP	67329	CBY	67347	CBY	67365	CBY	67383	CAN
67312	TSP	67330	CBY	67348	NAN	67366	CBY	67384	CAN
67313	TSP	67331	CBY	67349	NAN	67367	CBY	67385	CAN
67314	TSP	67332	CBY	67350	CBY	67368	CBY	67386	NAN
67315	TSP	67333	CBY	67351	NAN	67369	CBY	67387	NAN
67316	TSP	67334	CBY	67352	NAN	67370	CBY	67388	NAN
67317	TSP	67335	CBY	67353	CBY	67371	CAN	67389	NAN
67318	TSP	67336	CBY	67354	NAN	67372	CAN	67390	NAN

Old Numbers:

67371 (67082)	67375 (67116)	67379 (67113)	67383 (67119)	67387 (67124)
67372 (67107)	67376 (67095)	67380 (67100)	67384 (67099)	67388 (67096)
67373 (67110)	67377 (67104)	67381 (67111)	67385 (67105)	67389 (67093)
67374 (67109)	67378 (67098)	67382 (67101)	67386 (67094)	67390 (67291)

Name:67348 LA BERNERIE EN RETZ

BB 67400 CLASS   B–B

This class is the one a British visitor usually encounters first as they usually haul the boat trains from Calais and Boulogne. The class represents another development of the BB 67000 series. Three-phase transmission and e.t.h. fitted they can be found virtually all over the system on freight and passenger duties. One gear ratio.

Built: 1969–75.
Builders: Brissonneau and Lotz/MTE.
Engine: SEMT 16PA4 of 1765 kW.
Transmission: Three-phase electric.

Train Heating: Electric	**Weight in Full Working Order:** 83 tonnes.
Maximum Tractive Effort: 285 kN.	**Length over Buffers:** 1709 mm.
Driving Wheel Dia.: 1260 mm.	**Max. Speed:** 140 km/h.

Multiple working fitted within class and with BB 67300. 47 locomotives are push and pull fitted. 67419/537 have 160 km/h bogies. Some have snowploughs and/or rail greasers.

67401	NEV	67447	CAN	67494	MAR	67540	NEV	67586	STR
67402	BOR	67448	CAN	67495	MAR	67541	MAR	67587	STR
67403	CAN	67449	NEV	67496	MAR	67542	NEV	67588	STR
67404	CAN	67450	NEV	67497	NIM	67543	MAR	67589	LON
67405	MAR	67451	CAN	67498	STR	67544	CAN	67590	LON
67406	REN	67452	NEV	67499	STR	67545	MAR	67591	LON
67407	REN	67453	NEV	67500	REN	67546	NEV	67592	LON
67408	BOR	67454	CAN	67501	NIM	67547	NEV	67593	LON
67409	CLY	67455	NEV	67502	NIM	67548	NEV	67594	LON
67410	REN	67456	CLY	67503	NIM	67549	MAR	67595	LON
67411	CLY	67457	MAR	67504	NIM	67550	CAN	67596	LON
67412	BOR	67458	NEV	67505	NEV	67551	CAN	67597	LON
67413	CLY	67459	NEV	67506	NEV	67552	CAN	67598	LON
67414	LON	67460	NEV	67507	NEV	67553	CAN	67599	LON
67415	CAN	67461	CAN	67508	CAN	67554	NIM	67600	LON
67416	LON	67462	NEV	67509	CAN	67555	NIM	67601	LON
67417	REN	67463	NEV	67510	STR	67556	NIM	67602	LON
67418	NAN	67464	CLY	67511	STR	67557	NIM	67603	STR
67419	REN	67465	CAN	67512	STR	67558	NIM	67604	LON
67420	REN	67466	CAN	67513	STR	67559	NIM	67605	LON
67421	REN	67467	CAN	67514	STR	67560	NIM	67606	LON
67422	REN	67468	BOR	67515	STR	67561	NIM	67607	LON
67423	CLY	67469	NEV	67516	STR	67562	NEV	67608	LON
67424	REN	67470	BOR	67517	STR	67563	CAN	67609	LON
67425	REN	67471	BOR	67518	STR	67564	NEV	67610	LON
67426	REN	67472	CAN	67519	STR	67565	MAR	67611	LIM
67427	REN	67473	BOR	67520	STR	67566	NEV	67612	LIM
67428	REN	67474	CAN	67521	STR	67567	NEV	67613	LIM
67429	BOR	67475	REN	67522	STR	67568	NIM	67614	LIM
67430	REN	67476	REN	67523	STR	67569	STR	67615	LIM
67431	REN	67477	REN	67524	STR	67570	STR	67616	LIM
67432	REN	67478	NEV	67525	NEV	67571	STR	67617	LON
67433	CLY	67479	NEV	67526	CLY	67572	STR	67618	LON
67434	REN	67480	BOR	67527	CAN	67573	NEV	67619	LON
67435	BOR	67481	CAN	67528	NEV	67574	NEV	67620	LON
67436	BOR	67482	MAR	67529	CAN	67575	MAR	67621	LIM
67437	BOR	67483	LON	67530	CLY	67576	NEV	67622	LIM
67438	LON	67484	MAR	67531	NEV	67577	NEV	67623	LIM
67439	LON	67485	LON	67532	CAN	67578	NEV	67624	LIM
67440	CAN	67486	LON	67533	CAN	67579	NEV	67625	LIM
67441	CAN	67488	MAR	67534	CAN	67580	MAR	67626	LIM
67442	REN	67489	MAR	67535	NEV	67581	NEV	67627	LIM
67443	BOR	67490	CAN	67536	REN	67582	CLY	67628	LIM
67444	NIM	67491	CAN	67537	REN	67583	CLY	67629	LIM
67445	REN	67492	CAN	67538	REN	67584	CLY	67631	LIM
67446	CAN	67493	MAR	67539	REN	67585	NEV	67632	LIM

Names: 67428 DREUSE, 67530 ROMILLY-SUR-SEINE, 67580 MONTPELLIER, 67581 NEVERS, 67620 ABBEVILLE.

CC 6500 class No. CC 6558 having just arrived at Lyon Part-Dieu with a special train from Nice on 01/10/86. [Peter Fox

BB 9300 class No. BB 9325 at Bordeaux with a Paris–Tarbes working on 05/07/83. [Mike Godfrey

A1AA1A 68000 class No. 68001 at Vierzon on 14/04/83. [Brian Garvin

BB 71000 class No. BB 71028 at Tours St. Pierre Depot on 14/04/83. [E. Dunkling

A1AA1A 68000 CLASS

A1A–A1A

Introduced at the same time as BB 67000 but fitted with steam boilers for passenger train work. These have since been removed or isolated and the class is mostly relegated to freight work. Some BB 68500 have been re-engined and added to this series probably using the redundant engines ex BR Class 48 (re-engined class 47) Nos. D 1702–6, since the engines from these locos were sold to the SNCF.

Built: 1963–68.
Builders: CAFL/CEM/Fives-Lille.
Engine: Sulzer 12LVA24 of 1950 kW.
Transmission: Electric.
Train Heating: None.
Maximum Tractive Effort: 298 kN.
Driving Wheel Dia.: 1250 mm.

Weight in Full Working Order: 104 tonnes.
Length over Buffers: 17920 mm.
Max. Speed: 130 km/h.

Multiple working fitted. Rail greasers.

68001	NAN	68018	NAN	68036	PLP	68053	TSP	68070	TSP
68002	CLY	68019	CLY	68037	PLP	68054	TSP	68071	TSP
68003	CLY	68020	PLP	68038	PLP	68055	TSP	68072	TSP
68004	CLY	68021	PLP	68039	PLP	68056	TSP	68073	TSP
68005	CLY	68022	PLP	68040	PLP	68057	TSP	68074	TSP
68006	NAN	68023	PLP	68041	PLP	68058	TSP	68075	TSP
68007	NAN	68024	PLP	68042	PLP	68059	TSP	68076	TSP
68008	PLP	68025	NAN	68043	NAN	68060	TSP	68077	TSP
68009	NAN	68026	CLY	68044	NAN	68061	CLY	68078	TSP
68010	PLP	68027	CAN	68045	CLY	68063	TSP	68079	TSP
68011	NAN	68029	NAN	68046	PLP	68064	TSP	68080	TSP
68012	NAN	68030	PLP	68047	PLP	68065	TSP	68081	TSP
68013	NAN	68031	CLY	68048	NAN	68066	TSP	68082	TSP
68014	NAN	68032	CLY	68049	TSP	68067	TSP	68083	TSP
68015	PLP	68033	NAN	68050	TSP	68068	TSP	68084	CLY
68016	CLY	68034	CLY	68051	TSP	68069	TSP	68085	CLY
68017	CLY	68035	NAN	68052	TSP				

Old Numbers:

68005 (68501)	68082 (68529)	68083 (68525)	68084 (68508)	68085 (68510)

A1AA1A 68500 CLASS

A1A–A1A

Similar to A1AA1A 68000 but with a different engine. Mainly used on freights on the Paris–Chalindrey–Belfort line.

Built: 1964–68.
Builders: CAFL/CEM/SACM/Fives-Lille.
Engine: AGO 12DSHR of 1985 kW.
Transmission: Electric.
Train Heating: None.
Maximum Tractive Effort: 298 kN.
Driving Wheel Dia.: 1250 mm.

Weight in Full Working Order: 102 tonnes.
Length over Buffers: 17920 mm.
Max. Speed: 130 km/h.

68502	CLY	68507	CLY	68514	CLY	68519	CLY	68524	CLY
68503	CLY	68509	CLY	68515	CLY	68520	CLY	68526	CLY
68504	CLY	68511	CLY	68516	CLY	68521	CLY	68527	CLY
68505	CLY	68512	CLY	68517	CLY	68522	CLY	68528	CLY
68506	CLY	68513	CLY	68518	CLY	68523	CLY		

BB 71000 CLASS

B–B

With the demise of class C 61000 this is the only diesel left that sports coupling rods. Split for many years between Tours St.Pierre and Nevers depots, all are now congregated at the latter and are earmarked for early withdrawal. they are used on short trip workings and can be found working at Vichy and St. Germain des Fosses.

CC 14100 class No. CC 14131 passing Thionville station with a local steelworks service on 25/05/85.
[Roger Sanders

Dual voltage BB 20200 class No. BB 20209 in the new grey and yellow livery is seen on Mulhouse stabling point on 30/09/86.
[Peter Fox

CC 72000 class No. CC 72092 leaves Clermont Ferrand with the 08.27 to Paris Gare de Lyon on 08/06/86.
[Michael Jacob

RTG unit No. 2059/60 waits to leave Paris St. Lazare with the 14.34 to Caen on 01/11/80.
[Michael Jacob

Built: 1965–66.
Builders: Fives-Lille/CFD.
Engine: Poyaud V12 of 615 kW.
Transmission: Mechanical.
Train Heating: None.
Maximum Tractive Effort:　　　kN.
Driving Wheel Dia.: 860 mm.

Weight in Full Working Order: 55 tonnes.
Length over Buffers: 11850 mm.
Max. Speed: 80 km/h.

71002	NEV	71006	NEV	71010	NEV	71012	NEV	71014	NEV
71003	NEV	71007	NEV	71011	NEV	71013	NEV	71015	NEV
71005	NEV	71009	NEV						

CC 72000 CLASS   C–C

This is SNCF's really big diesel and features monomotor bogies with gear selection. The low gear is intended for freight work but is also used when hauling passenger trains over difficult routes such as Lyon–Roanne–St.Germain des Fosses. After surmounting the gradients out of Lyon the express gear ratio is selected whilst station duties are undertaken at Roanne.

Built: 1967–74.
Builders: Alsthom/SACM/SEMT.
Engine: AGO V16ESHR of 2650 kW. (Pielstick 12PA6280 of 3530 kWt).
Transmission: Electric.
Train Heating: Electric.
Maximum Tractive Effort: 362/189 kN.
Driving Wheel Dia.: 1140 mm.

Weight in Full Working Order: 114/118 tonnes.
Length over Buffers: 20190 mm.
Max. Speed: 85/160 (85/140*)km/h.

Electro-pneumatic braking. Press button emergency direct air brake. Driver-guard communication (not *).

72001*	VEN	72020*	REN	72038	CLY	72057	REN	72075†	REN
72002*	VEN	72021	VEN	72039	CLY	72058	VEN	72076	CLY
72003*	VEN	72022	CLY	72040	VEN	72059	REN	72077	CLY
72004*	VEN	72023	VEN	72041	CLY	72060	CLY	72078	CLY
72005*	VEN	72024	REN	72042	VEN	72061	VEN	72079	CLY
72006*	VEN	72025	VEN	72043	CLY	72062	VEN	72080	CLY
72007*	VEN	72026	CLY	72044	REN	72063	REN	72081	REN
72008*	VEN	72027	CLY	72045	CLY	72064	VEN	72082	CLY
72009*	VEN	72028	CLY	72047	CLY	72065	REN	72083	VEN
72010*	VEN	72029	CLY	72048	CLY	72066	REN	72084	VEN
72011*	VEN	72030	CLY	72049	CLY	72067	VEN	72085	VEN
72012*	VEN	72031	CLY	72050	VEN	72068	CLY	72086	VEN
72013*	VEN	72032	REN	72051	CLY	72069	REN	72087	VEN
72014*	VEN	72033	REN	72052	REN	72070	VEN	72088	VEN
72015*	VEN	72034	VEN	72053	CLY	72071	VEN	72089	REN
72016*	REN	72035	VEN	72054	VEN	72072	REN	72090	VEN
72017*	REN	72036	CLY	72055	VEN	72073	REN	72091	REN
72018*	REN	72037	REN	72056	VEN	72074	CLY	72092	VEN
72019*	REN								

Names:

72001 ANNONAY	72056 LA BOURBOULE
72010 BOURG ARGENTAL	72063 LA ROCHE-SUR-YON
72015 PARAY-LE-MONIAL	72071 MARSEILLE
72022 VILLEMOMBLE	72072 SAINT-MALO
72024 PONT AUDEMER	72074 TOULON
72026 LUXEUIL-LES-BAINS	72077 NOISY-LE-SEC
72036 THANN	72080 MULHOUSE
72043 LANGRES	72082 PROVINS
72052 LA BAULE	72090 BELFORT
72053 MAUTAUBAN DE BRETAGNE	

DIESEL RAILCARS AND MULTIPLE UNITS
X 2100 & XR 6000 CLASSES
SINGLE UNITS (B–B) & TRAILERS

A relatively new diesel railcar ordered to help replace the ageing X 2400 and X 3800 series. The units are able to work hauling R 6000 trailers and can work in multiple with X 2100 & X 2800. Livery is Massif Central blue and white. Some sets were built specially for area councils and are painted in special liveries. Numbers of these sets are prefixed with a 9.

X 2100 RAILCARS. XABD (DMBC).

Built: 1980–83.
Builder: ANF/Schneider.
Engine: Saurer S1DHR of 440 kW.　　**Transmission:** Hydraulic. Voith.
Seats: 8F 48S 1L.　　**Weight:** 44 tonnes.
Length over couplings: 22400 mm.　　**Max. Speed:** 140 km/h.

Hydrodynamic braking. Flange lubricator. Multiple working.

X 2101	TOU	X 2112	REN	X 2123	LYV	X 2135	REN	X 2145	REN
X 2102	TOU	X 2113	NAN	X 2124	LYV	X 2136	REN	X 2146	REN
X 2103	TOU	X 2114	NAN	X 2125	LYV	X 2137	REN	X 2147	REN
X 2104	TOU	X 2115	NAN	X 2126	LYV	X 2138	REN	X 2148	REN
X 2105	TOU	X 2116	LYV	X 2127	LYV	X 2139	REN	X 2149	REN
X 2106	TOU	X 2117	NAN	X 2128	LYV	X 2140	REN	X 2150	REN
X 2107	TOU	X 2118	NAN	X 2129	LYV	X 2141	REN	X 92101	NAN
X 2108	LYV	X 2119	LYV	X 2130	LYV	X 2142	REN	X 92102	NAN
X 2109	LYV	X 2120	LYV	X 2131	LYV	X 2143	REN	X 92103	NAN
X 2110	REN	X 2121	LYV	X 2132	LYV	X 2144	REN	X 92104	TOU
X 2111	LYV	X 2122	LYV	X 2134	REN				

Names: (also including X 2200 class).

X 2132	DUNIÈRES.	X 92201	NORMANDIE
X 92101-3	PAYS DE LA LOIRE	X 92202	MIDI PYRÉNÉES
X 92104	MIDI PYRÉNÉES	X 92203	LANGUEDOC ROUSSILLON

X 6000 TRAILERS. XRAB (TCO).

Built: 1980–83.
Builder: ANF/Schneider.
Seats: 16F 60S 1L.　　**Weight:** 24 tonnes.
Length over couplings: 24040 mm.　　**Max. Speed:** 140 km/h.

XR 6001	TOU	XR 6022	CLE	XR 6043	CLE	XR 6065	TOU	XR 6087	LIM
XR 6002	LIM	XR 6023	CLE	XR 6044	CLE	XR 6066	TOU	XR 6088	LYV
XR 6003	LIM	XR 6024	CLE	XR 6045	CLE	XR 6067	TOU	XR 6089	LYV
XR 6004	LIM	XR 6025	CLE	XR 6046	CLE	XR 6068	TOU	XR 6090	LYV
XR 6005	LIM	XR 6026	CLE	XR 6047	CLE	XR 6070	LIM	XR 6091	LYV
XR 6006	LIM	XR 6027	TOU	XR 6048	CLE	XR 6071	LIM	XR 6092	LYV
XR 6007	LIM	XR 6028	TOU	XR 6049	LYV	XR 6072	LIM	XR 6093	LYV
XR 6008	TOU	XR 6029	TOU	XR 6050	LYV	XR 6073	LIM	XR 6094	LYV
XR 6009	CLE	XR 6030	TOU	XR 6051	LYV	XR 6074	LIM	XR 6095	LYV
XR 6010	CLE	XR 6031	CLE	XR 6052	LYV	XR 6075	LIM	XR 6096	LYV
XR 6011	CLE	XR 6032	CLE	XR 6053	LYV	XR 6076	LIM	XR 6097	LYV
XR 6012	CLE	XR 6033	CLE	XR 6054	TOU	XR 6077	LIM	XR 6098	LYV
XR 6013	CLE	XR 6034	CLE	XR 6055	TOU	XR 6078	LIM	XR 6099	LYV
XR 6014	CLE	XR 6035	CLE	XR 6056	TOU	XR 6079	LIM	XR 6100	LYV
XR 6015	CLE	XR 6036	CLE	XR 6058	TOU	XR 6080	LIM	XR 96001	NAN
XR 6016	CLE	XR 6037	CLE	XR 6059	TOU	XR 6081	LIM	XR 96002	NAN
XR 6017	CLE	XR 6038	CLE	XR 6060	TOU	XR 6082	LIM	XR 96003	NAN
XR 6018	CLE	XR 6039	CLE	XR 6061	TOU	XR 6083	LIM	XR 96004	TOU
XR 6019	CLE	XR 6040	CLE	XR 6062	TOU	XR 6084	LIM	XR 96005	SOT
XR 6020	CLE	XR 6041	CLE	XR 6063	TOU	XR 6085	LIM	XR 96006	TOU
XR 6021	CLE	XR 6042	CLE	XR 6064	TOU	XR 6086	LIM		

A pair of TGV units is seen at Paris Sud-Est depot on 04/07/86. [Richard Pegler

A refurbished RGP set No. X 2728/XR 7728 at Marseille Blancarde depot on 01/07/86 having recently been used on the ''Alpazur'' service. [Mike Godfrey

A pair of X 2100 diesel railcars at Nantes depot with X 92101 in "Pays de la Loire" yellow livery nearest the camera and a standard liveried version in the background. (13/04/83).

[Michael Jacob

The latest SNCF diesel railcar is the X 2200 class. This view of No. X 2201 shows the "CONSEIL REGIONAL LIMOUSIN" marking on the white roof band.

[Patrick Olivain (SNCF, CAV)

X 2200 & XR 6100/6200 CLASSES SINGLE UNITS (B–B) & TRAILERS

An improved version of X 2100 but painted in a new red and white livery. Work with trailers of the XR 6100 series.

X 2200 RAILCARS. XABD (DMBCO).

Built: 1985 onwards.
Builder: ANF/Schneider.
Engine: Saurer S1DHR of 440 kW.   **Transmission:** Hydraulic. (Voith)
Seats: 8F 48S 1L.   **Weight:** 44 tonnes.
Length over couplings: 22400 mm.   **Max. Speed:** 140 km/h.

Hydrodynamic braking. Flange lubricator. Multiple working.

X 2201	LIM	X 2214	LIM	X 2227	X 2240	X 2252	
X 2202	LYV	X 2215	LIM	X 2228	X 2241	X 2253	
X 2203	LIM	X 2216	LIM	X 2229	X 2242	X 2254	
X 2204	LIM	X 2217	LIM	X 2230	X 2243	X 2255	
X 2205	TSP	X 2218	LIM	X 2231	X 2244	X 2256	
X 2206	TSP	X 2219	LIM	X 2232	X 2245	X 2257	
X 2207	TSP	X 2220		X 2233	X 2246	X 92201	SOT
X 2208	TSP	X 2221	LIM	X 2234	X 2247	X 92202	TOU
X 2209	TSP	X 2222	LIM	X 2235	X 2248	X 92203	LYV
X 2210	TSP	X 2223		X 2236	X 2249	X 92204	
X 2211	TSP	X 2224		X 2237	X 2250	X 92205	
X 2212	TSP	X 2225		X 2238	X 2251	X 92206	
X 2213	TSP	X 2226		X 2239			

X 6100 TRAILERS. XRAB (TCO).

Built: 1985 onwards.
Builder: ANF/Schneider.
Seats: 16F 60S 1L.   **Weight:** 24 tonnes.
Length over couplings: 24040 mm.   **Max. Speed:** 140 km/h.

XR 6101	REN	XR 6115	LYV	XR 6129	TSP	XR 6143	XR 6157
XR 6102	REN	XR 6116	LYV	XR 6130	TSP	XR 6144	XR 6158
XR 6103	REN	XR 6117	LIM	XR 6131	TSP	XR 6145	XR 6159
XR 6104	REN	XR 6118	LIM	XR 6132	TSP	XR 6146	XR 6160
XR 6105	REN	XR 6119	LIM	XR 6133	TSP	XR 6147	XR 6161
XR 6106	REN	XR 6120	LIM	XR 6134	TSP	XR 6148	XR 6162
XR 6107	REN	XR 6121	LIM	XR 6135	TSP	XR 6149	XR 6163
XR 6108	REN	XR 6122	LIM	XR 6136	TSP	XR 6150	XR 6164
XR 6109	REN	XR 6123	LIM	XR 6137	TSP	XR 6151	XR 6165
XR 6110	REN	XR 6124	LIM	XR 6138	LYV	XR 6152	XR 6166
XR 6111	LIM	XR 6125	LIM	XR 6139	LYV	XR 6153	XR 6167
XR 6112	LIM	XR 6126	LIM	XR 6140		XR 6154	XR 6168
XR 6113	LYV	XR 6127	LIM	XR 6141		XR 6155	XR 6169
XR 6114	LYV	XR 6128	LIM	XR 6142		XR 6156	XR 6170

X 6200 TRAILERS. On order. Details not yet available.

XR 6201	XR 6211	XR 6221	XR 6231	XR 6241
XR 6202	XR 6212	XR 6222	XR 6232	XR 6242
XR 6203	XR 6213	XR 6223	XR 6233	XR 6243
XR 6204	XR 6214	XR 6224	XR 6234	XR 6244
XR 6205	XR 6215	XR 6225	XR 6235	XR 6245
XR 6206	XR 6216	XR 6226	XR 6236	XR 6246
XR 6207	XR 6217	XR 6227	XR 6237	XR 6247
XR 6208	XR 6218	XR 6228	XR 6238	XR 6248
XR 6209	XR 6219	XR 6229	XR 6239	XR 6249
XR 6210	XR 6220	XR 6230	XR 6240	XR 6250

X 2400 CLASS   SINGLE UNITS (B–B)

These powerful railcars are now in the process of being withdrawn. They operate as single cars or hauling several standard trailers.

XABDP (DMBSO).

Built: 1951–56.
Builder: Decauville Aîné.
Engine: Two Renault 517G of 255 kW each (X 2401–2469), Two Saurer BZDS-B of 255 kWeach (X 2470–2478).
Transmission: Mechanical.
Seats: 12F 56S 1L.
Length over couplings: 27733 mm.
Weight: 43 tonnes.
Max. Speed: 120 km/h.

X 2401	REN	X 2412	LIM	X 2422	REN	X 2431	LIM	X 2465	REN
X 2402	REN	X 2413	LIM	X 2423	REN	X 2435	REN	X 2466	LIM
X 2403	REN	X 2414	LIM	X 2424	LIM	X 2440	REN	X 2467	LIM
X 2404	LIM	X 2415	LIM	X 2425	LIM	X 2448	LIM	X 2468	LIM
X 2405	LIM	X 2416	REN	X 2426	LIM	X 2457	REN	X 2469	LIM
X 2407	REN	X 2417	REN	X 2427	REN	X 2459	REN	X 2471	LIM
X 2408	LIM	X 2419	REN	X 2428	LIM	X 2463	REN	X 2478	LIM
X 2411	REN	X 2421	REN	X 2429	REN	X 2464	REN		

X 2700 CLASS   2-CAR UNITS (B–2+2–2)

Still known as RGPs (Rame à Grand Parcours) denoting that they were built for long distance services over non-electrified lines. Such services have now been taken over by turbotrains or are now loco-hauled, so the class is in the process of being withdrawn. The power cars from sets 2707/14 have been rebuilt at Bordeaux works into an ultrasonic rail testing unit which is numbered X 2700 and known as "V4".

XBD+XRADx (DMBSO–DTCO).

Built: 1954–55.
Builder: Decauville-Aîné.**Engine:** 2 Renault 517G of 250 kW each.
Transmission: Mechanical.
Seats: 48S 1L + 21F 44S 1L.
Length over couplings: 26630 +25530 mm.
Weight: 45 + 32 tonnes.
Max. Speed: 120 km/h.

X 2705	XR 7705	BOR	X 2713	XR 7713	MET	X 2717	XR 7717	BOR
X 2709	XR 7762	BOR	X 2716	XR 7719	BOR	X 2719	XR 7708	BOR

X 2720 & X 2770 CLASSES 2 CAR UNITS (B–2–+2–2)

These two classes are now being modernised and regrouped into one class. X 2720 started off as RGPs but with only one engine. The cabs are being rebuilt to X 2200 standard and a new livery applied similar to that on the X 2200 class. The trailers X 7721–32 have been renumbered X 7757–68 prior to refurbishing and are being renumbered back when refurbished. However they will not necessarily regain their original number. The X 2770 series were former TEE units long since downgraded in use. They will be renumbered in the series X 2739–49 when refurbished.

XBD+XRABx (DMBSO–DTCO).

Built: 1955–56.
Engine: MGO V12SH of 605 kW.
Seats: 60S (56S*) + 24F 52S.
Weight: 53 (48*) + 32 (29–33*) tonnes.
Length over couplings: 27630 + 26050 (26630 +25530*) mm.
Max. Speed: 140 km/h.
Builder: De Dietrich/SACM.
Transmission: Hydraulic.

X 2721	XR 7721	LYV	X 2731	XR 7731	MET	X 2773	XR 7773	LYV
X 2722	XR 7722 r	MET	X 2732	XR 7732	LYV	X 2774	XR 7774	LYV
X 2723	XR 7723 r	MET	X 2733	XR 7733	LYV	X 2775	XR 7775	LYV
X 2724	XR 7724	LYV	X 2734	XR 7734	LYV	X 2776	XR 7776	LYV
X 2725	XR 7725	LYV	X 2735	XR 7735 r	MET	X 2777	XR 7772	LYV
X 2726	XR 7726	LYV	X 2736	XR 7736 r	MET	X 2778	XR 7751	MET
X 2727	XR 7727	LYV	X 2737	XR 7737	LYV	X 2779	XR 7757	LYV
X 2728	XR 7728 r	LYV	X 2738	XR 7738	LYV	X 2780	XR 7780	LYV
X 2729	XR 7729	LYV	X 2771	XR 7771	LYV	X 2781	XR 7781	LYV
X 2730	XR 7730	LYV	X 2772	XR 7777	LYV			

Double Decker Z 5600 class e.m.u. No. 5603 in the new white, blue and red livery,
[Patrick Olivain (SNCF, CAV)

Z2 e.m.u. No. Z 9634/ZR 19634 arrives at Lyon Perrache on 01/10/86.   [Peter Fox

Two Cerdagne line trains are seen at Font Romeu, the one on the left being a refurbished unit and the one on the right an unrefurbished one.   [Peter Heppenstall

Two Z 600 class metre gauge "Savoie" units Nos. Z 605 and Z 607 are seen at St. Gervais on 29/05/84.   [Michael Jacob

X 2400 class diesel railcar No. X 2404 hauling trailer XR 7987 prepares to leave Sarlat on the 15.10 to Libourne on 13/08/84.   [G.J. Wiseman

X 2700 class (RGP) unit No. X 2701 at Bordeaux St. Jean station on 16/04/81.   [Brian Garvin

X 2800 & XR 7300/7800 CLASSES
SINGLE UNITS (B–2) & TRAILERS

These sets are similar to class X 2400 but with more powerful engines and hydraulic transmission. They have all been refurbished and are known as "Massif Central sets", although they do also work elsewhere. On refurbishment the sets were painted blue and white. They can work in multiple with other d.m.u.s.

X 2800 RAILCARS. XABD (DMBCO).

Built: 1957–62.
Builder: Decauville/Renault.
Engine: MGO V12SH of 605 kW.
Transmission: Hydraulic (Maybach).
Seats: 12F 50S 1L.
Weight: 54 tonnes.
Length over couplings: 27730 mm.
Max. Speed: 120 km/h.

X 2801	LIM	X 2826	LYV	X 2850	LYV	X 2874	LYV	X 2897	LYV
X 2802	LYV	X 2827	LYV	X 2851	LIM	X 2875	LIM	X 2898	LYV
X 2803	LYV	X 2828	LYV	X 2852	LYV	X 2876	LIM	X 2899	LYV
X 2804	LIM	X 2829	LYV	X 2853	TOU	X 2877	LYV	X 2900	LIM
X 2805	LIM	X 2830	LYV	X 2854	TOU	X 2878	LYV	X 2901	LIM
X 2806	LYV	X 2831	TOU	X 2855	LYV	X 2879	LIM	X 2902	LIM
X 2807	LYV	X 2832	LIM	X 2856	LYV	X 2880	LIM	X 2903	TOU
X 2808	LIM	X 2833	TOU	X 2857	LIM	X 2881	TOU	X 2904	LIM
X 2809	LIM	X 2834	LYV	X 2858	LYV	X 2882	LIM	X 2905	LIM
X 2810	LYV	X 2835	LYV	X 2859	LYV	X 2883	LIM	X 2906	LIM
X 2811	LYV	X 2836	LYV	X 2860	LYV	X 2884	LIM	X 2907	LIM
X 2812	LIM	X 2837	LYV	X 2861	LIM	X 2885	LYV	X 2908	LIM
X 2813	LIM	X 2838	LYV	X 2862	LYV	X 2886	LIM	X 2909	TOU
X 2814	LIM	X 2839	LIM	X 2863	LYV	X 2887	TOU	X 2910	TOU
X 2815	LIM	X 2840	LYV	X 2864	LYV	X 2888	LIM	X 2911	LYV
X 2816	LYV	X 2841	TOU	X 2865	LIM	X 2889	LIM	X 2912	LYV
X 2817	TOU	X 2842	LYV	X 2866	LYV	X 2890	LIM	X 2913	LYV
X 2818	LYV	X 2843	LYV	X 2867	LIM	X 2891	TOU	X 2914	LYV
X 2819	LYV	X 2844	LYV	X 2868	LYV	X 2892	LIM	X 2915	LIM
X 2820	TOU	X 2845	LYV	X 2869	LYV	X 2893	LYV	X 2916	LYV
X 2822	LIM	X 2846	LYV	X 2870	LYV	X 2894	LYV	X 2917	LYV
X 2823	LYV	X 2847	LIM	X 2871	LIM	X 2895	LYV	X 2918	LIM
X 2824	LYV	X 2848	LYV	X 2872	LIM	X 2896	LYV	X 2919	LIM
X 2825	LYV	X 2849	LIM	X 2873	LYV				

X 7300 TRAILERS. XRABD (TBCO) 12F 65S 1L. 18–20 tonnes. 21190 mm.

These trailers are numbered in the range XR 7301–7581. 82 still in existence, allocated to BOR (17), CAN (1), DIJ (9), LIM (5), LON (3), LYV (12), MOH (9), NAN (7), REN (19). Individual numbers not known.

X 7800 TRAILERS. XRBD (TBSO) 66S 1L or 81S 1L*. 18–20 tonnes. 21190 mm.

These trailers are numbered in the range XR 7801–8018 and XR 8101–8293*. 162 still in existence, allocated to BOR (25), CAN (3), CLE (13), DIJ (9), LIM (15), LON (8), LYV (6), MOH (8), NAN (6), REN (37), TOU (32). Individual numbers not known.

X 3800 CLASS (PICASSO) SINGLE UNITS (B–2)

An SNCF classic diesel railcar known as "Picassos" because of the strange location of the driving cab (on the roof!) and the fact that the driver has to sit side on instead of facing the direction of travel! They were built with one cab as a means of providing a cheap unit that would help to keep branch lines open, the roof cab meaning that the driver did not have to change ends during reversals en route. They are medium powered but can haul trailers. Now being withdrawn but could last in traffic until 1989 depending upon the delivery of new units. Sotteville and Bordeaux depots will be next to lose their allocations.

XBD (DMBSO) or XABD (DMBCO).

Built: 1951–62.
Builder: ANF/De Dietrich/Renault/Saurer.

Two views of the Chemins de Fer de la Provence: CAV-Montmirail diesel railcar No. SY 06 stands at Digne on 03/10/86 having arrived with the 08.40 from Nice. [Peter Fox

Pre-war Renault railcar No. ZZ 6 approaches Colomars with the 17.00 St. Martin du Var–Nice on the same date. [Peter Fox

Engine: Renault 517G of 250 kW.
Transmission: Mechanical.
Seats: 62S (Some 12F 32S 1L). **Weight:** 53 tonnes.
Length over couplings: 27730 mm. **Max. Speed:** 120 km/h.

X 3896, 3900 are fitted out as inspection saloons. X 3997 is also in departmental use.

X 3801	BOR	X 3830	NEV	X 3866	NEV	X 3896	MOH	X 3951	MOH
X 3812	SOT	X 3835	BOR	X 3867	NEV	X 3897	MOH	X 3968	BOR
X 3814	MOH	X 3838	MOH	X 3869	BOR	X 3900	MOH	X 3970	BOR
X 3817	SOT	X 3840	NEV	X 3876	NEV	X 3914	SOT	X 3973	NEV
X 3818	BOR	X 3850	MOH	X 3881	NEV	X 3934	MOH	X 3974	SOT
X 3819	BOR	X 3853	MOH	X 3886	BOR	X 3942	NEV	X 3995	MOH
X 3823	SOT	X 3864	NEV	X 3891	NEV	X 3943	NEV	X 4013	NEV
X 3824	BOR	X 3865	BOR	X 3895	MOH	X 3944	MOH	X 4032	NEV
X 3827	NEV								

X 4300 CLASS 2 CAR UNITS (B–2+2–2)

These two-car d.m.u.s represent the 1960s generation of d.m.u.s. Introduced in 1963 similar units continued to be built until the early 1980s. Their introduction led to mass withdrawals of old units many of which dated from pre-war days. The units now operate with either an XR 8300 or an XR 8500 driving trailer to match demand depending on the proportions of first and second class accommodation required. Formations now tend to be permanent after several years of changes. This class together with the X 4500 are to be refurbished from 1987. Externally the ends will be altered to resemble the refurbished RGPs and the recently-delivered RRR push & pull sets with a sloping front and one large and one small window. X 4372 is expected to be the first of the class in April 1987.

XBD+XRABDx (DMBSO–DTCO).

Built: 1963–70.
Builder: ANF.
Engine: Poyaud of 320 kW.
Transmission: Mechanical.
Seats: 60S 1L+ 12F 69S 1L (24F 49S* 1L). **Weight:** 34 + 23 tonnes.
Length over couplings: 21240 +21240 mm. **Max. Speed:** 120 km/h.

X 4347/85 were withdrawn during 1973. X 4365 became a turbotrain prototype.

X 4301	XR 8301	TSP	X 4326	XR 8316	MET	X 4353	XR 8343	MET
X 4302	XR 8302	TSP	X 4327	XR 8317	MET	X 4354	XR 8524*	MET
X 4303	XR 8557*	NAN	X 4328	XR 8318	MET	X 4355	XR 8345	MET
X 4304	XR 8559*	NAN	X 4329	XR 8540*	NEV	X 4356	XR 8344	TSP
X 4305	XR 8505*	NAN	X 4330	XR 8543*	MET	X 4357	XR 8347	MET
X 4306	XR 8504*	MET	X 4331	XR 8319	MET	X 4358	XR 8581*	MET
X 4307	XR 8507*	TSP	X 4332	XR 8320	MET	X 4359	XR 8568*	MET
X 4308	XR 8303	TSP	X 4333	XR 8544*	NAN	X 4360	XR 8527*	TSP
X 4309	XR 8330	TSP	X 4334	XR 8545*	NAN	X 4361	XR 8576*	TSP
X 4310	XR 8331	TSP	X 4335	XR 8321	TSP	X 4362	XR 8570*	TSP
X 4311	XR 8621*	TSP	X 4336	XR 8322	TSP	X 4363	XR 8577*	MET
X 4312	XR 8306	TSP	X 4337	XR 8554*	NAN	X 4364	XR 8354	MET
X 4313	XR 8309	TSP	X 4338	XR 8536*	MET	X 4365	XR 8356	MET
X 4314	XR 8310	TSP	X 4339	XR 8324	MET	X 4366	XR 8356	MET
X 4315	XR 8311	TSP	X 4340	XR 8325	TSP	X 4367	XR 8362	TSP
X 4316	XR 8312	TSP	X 4341	XR 8326	MET	X 4368	XR 8357	MET
X 4317	XR 8517*	MET	X 4342	XR 8340	MET	X 4369	XR 8361	MET
X 4318	XR 8349	MET	X 4343	XR 8337	MET	X 4370	XR 8355	TSP
X 4319	XR 8519*	MET	X 4344	XR 8342	MET	X 4372	XR 8348	MET
X 4320	XR 8520*	MET	X 4345	XR 8327	MET	X 4373	XR 8518*	MET
X 4321	XR 8521*	MET	X 4346	XR 8555*	TSP	X 4374	XR 8350	MET
X 4322	XR 8313	MET	X 4348	XR 8328	MET	X 4375	XR 8351	MET
X 4323	XR 8314	MET	X 4349	XR 8598*	MET	X 4376	XR 8352	TSP
X 4324	XR 8533*	NAN	X 4350	XR 8329	MET	X 4377	XR 8359	MET
X 4325	XR 8315	MET	X 4352	XR 8339	MET	X 4378	XR 8578*	MET
						X 4379	XR 8588*	TSP

Class X 2800 d.m.u. No. X 2807 at Avignon on 15/04/81.   G.J. Wiseman

Class X 3800 ("Picasso") No. X 4051 arrives at St. Germain des Fosses from Vichy on 03/09/82.
[G.J. Wiseman

X 4380	XR 8580*	MET	X 4406	XR 8506*	NAN	X 4429	XR 8394	MET
X 4381	XR 8582*	MET	X 4407	XR 8626*	TSP	X 4430	XR 8395	TSP
X 4383	XR 8602*	NAN	X 4408	XR 8573*	MET	X 4431	XR 8396	TSP
X 4384	XR 8603*	MET	X 4409	XR 8628*	MET	X 4432	XR 8593*	MET
X 4386	XR 8539*	MET	X 4410	XR 8569*	MET	X 4433	XR 8584*	MET
X 4387	XR 8606*	TSP	X 4411	XR 8532*	MET	X 4434	XR 8523*	MET
X 4388	XR 8607*	MET	X 4412	XR 8631*	NAN	X 4435	XR 8632*	MET
X 4389	XR 8608*	MET	X 4413	XR 8591*	TSP	X 4436	XR 8541*	MET
X 4390	XR 8609*	TSP	X 4414	XR 8558*	MET	X 4437	XR 8597*	MET
X 4391	XR 8610*	MET	X 4415	XR 8586*	MET	X 4438	XR 8418	MET
X 4392	XR 8611*	TSP	X 4416	XR 8381	TSP	X 4439	XR 8531*	MET
X 4393	XR 8612*	MET	X 4417	XR 8382	MET	X 4440	XR 8420	TSP
X 4394	XR 8501*	NAN	X 4418	XR 8383	TSP	X 4441	XR 8421	TSP
X 4395	XR 8549*	MET	X 4419	XR 8587*	MET	X 4442	XR 8422	MET
X 4396	XR 8363	MET	X 4420	XR 8552*	MET	X 4443	XR 8423	MET
X 4397	XR 8560*	MET	X 4421	XR 8526*	MET	X 4444	XR 8424	MET
X 4398	XR 8605*	MET	X 4422	XR 8387	MET	X 4445	XR 8425	MET
X 4399	XR 8613*	TSP	X 4423	XR 8388	MET	X 4446	XR 8426	MET
X 4400	XR 8542*	NAN	X 4424	XR 8386	MET	X 4447	XR 8427	MET
X 4401	XR 8367	TSP	X 4425	XR 8390	MET	X 4448	XR 8428	MET
X 4402	XR 8502*	TSP	X 4426	XR 8391	TSP	X 4449	XR 8429	MET
X 4403	XR 8369	TSP	X 4427	XR 8392	MET	X 4450	XR 8430	MET
X 4404	XR 8366	TSP	X 4428	XR 8393	MET	X 4451	XR 8431	MET
X 4405	XR 8513*	MET						

X 4500 CLASS   2 CAR UNITS (B–2+2–2)

Similar to class X 4300 except fitted with a different engine and slightly heavier.

XBD+XRABx (DMBSO–DTCO).

Built: 1963–70.
Builder: ANF.
Engine: Saurer SDHR of 320 kW.
Transmission: Mechanical.
Seats: 60S 1L + 12F 69S 1L (24F 49S 1L*).**Weight**: 35 + 23 tonnes.
Length over couplings: 21240 + 21240 mm.**Max. Speed**: 120 km/h.

X 4562 was withdrawn in 1973. X 4624/5/6 were rebuilt from X 4351/71/85 respectively.

X 4501	XR 8503*	SOT	X 4523	XR 8360	LON	X 4545	XR 8601*	LON
X 4502	XR 8365	MAR	X 4524	XR 8534*	LON	X 4546	XR 8385	LON
X 4503	XR 8509*	LON	X 4525	XR 8535*	LON	X 4547	XR 8379	LON
X 4504	XR 8304	LON	X 4526	XR 8364	LON	X 4548	XR 8561*	LON
X 4505	XR 8511*	LON	X 4527	XR 8537*	LON	X 4549	XR 8353	MAR
X 4506	XR 8615*	LON	X 4528	XR 8538*	LON	X 4550	XR 8563*	LON
X 4507	XR 8370	LON	X 4529	XR 8371	LON	X 4551	XR 8553*	LON
X 4508	XR 8346	LON	X 4530	XR 8416	LON	X 4552	XR 8334	MAR
X 4509	XR 8512*	SOT	X 4531	XR 8529*	MAR	X 4553	XR 8565*	LON
X 4510	XR 8514*	LON	X 4532	XR 8546*	LON	X 4554	XR 8564*	MAR
X 4511	XR 8515*	LON	X 4533	XR 8547*	SOT	X 4555	XR 8567*	LON
X 4512	XR 8432	LON	X 4534	XR 8548*	LON	X 4556	XR 8551*	SOT
X 4513	XR 8522*	LON	X 4535	XR 8307	LON	X 4557	XR 8571*	LON
X 4514	XR 8414	LON	X 4536	XR 8530*	LON	X 4558	XR 8572*	MAR
X 4515	XR 8332	MAR	X 4537	XR 8368	MAR	X 4559	XR 8372	LON
X 4516	XR 8525*	MAR	X 4538	XR 8508*	LON	X 4560	XR 8622*	MAR
X 4517	XR 8389	LON	X 4539	XR 8510*	LON	X 4561	XR 8575*	SOT
X 4518	XR 8629*	LON	X 4540	XR 8550*	SOT	X 4563	XR 8341	LON
X 4519	XR 8528*	SOT	X 4541	XR 8566*	MAR	X 4564	XR 8630*	LON
X 4520	XR 8604*	MAR	X 4542	XR 8333	MAR	X 4565	XR 8583*	LON
X 4521	XR 8614*	MAR	X 4543	XR 8562*	SOT	X 4566	XR 8585*	LON
X 4522	XR 8419	LON	X 4544	XR 8335	MAR	X 4567	XR 8380	LON

X 4568	XR 8384	LON	X 4588	XR 8617*	SOT	X 4608	XR 8633*	MAR
X 4569	XR 8413	LON	X 4589	XR 8618*	LON	X 4609	XR 8634*	LON
X 4570	XR 8589*	SOT	X 4590	XR 8619*	SOT	X 4610	XR 8635*	SOT
X 4571	XR 8590*	LON	X 4591	XR 8620*	SOT	X 4611	XR 8636*	MAR
X 4572	XR 8378	LON	X 4592	XR 8305	LON	X 4612	XR 8637*	MAR
X 4573	XR 8592*	LON	X 4593	XR 8641*	SOT	X 4613	XR 8638*	MAR
X 4574	XR 8412	LON	X 4594	XR 8627*	SOT	X 4614	XR 8639*	MAR
X 4575	XR 8594*	LON	X 4595	XR 8624*	LON	X 4615	XR 8640*	MAR
X 4576	XR 8308	LON	X 4596	XR 8625*	LON	X 4616	XR 8516*	MAR
X 4577	XR 8596*	LON	X 4597	XR 8397	LON	X 4617	XR 8407	LON
X 4578	XR 8417	LON	X 4598	XR 8398	LON	X 4618	XR 8358	LON
X 4579	XR 8338	LON	X 4599	XR 8399	LON	X 4619	XR 8409	LON
X 4580	XR 8599*	SOT	X 4600	XR 8556*	LON	X 4620	XR 8410	LON
X 4581	XR 8600*	LON	X 4601	XR 8401	LON	X 4621	XR 8411	LON
X 4582	XR 8373	LON	X 4602	XR 8402	LON	X 4622	XR 8574*	MAR
X 4583	XR 8374	LON	X 4603	XR 8323	LON	X 4623	XR 8433	MAR
X 4584	XR 8375	LON	X 4604	XR 8404	LON	X 4624	XR 8336	MAR
X 4585	XR 8376	LON	X 4605	XR 8405	LON	X 4625	XR 8623*	SOT
X 4586	XR 8377	LON	X 4606	XR 8406	LON	X 4626	XR 8408	LON
X 4587	XR 8616*	LON	X 4607	XR 8415	LON			

X 4630 CLASS   2-CAR UNITS (B–2+2–2)

A development of the preceding classes but featuring hydraulic transmission. Many of the Nantes units are being refurbished internally and reliveried in all over white with a blue band below the windows and carry "Pays de la Loire" markings. They have not been renumbered.

XBD+XRABx (DMBSO–DTCO).

Built: 1974–77.
Builder: ANF.
Engine: Saurer SDHR of 320 kW.
Transmission: Hydraulic. Voith.
Seats: 60S 1L + 24F 49S 1L (89S 1L*).   **Weight:** 39 + 24 tonnes.
Length over couplings: 21240 + 21240 mm.**Max. Speed:** 120 km/h.

X 4630	XR 8642	LON	X 4658	XR 8447	NEV	X 4686	XR 8683	LYV
X 4631	XR 8643	NEV	X 4659	XR 8448	NEV	X 4687	XR 8684	LYV
X 4632	XR 8644	NEV	X 4660	XR 8657	NEV	X 4688	XR 8685	NAN
X 4633	XR 8645	NEV	X 4661	XR 8658	NEV	X 4689	XR 8686	LYV
X 4634	XR 8646	NEV	X 4662	XR 8659	NEV	X 4690	XR 8687	LYV
X 4635	XR 8647	NEV	X 4663	XR 8660	NEV	X 4691	XR 8688	LYV
X 4636	XR 8648	NAN	X 4664	XR 8661	NEV	X 4692	XR 8689	LYV
X 4637	XR 8649	NAN	X 4665	XR 8662	NEV	X 4693	XR 8690	LYV
X 4638	XR 8650	NEV	X 4666	XR 8663	NEV	X 4694	XR 8691	LYV
X 4639	XR 8651	NEV	X 4667	XR 8664	NEV	X 4695	XR 8692	LYV
X 4640	XR 8652	NEV	X 4668	XR 8665	NAN	X 4696	XR 8693	LON
X 4641	XR 8653	NEV	X 4669	XR 8666	LYV	X 4697	XR 8694	LON
X 4642	XR 8654	NEV	X 4670	XR 8667	NAN	X 4698	XR 8695	LYV
X 4643	XR 8655	NEV	X 4671	XR 8668	NAN	X 4699	XR 8696	LYV
X 4644	XR 8656	NEV	X 4672	XR 8669	NAN	X 4700	XR 8697	LYV
X 4645	XR 8434	NEV	X 4673	XR 8670	NAN	X 4701	XR 8698	LYV
X 4646	XR 8435	NEV	X 4674	XR 8671	NAN	X 4702	XR 8699	LYV
X 4647	XR 8436	NEV	X 4675	XR 8672	NAN	X 4703	XR 8700	LYV
X 4648	XR 8437	NEV	X 4676	XR 8673	NAN	X 4704	XR 8701	LYV
X 4649	XR 8444	NEV	X 4677	XR 8674	LYV	X 4705	XR 8702	LYV
X 4650	XR 8439	NEV	X 4678	XR 8675	NAN	X 4706	XR 8703	LYV
X 4651	XR 8440	NEV	X 4679	XR 8676	LYV	X 4707	XR 8704	LYV
X 4652	XR 8441	NEV	X 4680	XR 8677	NAN	X 4708	XR 8705	LYV
X 4653	XR 8442	NEV	X 4681	XR 8678	NAN	X 4709	XR 8706	LYV
X 4654	XR 8443	NEV	X 4682	XR 8679	NAN	X 4710	XR 8707	LYV
X 4655	XR 8445	NEV	X 4683	XR 8680	LYV	X 4711	XR 8708	LYV
X 4656	XR 8438	NAN	X 4684	XR 8681	NAN	X 4712	XR 8709	LYV
X 4657	XR 8446	NEV	X 4685	XR 8682	LYV	X 4713	XR 8710	NEV

X 4714	XR 8711	LON	X 4724	XR 8721	LON	X 4734	XR 8731	NEV
X 4715	XR 8712	LYV	X 4725	XR 8722	NEV	X 4735	XR 8732	NEV
X 4716	XR 8713	LON	X 4726	XR 8723	NEV	X 4736	XR 8733	NEV
X 4717	XR 8714	LON	X 4727	XR 8724	NEV	X 4737	XR 8734	NEV
X 4718	XR 8715	LON	X 4728	XR 8725	NEV	X 4738	XR 8735	NEV
X 4719	XR 8716	LON	X 4729	XR 8726	NEV	X 4739	XR 8736	NEV
X 4720	XR 8717	LON	X 4730	XR 8727	NEV	X 4740	XR 8737	NEV
X 4721	XR 8718	LON	X 4731	XR 8728	NEV	X 4741	XR 8738	NEV
X 4722	XR 8719	LON	X 4732	XR 8729	LON	X 4742	XR 8739	NEV
X 4723	XR 8720	LON	X 4733	XR 8730	NEV	X 94630	X 98630	MAR

X 4750 CLASS   2-CAR UNITS (B–2+2–2)

The last of the two car sets to appear were this series having a more powerful engine and a higher maximum speed.

XBD+XRABx (DMBSO–DTSO).

Built: 1977–81.
Builder: ANF.
Engine: Saurer of 440 kW.
Transmission: Hydraulic. Voith.
Seats: 60S 1L + 24F 49S 1L.   **Weight:** 39 + 24 tonnes.
Length over couplings: 21240 + 21240 mm. **Max. Speed:** 140 km/h.

X 4750	XR 8750	MET	X 4764	XR 8764	SOT	X 4777	XR 8777	MET
X 4751	XR 8751	MET	X 4765	XR 8765	SOT	X 4778	XR 8778	MET
X 4752	XR 8752	MET	X 4766	XR 8766	SOT	X 4779	XR 8779	MET
X 4753	XR 8753	MET	X 4767	XR 8767	SOT	X 4780	XR 8780	MET
X 4754	XR 8754	MET	X 4768	XR 8768	SOT	X 4781	XR 8781	MET
X 4755	XR 8755	SOT	X 4769	XR 8769	SOT	X 4782	XR 8782	MET
X 4756	XR 8756	SOT	X 4770	XR 8770	SOT	X 4783	XR 8783	MET
X 4757	XR 8757	SOT	X 4771	XR 8771	SOT	X 4784	XR 8784	MET
X 4758	XR 8758	SOT	X 4772	XR 8772	SOT	X 4785	XR 8785	MET
X 4759	XR 8759	SOT	X 4773	XR 8773	SOT	X 4786	XR 8786	MET
X 4760	XR 8760	SOT	X 4774	XR 8774	SOT	X 4787	XR 8787	MET
X 4761	XR 8761	SOT	X 4775	XR 8775	MET	X 4788	XR 8788	MET
X 4762	XR 8762	SOT	X 4776	XR 8776	MET	X 4789	XR 8789	SOT
X 4763	XR 8763	SOT						

X 4790 CLASS   2-CAR UNITS (B–2+2–2)

As class 4750 but with better seats and finished off in orange/grey livery for the Paris–Granville services. However this service has become so popular that it has now gone loco-hauled and the units are being used on other services in the Basse-Normandie region.

XBD+XRABx (DMBSO–DTSO).

Built: 1977–81.
Builder: ANF.
Engine: Saurer.
Transmission: Hydraulic. Voith.
Seats: 47S 1L + 24F 36S 1L.   **Weight:** 39 + 24 tonnes.
Length over couplings: 21240 + 21240 mm. **Max. Speed:** 140 km/h.

X 4790	XR 8790	BAGNOLES-DE-L'ORNE	SOT	X 4794	XR 8794	L'AIGLE	SOT
X 4791	XR 8791	GRANVILLE	SOT	X 4795	XR 8795	FLERS	SOT
X 4792	XR 8792	VILLEDIEU-LES-POEULES	SOT	X 4796	XR 8796	ARGENTAN	SOT
X 4793	XR 8793	VIRE	SOT				

X 4900 CLASS   3-CAR UNITS (B–2+2–2+2–B)

These are 3-car versions of X 4630 and are intended for long distance work as a higher standard of comfort is provided. They are in the modern blue and white d.m.u. livery as applied to X 2800 and are known as EATs ("Élements automoteurs triples").

XBD+XRAB+XBD (DMBSO–TCO–DMBSO).

Built: 1975–77.
Builder: ANF.
Engine: Saurer SHDR of 320 kW.
Transmission: Hydraulic. Voith.
Seats: 47S 1L + 32F 28S 1L + 47S 1L. **Weight:** 39 + 28 + 39 tonnes.
Length over couplings: 21240 + 20750 + 21240 mm.**Max. Speed:** 140 km/h.

X 4901 XR 8901X 4902 VEYNES	MAR		X 4915 XR 8908X 4916	SOT
X 4903 XR 8902X 4904 MANOSQUE	MAR		X 4917 XR 8909X 4918	SOT
X 4905 XR 8903X 4906	MAR		X 4919 XR 8910X 4920 *	SOT
X 4907 XR 8904X 4908	MAR		X 4921 XR 8911X 4922	SOT
X 4909 XR 8905X 4910	MAR		X 4923 XR 8912X 4924	SOT
X 4911 XR 8906X 4912	MAR		X 4925 XR 8913X 4926	SOT
X 4913 XR 8907X 4914	SOT			

* Name: SOTTEVILLE-LES-ROUEN

X 94750 CLASS   2-CAR UNITS (B–2+2–2)

These 2-car units belong to the postal authorities and are used exclusively as mail grains. There is plenty of stowage space and the units are finished off in a special livery with maroon replacing the usual red of other units. All are based at Sotteville for work over a wide area of Northern France and can often be seen at Lille and Caen as well as Paris.

XP+XRPx (DMP–TP).

Built: 1978–79.
Builder: ANF.
Engine: Saurer of 440 kW.
Transmission: Hydraulic. Voith.
Seats: None.   **Weight:** 39 + 23 tonnes.
Length over couplings: 21240 + 21240 mm.**Max. Speed:** 140 km/h.

X 94750	XR 98750	SOT		X 94753	XR 98753	SOT		X 94756 XR 98756 SOT
X 94751	XR 98751	SOT		X 94754	XR 98754	SOT		X 94757 XR 98757 SOT
X 94752	XR 98752	SOT		X 94755	XR 98755	SOT		

X 4630 class 2-car d.m.u. Nos. X 4713/XR 8710 at Bellegarde with a local for Évian on 14/04/81.
G.J. Wiseman

SMALL DIESEL SHUNTERS

These small diesel shunters are known as tractors *(locotracteurs)* in France and canbe operated by station staff as well as locomen.

Y 2200 CLASS   B

This series of light shunters is mostly in use as depots/works shunters. They rarely get out on main line but some are allowed to and are fitted with scrapers to ensure the operation of track circuits. Some are fitted with a form of automatic coupling for shunting work. The class is now being withdrawn.

Built: 1956–60.
Builder: Moyse/Decauville/Alsthom.
Engine: Poyaud 2BDT of 44 kW (* Agron 40 kW).
Transmission: Mechanical.
Train Heating: None
Maximum Tractive Effort: kN.
Wheel Dia.: 1050 mm.
Weight in Full Working Order: 16 tonnes.
Length over Buffers: 5780 mm.
Max. Speed: 50 km/h.

Y 2203 STR	Y 2243 CLY	Y 2272 ACH	Y 2308 CBY	Y 2321* PLV
Y 2206 CLY	Y 2247 CLY	Y 2280 LIM	Y 2309 AVI	Y 2322* MET
Y 2208 CLY	Y 2255 PLP	Y 2282 HEN	Y 2310 VEN	Y 2330* NAN
Y 2209 VEN	Y 2257 NIM	Y 2285 TAR	Y 2311 CBY	Y 2331* SOT
Y 2215 CLY	Y 2259 MAR	Y 2291 STR	Y 2314 AVI	Y 2334* NIM
Y 2219 STR	Y 2260 CBY	Y 2296 CAN	Y 2315 MAR	Y 2336* AVI
Y 2237 NEV	Y 2261 VEN	Y 2298 CBY	Y 2316 AVI	Y 2337* MAR
Y 2240 DIJ	Y 2266 NEV	Y 2301 MAR	Y 2317 VEN	Y 2340* MAR
Y 2242 CBY	Y 2267 PLP	Y 2306 SOT	Y 2319 LMS	

Y 2400 CLASS   B

Another small light duty shunter with almost all being used within depot and carriage siding limits.

Built: 1962–69.
Builder: Decauville.
Engine: Agron 45 kW.
Transmission: Mechanical.
Train Heating: None
Maximum Tractive Effort: kN.
Wheel Dia.: 1050 mm.
Weight in Full Working Order: 17 tonnes.
Length over Buffers: 7180 mm.
Max. Speed: 50 km/h.

Y 2401 ACH	Y 2426 CBY	Y 2452 VEN	Y 2478 DIJ	Y 2500 MAR	
Y 2403 TOU	Y 2427 NEV	Y 2453 AVI	Y 2479 DIJ	Y 2501 MAR	
Y 2404 LIM	Y 2428 AVI	Y 2454 CBY	Y 2480 LON	Y 2502 TSP	
Y 2405 TAR	Y 2429 SOT	Y 2455 VEN	Y 2481 ACH	Y 2503 MAR	
Y 2406 NEV	Y 2431 SOT	Y 2456 MAR	Y 2482 TOU	Y 2504 NIM	
Y 2407 TOU	Y 2433 PSO	Y 2459 MAR	Y 2483 VSG	Y 2505 REN	
Y 2409 CLY	Y 2435 NEV	Y 2460 VSG	Y 2484 AVI	Y 2506 VSG	
Y 2412 NEV	Y 2436 TSP	Y 2461 DIJ	Y 2485 LIM	Y 2507 VSG	
Y 2413 CBY	Y 2438 DIJ	Y 2464 MAR	Y 2486 REN	Y 2508 TAR	
Y 2414 CBY	Y 2439 NIM	Y 2465 VSG	Y 2487 TSP	Y 2509 VEN	
Y 2415 NEV	Y 2440 VEN	Y 2466 NEV	Y 2488 NEV	Y 2510 LIM	
Y 2416 LIM	Y 2441 DIJ	Y 2467 CBY	Y 2490 REN	Y 2511 NIM	
Y 2417 NIM	Y 2442 PLP	Y 2468 NIM	Y 2492 ACH	Y 2512 CBY	
Y 2418 LIM	Y 2443 PSO	Y 2469 NIM	Y 2493 LIM	Y 2513 VEN	
Y 2419 LIM	Y 2444 AVI	Y 2470 MAR	Y 2494 BOR	Y 2514 VSG	
Y 2420 PSO	Y 2445 MAR	Y 2472 VSG	Y 2495 NEV	Y 2515 VEN	
Y 2421 TOU	Y 2447 MAR	Y 2473 VEN	Y 2496 CLY	Y 2516 CBY	
Y 2422 ACH	Y 2448 VEN	Y 2474 CBY	Y 2497 STR	Y 2517 CBY	
Y 2423 BOR	Y 2449 DIJ	Y 2475 VEN	Y 2498 STR	Y 2518 VEN	
Y 2424 NIM	Y 2450 VEN	Y 2476 CBY	Y 2499 CLY	Y 2519 CBY	
Y 2425 VEN	Y 2451 MAR	Y 2477 NEV			

Y 2300 class No. Y 2330 at Nantes shed on 13/04/83. The rail scrapers *("frotteurs")* areclearly visible close to the wheels.
[Brian Garvin

Y 2400 class No. Y 2425 at Lyon Venisssieux depot.
[E. Dunkling

Y 5100 CLASS B

Another small, light duty shunter virtually all being used as depot/workshops shunters. Being so small they can often fit on a turntable or traverser with a locomotive or carriage.

Built: 1960–63.
Builder: De Dietrich.
Engine: Poyaud 4PYT of 81 kW.
Transmission: Hydraulic.
Train Heating: None
Maximum Tractive Effort: kN.
Driving Wheel Dia.: 1050 mm.
Weight in Full Working Order: 20 tonnes.
Length over Buffers: 718 mm.
Max. Speed: 18 km/h.

Y 5101	VEN	Y 5116	NEV	Y 5131	STR	Y 5146	PLP	Y 5162	PLV
Y 5102	LMS	Y 5117	LON	Y 5132	THI	Y 5147	LON	Y 5201	REN
Y 5103	ACH	Y 5118	LEN	Y 5133	MOH	Y 5148	LEN	Y 5202	PLP
Y 5104	LAR	Y 5119	LON	Y 5134	LEN	Y 5149	LMS	Y 5203	PLP
Y 5105	ACH	Y 5120	NAN	Y 5135	LEN	Y 5150	LMS	Y 5204	TAR
Y 5106	PSO	Y 5121	SOT	Y 5136	LEN	Y 5151	VSG	Y 5205	LIM
Y 5107	LAB	Y 5122	ACH	Y 5137	CAN	Y 5152	VSG	Y 5207	VEN
Y 5108	TOU	Y 5123	BOR	Y 5138	REN	Y 5154	LEN	Y 5208	NIM
Y 5109	PSO	Y 5124	LIM	Y 5139	LMS	Y 5155	PLP	Y 5209	STR
Y 5110	LIM	Y 5125	LAB	Y 5140	VSG	Y 5156	LEN	Y 5210	STR
Y 5111	NIM	Y 5126	TOU	Y 5141	VEN	Y 5157	LON	Y 5211	LON
Y 5112	MAR	Y 5127	PSO	Y 5142	NEV	Y 5158	PLP	Y 5212	LEN
Y 5113	LEN	Y 5128	MET	Y 5143	PLV	Y 5159	THI	Y 5213	TSP
Y 5114	DIJ	Y 5129	MET	Y 5144	MET	Y 5160	NAN	Y 5214	PLP
Y 5115	VSG	Y 5130	MOH	Y 5145	CLY	Y 5161	AVI	Y 5215	LEN

Y 6200 CLASS B

This is another class that can be considered to be in departmental use as most of them seem to be used on short ballast trains etc. Series now being withdrawn.

Built: 1949–58.
Builders: Billard/Moyse.
Engine: Poyaud 6PDT of 132 kW.
Transmission: Electric.
Train Heating: None
Maximum Tractive Effort: kN.
Wheel Dia.: 1050 mm.
Weight in Full Working Order: 30 tonnes.
Length over Buffers: 8900 mm.
Max. Speed: 60 km/h.

Y 6201	MET	Y 6219	LAB	Y 6244	PSO	Y 6262	MAR	Y 6281	TSP
Y 6202	LIM	Y 6220	TSP	Y 6245	VEN	Y 6264	VEN	Y 6286	VSG
Y 6203	BOR	Y 6223	STR	Y 6246	MOH	Y 6267	MAR	Y 6288	MET
Y 6205	MET	Y 6225	PLP	Y 6248	VEN	Y 6269	MAR	Y 6289	PLV
Y 6206	TOU	Y 6226	LON	Y 6252	VSG	Y 6270	TOU	Y 6292	MOH
Y 6207	NEV	Y 6229	PSO	Y 6255	VEN	Y 6271	TOU	Y 6293	LMS
Y 6211	ACH	Y 6230	LEN	Y 6261	NEV	Y 6276	TOU	Y 6297	CLY
Y 6213	VSG	Y 6235	VSG						

Y 6300 & Y 6400 CLASSES B

These low powered shunters are found all over France on light shunting duties and works trains.

Built: 1949–58.
Builders: Billard (Y 6300), De Dietrich/Decauville/SNCF (Y 6400).
Engine: Poyaud 6PDT of 132 kW.
Transmission: Electric.
Train Heating: None
Maximum Tractive Effort: kN.
Wheel Dia.: 1050 mm.
Weight in Full Working Order: 30 tonnes.
Length over Buffers: 8900 mm.
Max. Speed: 60 km/h.

Y 5100 class No. Y 5122 at Achères Depot on 10/04/83.   [E. Dunkling

Y 6200 class No. Y 6255 at Lyon Venissieux Depot on 30/03/83.   [E. Dunkling

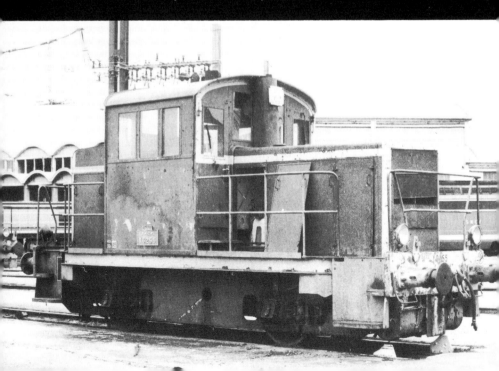

Y 6300 CLASS

Y 6302	NEV	Y 6308	NEV	Y 6315	LAR	Y 6320	PLV	Y 6324	VSG
Y 6303	CBY	Y 6311	LEN	Y 6316	LAR	Y 6321	MET	Y 6327	CLY
Y 6304	VEN	Y 6312	LEN	Y 6317	LAR	Y 6322	MOH	Y 6329	STR
Y 6307	VSG	Y 6314	LAR	Y 6318	LAR	Y 6323	MOH	Y 6330	LEN

Y 6400 CLASS

Y 6401	MET	Y 6445	TOU	Y 6494	VSG	Y 6538	BOR	Y 6582	LAB
Y 6404	PLP	Y 6446	TOU	Y 6495	CBY	Y 6539	TOU	Y 6583	TOU
Y 6405	MOH	Y 6449	LAB	Y 6496	REN	Y 6540	TAR	Y 6585	SOT
Y 6407	LEN	Y 6450	TOU	Y 6497	NEV	Y 6542	LIM	Y 6587	PSO
Y 6408	PLP	Y 6451	TSP	Y 6498	CBY	Y 6543	NEV	Y 6588	TSP
Y 6409	LEN	Y 6452	BOR	Y 6499	LMS	Y 6545	TSP	Y 6590	VEN
Y 6410	LEN	Y 6454	CAN	Y 6500	DIJ	Y 6546	NAN	Y 6591	LAB
Y 6411	CLY	Y 6456	ACH	Y 6501	MET	Y 6547	SOT	Y 6594	PLP
Y 6412	MET	Y 6457	REN	Y 6502	MOH	Y 6548	LMS	Y 6595	CAN
Y 6413	ACH	Y 6458	CAN	Y 6503	CLY	Y 6549	REN	Y 6596	REN
Y 6414	NAN	Y 6459	SOT	Y 6504	CLY	Y 6550	SOT	Y 6599	LMS
Y 6416	ACH	Y 6460	CAN	Y 6506	PLP	Y 6552	LEN	Y 6600	SOT
Y 6417	BOR	Y 6461	REN	Y 6507	LEN	Y 6553	MET	Y 6601	SOT
Y 6418	DIJ	Y 6463	ACH	Y 6508	LEN	Y 6554	BOR	Y 6604	CAN
Y 6419	LIM	Y 6464	NAN	Y 6509	LON	Y 6555	REN	Y 6605	REN
Y 6421	CBY	Y 6465	BOR	Y 6510	LEN	Y 6556	LEN	Y 6606	PLP
Y 6422	VEN	Y 6466	ACH	Y 6511	DIJ	Y 6557	LON	Y 6607	PSO
Y 6423	VSG	Y 6467	CAN	Y 6512	VEN	Y 6559	LMS	Y 6608	TSP
Y 6424	CBY	Y 6468	VSG	Y 6513	VSG	Y 6560	PLP	Y 6609	LAB
Y 6425	CBY	Y 6472	MAR	Y 6514	DIJ	Y 6561	PLP	Y 6610	SOT
Y 6426	VSG	Y 6473	NIM	Y 6517	MAR	Y 6562	BOR	Y 6612	BOR
Y 6428	VEN	Y 6474	NIM	Y 6518	MAR	Y 6563	MOH	Y 6613	PSO
Y 6429	VEN	Y 6475	NIM	Y 6519	MAR	Y 6564	CLY	Y 6614	LON
Y 6430	VEN	Y 6476	NIM	Y 6520	MAR	Y 6565	VSG	Y 6615	PSO
Y 6431	MOH	Y 6477	NIM	Y 6521	REN	Y 6566	MOH	Y 6616	PSO
Y 6432	MOH	Y 6478	CLY	Y 6522	SOT	Y 6567	PLP	Y 6617	LAB
Y 6433	CLY	Y 6479	AVI	Y 6523	SOT	Y 6569	PLP	Y 6618	MAR
Y 6435	MOH	Y 6480	NIM	Y 6524	VEN	Y 6571	PLV	Y 6619	TAR
Y 6436	STR	Y 6482	VEN	Y 6525	CAN	Y 6573	LON	Y 6620	SOT
Y 6437	BOR	Y 6483	VSG	Y 6527	SOT	Y 6574	CBY	Y 6621	SOT
Y 6438	PSO	Y 6485	DIJ	Y 6528	SOT	Y 6575	PLP	Y 6622	REN
Y 6439	BOR	Y 6487	VEN	Y 6531	SOT	Y 6576	LEN	Y 6623	LEN
Y 6440	TOU	Y 6488	VEN	Y 6532	NAN	Y 6577	LAB	Y 6624	SOT
Y 6441	BOR	Y 6489	DIJ	Y 6533	CAN	Y 6578	BOR	Y 6625	NAN
Y 6442	TOU	Y 6490	DIJ	Y 6535	CAN	Y 6580	DIJ	Y 6626	LEN
Y 6443	TOU	Y 6491	MAR	Y 6536	TOU	Y 6581	PSO	Y 6627	LON
Y 6444	LIM	Y 6493	DIJ	Y 6537	LIM				

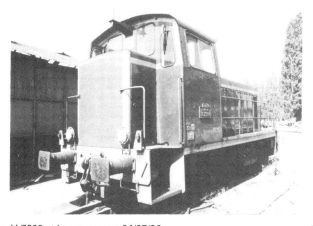

Y 7100 class No. Y 7299 at Longueau on 04/07/86.

Richard Pegler

Y 7100 CLASS   B

The Y 6xxx series were built after World War Two and virtually continued pre-war designs. The Y 7100 series was a completely fresh design and featured hydraulic transmission. However this form of transmission was dropped for future classes after Y 7192 had been converted to mechanical transmission and renumbered Y 7001.

Built: 1958–62.
Builder: Billard/Decauville.
Engine: Poyaud 6PYT of 150 kW.
Transmission: Hydraulic.
Train Heating: None
Maximum Tractive Effort: 73 kN.
Wheel Dia.: 1050 mm.

Weight in Full Working Order: 32 tonnes.
Length over Buffers: 8940 mm.
Max. Speed: 54 km/h.

Y 7101	MOH	Y 7143	LIM	Y 7185	ACH	Y 7228	MAR	Y 7270	VEN
Y 7102	MOH	Y 7144	MET	Y 7186	HEN	Y 7229	AVI	Y 7271	PLP
Y 7103	MET	Y 7145	DIJ	Y 7187	LIM	Y 7230	NIM	Y 7272	LEN
Y 7104	MET	Y 7146	LEN	Y 7188	LEN	Y 7231	MOH	Y 7273	LON
Y 7105	NIM	Y 7147	LON	Y 7189	ACH	Y 7232	MET	Y 7274	PLP
Y 7106	NIM	Y 7148	DIJ	Y 7190	MOH	Y 7233	MET	Y 7275	MAR
Y 7107	LEN	Y 7149	SOT	Y 7191	LEN	Y 7234	DIJ	Y 7276	VEN
Y 7108	PLP	Y 7150	PLP	Y 7193	LON	Y 7235	VEN	Y 7277	AVI
Y 7109	SOT	Y 7151	NEV	Y 7194	MOH	Y 7236	LEN	Y 7278	VEN
Y 7110	SOT	Y 7152	PLP	Y 7195	MET	Y 7237	LEN	Y 7279	CBY
Y 7111	MOH	Y 7153	TSP	Y 7196	MOH	Y 7238	LEN	Y 7280	VSG
Y 7112	MET	Y 7154	TAR	Y 7197	VEN	Y 7239	TAR	Y 7281	SOT
Y 7113	MOH	Y 7155	NIM	Y 7198	LON	Y 7240	LIM	Y 7282	SOT
Y 7114	MOH	Y 7156	VEN	Y 7199	PLP	Y 7241	HEN	Y 7283	LON
Y 7115	MOH	Y 7157	NIM	Y 7200	MET	Y 7242	NIM	Y 7284	PLP
Y 7116	MOH	Y 7158	MET	Y 7201	MOH	Y 7243	AVI	Y 7285	LEN
Y 7117	MOH	Y 7159	NEV	Y 7202	SOT	Y 7244	AVI	Y 7286	PLP
Y 7118	SOT	Y 7160	TSP	Y 7203	SOT	Y 7245	MET	Y 7287	MAR
Y 7119	MAR	Y 7161	LEN	Y 7204	MOH	Y 7246	MET	Y 7288	MAR
Y 7120	NIM	Y 7162	ACH	Y 7205	MOH	Y 7247	MET	Y 7289	VEN
Y 7121	NIM	Y 7163	TSP	Y 7206	LON	Y 7248	MOH	Y 7290	MOH
Y 7122	LEN	Y 7164	BOR	Y 7207	PLP	Y 7249	VSG	Y 7291	MOH
Y 7123	LEN	Y 7165	ACH	Y 7208	NIM	Y 7250	DIJ	Y 7292	SOT
Y 7124	LON	Y 7166	ACH	Y 7209	NIM	Y 7251	LON	Y 7293	ACH
Y 7125	MET	Y 7167	VEN	Y 7210	LON	Y 7252	LEN	Y 7294	SOT
Y 7126	LON	Y 7168	TSP	Y 7211	PLP	Y 7253	LON	Y 7295	ACH
Y 7127	LEN	Y 7169	HEN	Y 7212	BOR	Y 7254	NEV	Y 7296	LEN
Y 7128	SOT	Y 7170	SOT	Y 7213	LIM	Y 7255	HEN	Y 7297	LEN
Y 7129	ACH	Y 7171	MET	Y 7214	NEV	Y 7256	NEV	Y 7298	LON
Y 7130	SOT	Y 7172	MET	Y 7215	VEN	Y 7257	TSP	Y 7299	LON
Y 7131	NIM	Y 7173	NIM	Y 7216	LEN	Y 7258	NIM	Y 7300	VSG
Y 7132	MET	Y 7174	LEN	Y 7217	LEN	Y 7259	MAR	Y 7301	CBY
Y 7133	MET	Y 7175	NIM	Y 7218	SOT	Y 7260	MAR	Y 7302	VSG
Y 7134	MET	Y 7176	NIM	Y 7219	TSP	Y 7261	MAR	Y 7303	AVI
Y 7135	MET	Y 7177	MAR	Y 7220	LIM	Y 7262	MET	Y 7304	MAR
Y 7136	MOH	Y 7178	CAN	Y 7221	NEV	Y 7263	MOH	Y 7305	NIM
Y 7137	MAR	Y 7179	DIJ	Y 7222	NEV	Y 7264	MET	Y 7306	NIM
Y 7138	MAR	Y 7180	PSO	Y 7223	NEV	Y 7265	HEN	Y 7307	MAR
Y 7139	NIM	Y 7181	NIM	Y 7224	PLP	Y 7266	TSP	Y 7308	VSG
Y 7140	AVI	Y 7182	MAR	Y 7225	LON	Y 7267	LIM	Y 7309	DIJ
Y 7141	MAR	Y 7183	LIM	Y 7226	CAN	Y 7268	NIM	Y 7310	VSG
Y 7142	MAR	Y 7184	LEN	Y 7227	ACH	Y 7269	ACH		

Y 7400 CLASS   B

After succesful trials the mechanical transmission applied to 7001 became standard and the production run lasted nearly 10 years. They are found all over the network on a variety of shunting and trip duties. The original green livery is now giving way to the yellow livery first applied to the Y 8000 series.

Built: 1959/1963–72.
Builder: Decauville/De Dietrich.
Engine: Poyaud 6PYT of 150 kW.
Transmission: Mechanical.
Train Heating: None
Maximum Tractive Effort: 73 kN.
Wheel Dia.: 1050 mm.

Weight in Full Working Order: 32 tonnes.
Length over Buffers: 8940 mm.
Max. Speed: 60 km/h.

No.	Code	No.	Code	No.	Code	No.	Code	No.	Code
Y 7001	ACH	Y 7457	ACH	Y 7514	PLP	Y 7571	PLV	Y 7628	PSO
Y 7401	PLV	Y 7458	PLP	Y 7515	LIM	Y 7572	VSG	Y 7629	PSO
Y 7402	PLP	Y 7459	NIM	Y 7516	ACH	Y 7573	LIM	Y 7630	PSO
Y 7403	PLV	Y 7460	NIM	Y 7517	ACH	Y 7574	BOR	Y 7631	BOR
Y 7404	PLV	Y 7461	VEN	Y 7518	STR	Y 7575	CBY	Y 7632	BOR
Y 7405	PLV	Y 7462	MAR	Y 7519	CAN	Y 7576	DIJ	Y 7633	CLY
Y 7406	LON	Y 7463	VEN	Y 7520	STR	Y 7577	CLY	Y 7634	STR
Y 7407	REN	Y 7464	NEV	Y 7521	CLY	Y 7578	STR	Y 7635	LEN
Y 7408	LEN	Y 7465	CBY	Y 7522	CLY	Y 7579	STR	Y 7636	LEN
Y 7409	REN	Y 7466	AVI	Y 7523	CLY	Y 7580	STR	Y 7637	PLP
Y 7410	REN	Y 7467	PLV	Y 7524	CLY	Y 7581	SOT	Y 7638	REN
Y 7411	ACH	Y 7468	REN	Y 7525	LEN	Y 7582	CAN	Y 7639	ACH
Y 7412	TSP	Y 7469	VSG	Y 7526	LEN	Y 7583	ACH	Y 7640	LAB
Y 7413	BOR	Y 7470	ACH	Y 7527	TSP	Y 7584	CAN	Y 7641	VSG
Y 7414	TOU	Y 7471	PLV	Y 7528	BOR	Y 7585	LON	Y 7642	VEN
Y 7415	TSP	Y 7472	VSG	Y 7529	CBY	Y 7586	LEN	Y 7643	NEV
Y 7416	TSP	Y 7473	PLP	Y 7530	VSG	Y 7587	LEN	Y 7644	VEN
Y 7417	DIJ	Y 7474	PLP	Y 7531	NEV	Y 7588	LEN	Y 7645	NIM
Y 7418	DIJ	Y 7475	LIM	Y 7532	NIM	Y 7589	AVI	Y 7646	NEV
Y 7419	VSG	Y 7476	LIM	Y 7533	NEV	Y 7590	NIM	Y 7647	LIM
Y 7420	NEV	Y 7477	NEV	Y 7534	STR	Y 7591	CBY	Y 7648	TSP
Y 7421	NEV	Y 7478	DIJ	Y 7535	STR	Y 7592	BOR	Y 7649	PSO
Y 7422	VSG	Y 7479	NIM	Y 7536	STR	Y 7593	LIM	Y 7650	PSO
Y 7423	VEN	Y 7480	AVI	Y 7537	STR	Y 7594	TSP	Y 7651	PSO
Y 7424	AVI	Y 7481	REN	Y 7538	LEN	Y 7595	ACH	Y 7652	CLY
Y 7425	MAR	Y 7482	DIJ	Y 7539	PLP	Y 7596	DIJ	Y 7653	NAN
Y 7426	NIM	Y 7483	LON	Y 7540	REN	Y 7597	DIJ	Y 7654	VEN
Y 7427	NIM	Y 7484	LEN	Y 7541	TSP	Y 7598	CBY	Y 7655	PLP
Y 7428	AVI	Y 7485	BOR	Y 7542	CBY	Y 7599	CLY	Y 7656	LON
Y 7429	NIM	Y 7486	BOR	Y 7543	VEN	Y 7600	STR	Y 7657	PLP
Y 7430	NEV	Y 7487	NEV	Y 7544	MAR	Y 7601	REN	Y 7658	LEN
Y 7431	MAR	Y 7488	VSG	Y 7545	NIM	Y 7602	NAN	Y 7659	ACH
Y 7432	PLV	Y 7489	NIM	Y 7546	CLY	Y 7603	REN	Y 7660	ACH
Y 7433	VSG	Y 7490	NIM	Y 7547	CLY	Y 7604	LAB	Y 7661	CAN
Y 7434	NEV	Y 7491	STR	Y 7548	STR	Y 7605	NAN	Y 7662	DIJ
Y 7435	DIJ	Y 7492	PLV	Y 7549	PLV	Y 7606	LEN	Y 7663	DIJ
Y 7436	VSG	Y 7493	PSO	Y 7550	LON	Y 7607	PLP	Y 7664	NEV
Y 7437	PLV	Y 7494	LON	Y 7551	TOU	Y 7608	LEN	Y 7665	NEV
Y 7438	PLV	Y 7495	BOR	Y 7552	TSP	Y 7609	VEN	Y 7666	NIM
Y 7439	LEN	Y 7496	NEV	Y 7553	CBY	Y 7610	VEN	Y 7667	MAR
Y 7440	TSP	Y 7497	DIJ	Y 7554	DIJ	Y 7611	AVI	Y 7668	NIM
Y 7441	TSP	Y 7498	CBY	Y 7555	MAR	Y 7612	BOR	Y 7669	PLP
Y 7442	TSP	Y 7499	MAR	Y 7556	STR	Y 7613	BOR	Y 7670	PSO
Y 7443	BOR	Y 7500	CBY	Y 7557	STR	Y 7614	BOR	Y 7671	LAB
Y 7444	LEN	Y 7501	PLP	Y 7558	STR	Y 7615	BOR	Y 7672	BOR
Y 7445	PLP	Y 7502	DIJ	Y 7559	STR	Y 7616	VSG	Y 7673	BOR
Y 7446	CBY	Y 7503	CBY	Y 7560	TOU	Y 7617	VSG	Y 7674	PLV
Y 7447	REN	Y 7504	NIM	Y 7561	TOU	Y 7618	VSG	Y 7675	CLY
Y 7448	NAN	Y 7505	NIM	Y 7562	VSG	Y 7619	NEV	Y 7676	ACH
Y 7449	NAN	Y 7506	VSG	Y 7563	VSG	Y 7620	PLV	Y 7677	PLP
Y 7450	REN	Y 7507	LEN	Y 7564	STR	Y 7621	CLY	Y 7678	PLP
Y 7451	VEN	Y 7508	NIM	Y 7565	STR	Y 7622	ACH	Y 7679	PLP
Y 7452	VEN	Y 7509	NEV	Y 7566	CLY	Y 7623	CLY	Y 7680	REN
Y 7453	VEN	Y 7510	LON	Y 7567	CLY	Y 7624	STR	Y 7681	NAN
Y 7454	NEV	Y 7511	LON	Y 7568	REN	Y 7625	BOR	Y 7682	ACH
Y 7455	PLP	Y 7512	VEN	Y 7569	LAR	Y 7626	LIM	Y 7683	BOR
Y 7456	LON	Y 7513	ACH	Y 7570	NAN	Y 7627	DIJ	Y 7684	LIM

Y 7400 class No. Y 7431 at Marseille Blancarde on 31/03/86. [E. Dunkling

Y 8000 class No. Y 8110 at Charleville-Mézières station on 22/02/85. [E. Dunkling

Y 7685	TOU	Y 7726	BOR	Y 7767	LIM	Y 7808	LAB	Y 7849	VSG
Y 7686	TSP	Y 7727	TOU	Y 7768	BOR	Y 7809	TSP	Y 7850	VSG
Y 7687	BOR	Y 7728	BOR	Y 7769	PLP	Y 7810	LIM	Y 7851	VEN
Y 7688	NEV	Y 7729	STR	Y 7770	CLY	Y 7811	STR	Y 7852	CLY
Y 7689	VEN	Y 7730	CLY	Y 7771	NAN	Y 7812	LAR	Y 7853	CLY
Y 7690	VSG	Y 7731	PLP	Y 7772	LEN	Y 7813	NAN	Y 7854	PLP
Y 7691	CBY	Y 7732	LON	Y 7773	DIJ	Y 7814	REN	Y 7855	CAN
Y 7692	MAR	Y 7733	PLP	Y 7774	LEN	Y 7815	CLY	Y 7856	NAN
Y 7693	VEN	Y 7734	REN	Y 7775	NAN	Y 7816	STR	Y 7857	NAN
Y 7694	NIM	Y 7735	REN	Y 7776	NAN	Y 7817	CLY	Y 7858	ACH
Y 7695	NIM	Y 7736	TOU	Y 7777	SOT	Y 7818	PLP	Y 7859	CAN
Y 7696	NIM	Y 7737	TOU	Y 7778	LIM	Y 7819	LON	Y 7860	NEV
Y 7697	TOU	Y 7738	TOU	Y 7779	LIM	Y 7820	LEN	Y 7861	CBY
Y 7698	LIM	Y 7739	VSG	Y 7780	TAR	Y 7821	STR	Y 7862	VEN
Y 7699	LIM	Y 7740	CLY	Y 7781	NEV	Y 7822	REN	Y 7863	REN
Y 7700	PSO	Y 7741	NEV	Y 7782	DIJ	Y 7823	REN	Y 7864	CAN
Y 7701	LAR	Y 7742	NIM	Y 7783	CBY	Y 7824	SOT	Y 7865	SOT
Y 7702	REN	Y 7743	AVI	Y 7784	AVI	Y 7825	HEN	Y 7866	NAN
Y 7703	CLY	Y 7744	TOU	Y 7785	VEN	Y 7826	TSP	Y 7867	LIM
Y 7704	NEV	Y 7745	LAB	Y 7786	MAR	Y 7827	BOR	Y 7868	PSO
Y 7705	CAN	Y 7746	LAB	Y 7787	LIM	Y 7828	HEN	Y 7869	TSP
Y 7706	LAB	Y 7747	BOR	Y 7788	PSO	Y 7829	TOU	Y 7870	CAN
Y 7707	STR	Y 7748	CLY	Y 7789	LIM	Y 7830	VSG	Y 7871	NAN
Y 7708	CLY	Y 7749	STR	Y 7790	TSP	Y 7831	NEV	Y 7872	REN
Y 7709	CLY	Y 7750	LON	Y 7791	BOR	Y 7832	NEV	Y 7873	REN
Y 7710	BOR	Y 7751	LON	Y 7792	TOU	Y 7833	DIJ	Y 7874	STR
Y 7711	TOU	Y 7752	LON	Y 7793	CLY	Y 7834	CLY	Y 7875	STR
Y 7712	PLP	Y 7753	PLP	Y 7794	CLY	Y 7835	CLY	Y 7876	STR
Y 7713	ACH	Y 7754	REN	Y 7795	TSP	Y 7836	LEN	Y 7877	VSG
Y 7714	BOR	Y 7755	NAN	Y 7796	STR	Y 7837	LON	Y 7878	NEV
Y 7715	NAN	Y 7756	NAN	Y 7797	STR	Y 7838	REN	Y 7879	REN
Y 7716	LAB	Y 7757	BOR	Y 7798	STR	Y 7839	CAN	Y 7880	REN
Y 7717	TSP	Y 7758	PSO	Y 7799	PLP	Y 7840	REN	Y 7881	CAN
Y 7718	TOU	Y 7759	PSO	Y 7800	PLP	Y 7841	REN	Y 7882	ACH
Y 7719	CBY	Y 7760	VEN	Y 7801	LAR	Y 7842	TOU	Y 7883	DIJ
Y 7720	VSG	Y 7761	VSG	Y 7802	TOU	Y 7843	TOU	Y 7884	DIJ
Y 7721	VSG	Y 7762	VEN	Y 7803	NAN	Y 7844	PSO	Y 7885	VEN
Y 7722	VEN	Y 7763	MAR	Y 7804	NIM	Y 7845	LIM	Y 7886	NEV
Y 7723	NIM	Y 7764	NIM	Y 7805	CBY	Y 7846	BOR	Y 7887	CBY
Y 7724	AVI	Y 7765	VEN	Y 7806	NEV	Y 7847	CBY	Y 7888	VEN
Y 7725	LIM	Y 7766	NEV	Y 7807	PSO	Y 7848	DIJ		

Y 8000 CLASS   B

This is the new standard hydraulic shunter in the new yellow livery. Being more powerful and with a higher speed than previous designs the class sees more main line use on trip workings and they are allocated to fewer depots. Those at AVI are maintained by MAR, those at CBY by VEN and thhose at VSG by NEV. Radio fitted for "manoeuvres" use in stations.

Built: 1977 onwards. (Still under construction).
Builder: Moyse/Fauvet Giral.
Engine: Poyaud Y12-520NS of 290 kW.
Transmission: Hydraulic. Voith.

Train Heating: None	**Weight in Full Working Order:** 36 tonnes.
Maximum Tractive Effort: 66 kN.	**Length over Buffers:** 10140 mm.
Wheel Dia.: 1050 mm.	**Max. Speed:** 60 km/h.

Y 8001	TSP	Y 8009	MET	Y 8017	AVI	Y 8025	REN	Y 8033	REN
Y 8002	MET	Y 8010	MET	Y 8018	MAR	Y 8026	NIM	Y 8034	VSG
Y 8003	MET	Y 8011	MET	Y 8019	AVI	Y 8027	DIJ	Y 8035	VSG
Y 8004	MET	Y 8012	MET	Y 8020	TSP	Y 8028	VEN	Y 8036	CBY
Y 8005	MET	Y 8013	MET	Y 8021	DIJ	Y 8029	VEN	Y 8037	CBY
Y 8006	MET	Y 8014	MET	Y 8022	DIJ	Y 8030	REN	Y 8038	ACH
Y 8007	MET	Y 8015	MET	Y 8023	REN	Y 8031	REN	Y 8039	REN
Y 8008	MET	Y 8016	MAR	Y 8024	SOT	Y 8032	REN	Y 8040	REN

Y 8041	REN	Y 8102	ACH	Y 8163	ACH	Y 8224	LON	Y 8285	REN
Y 8042	AVI	Y 8103	NIM	Y 8164	SOT	Y 8225	SOT	Y 8286	
Y 8043	AVI	Y 8104	MAR	Y 8165	SOT	Y 8226	REN	Y 8287	
Y 8044	MAR	Y 8105	NIM	Y 8166	BOR	Y 8227	REN	Y 8288	
Y 8045	NIM	Y 8106	DIJ	Y 8167	BOR	Y 8228	REN	Y 8289	
Y 8046	DIJ	Y 8107	REN	Y 8168	BOR	Y 8229	ACH	Y 8290	
Y 8047	DIJ	Y 8108	MET	Y 8169	LON	Y 8230	ACH	Y 8291	
Y 8048	REN	Y 8109	MET	Y 8170	LON	Y 8231	NEV	Y 8292	
Y 8049	ACH	Y 8110	MET	Y 8171	LON	Y 8232	CBY	Y 8293	
Y 8050	ACH	Y 8111	BOR	Y 8172	MAR	Y 8233	NIM	Y 8294	
Y 8051	ACH	Y 8112	MET	Y 8173	MAR	Y 8234	BOR	Y 8295	
Y 8052	DIJ	Y 8113	VEN	Y 8174	NIM	Y 8235	VSG	Y 8296	
Y 8053	DIJ	Y 8114	CBY	Y 8175	NEV	Y 8236	VSG	Y 8297	
Y 8054	VEN	Y 8115	PLP	Y 8176	VEN	Y 8237	NIM	Y 8298	
Y 8055	VEN	Y 8116	MET	Y 8177	VSG	Y 8238	NEV	Y 8299	
Y 8056	ACH	Y 8117	MET	Y 8178	AVI	Y 8239	MAR	Y 8300	
Y 8057	SOT	Y 8118	MET	Y 8179	MAR	Y 8240	NIM	Y 8301	
Y 8058	SOT	Y 8119	DIJ	Y 8180	DIJ	Y 8241	LON	Y 8302	
Y 8059	SOT	Y 8120	CBY	Y 8181	MET	Y 8242	LON	Y 8303	
Y 8060	SOT	Y 8121	NEV	Y 8182	MET	Y 8243	LON	Y 8304	
Y 8061	MAR	Y 8122	ACH	Y 8183	PLP	Y 8244	MET	Y 8305	
Y 8062	NIM	Y 8123	MET	Y 8184	MET	Y 8245	REN	Y 8306	
Y 8063	MAR	Y 8124	MET	Y 8185	MET	Y 8246	REN	Y 8307	
Y 8064	DIJ	Y 8125	MET	Y 8186	MET	Y 8247	SOT	Y 8308	
Y 8065	AVI	Y 8126	PLP	Y 8187	MET	Y 8248	REN	Y 8309	
Y 8066	DIJ	Y 8127	PLP	Y 8188	PLP	Y 8249	REN	Y 8310	
Y 8067	TSP	Y 8128	PLP	Y 8189	BOR	Y 8250	SOT	Y 8311	
Y 8068	TSP	Y 8129	PLP	Y 8190	TSP	Y 8251	REN	Y 8312	
Y 8069	TSP	Y 8130	BOR	Y 8191	TSP	Y 8252	ACH	Y 8313	
Y 8070	LON	Y 8131	TSP	Y 8192	BOR	Y 8253	SOT	Y 8314	
Y 8071	LON	Y 8132	TSP	Y 8193	TSP	Y 8254	ACH	Y 8315	
Y 8072	BOR	Y 8133	TSP	Y 8194	BOR	Y 8255	SOT	Y 8316	
Y 8073	BOR	Y 8134	MET	Y 8195	BOR	Y 8256	CBY	Y 8317	
Y 8074	LON	Y 8135	PLP	Y 8196	BOR	Y 8257	MAR	Y 8318	
Y 8075	LON	Y 8136	MET	Y 8197	BOR	Y 8258	CBY	Y 8319	
Y 8076	TSP	Y 8137	MET	Y 8198	BOR	Y 8259	NEV	Y 8320	
Y 8077	TSP	Y 8138	NIM	Y 8199	TSP	Y 8260	VEN	Y 8321	
Y 8078	BOR	Y 8139	CBY	Y 8200	PLP	Y 8261	LON	Y 8322	
Y 8079	LON	Y 8140	REN	Y 8201	PLP	Y 8262	LON	Y 8323	
Y 8080	BOR	Y 8141	VSG	Y 8202	PLP	Y 8263	TSP	Y 8324	
Y 8081	TSP	Y 8142	VEN	Y 8203	SOT	Y 8264	BOR	Y 8325	
Y 8082	LON	Y 8143	REN	Y 8204	REN	Y 8265	BOR	Y 8326	
Y 8083	LON	Y 8144	SOT	Y 8205	SOT	Y 8266	LON	Y 8327	
Y 8084	BOR	Y 8145	ACH	Y 8206	VSG	Y 8267	LON	Y 8328	
Y 8085	BOR	Y 8146	ACH	Y 8207	NEV	Y 8268	LON	Y 8329	
Y 8086	LON	Y 8147	MAR	Y 8208	NIM	Y 8269	TSP	Y 8330	
Y 8087	LON	Y 8148	NIM	Y 8209	CBY	Y 8270	BOR	Y 8331	
Y 8088	LON	Y 8149	PLP	Y 8210	MAR	Y 8271	BOR	Y 8332	
Y 8089	TSP	Y 8150	PLP	Y 8211	MET	Y 8272	BOR	Y 8333	
Y 8090	BOR	Y 8151	PLP	Y 8212	MET	Y 8273	VSG	Y 8334	
Y 8091	VEN	Y 8152	MET	Y 8213	MET	Y 8274	VSG	Y 8335	
Y 8092	VEN	Y 8153	PLP	Y 8214	MET	Y 8275		Y 8336	
Y 8093	VEN	Y 8154	TSP	Y 8215	PLP	Y 8276		Y 8337	
Y 8094	CBY	Y 8155	TSP	Y 8216	MET	Y 8277		Y 8338	
Y 8095	NEV	Y 8156	TSP	Y 8217	TSP	Y 8278	LON	Y 8339	
Y 8096	VEN	Y 8157	BOR	Y 8218	TSP	Y 8279		Y 8340	
Y 8097	REN	Y 8158	TSP	Y 8219	BOR	Y 8280	LON	Y 8341	
Y 8098	REN	Y 8159	TSP	Y 8220	BOR	Y 8281	LON	Y 8342	
Y 8099	REN	Y 8160	REN	Y 8221	PLP	Y 8282		Y 8343	
Y 8100	ACH	Y 8161	REN	Y 8222	LON	Y 8283	NIM	Y 8344	
Y 8101	REN	Y 8162	SOT	Y 8223	LON	Y 8284	NIM	Y 8345	

In addition to the above, there are two small tractors for which details are not available which work at the bogie changing shed at Hendaye:

Y BL 160 HEN   Y BL 161   HEN

80

ELECTRIC MULTIPLE UNITS

Z 3700 CLASS   SINGLE UNIT (Bo–Bo–Bo)

This is the last unit of a small series built for the Paris–Le Mans route. The two-car unit is articulated and was used originally on express services but is now out of use after working staff trains between Paris Montparnasse and Montrouge. American influence is reflected in the Budd stainless steel finish.

ZABD (DMBCO).

System: 1500 V dc.
Built: 1937–39.
Builder-Mech. Parts: Carel & Fouché.
Builder-Elec. Parts: Schneider-Jeumont.
Traction Motors: 6 x 172 kW.
Seats: 28F 94S 1L.
Weight: 78 tonnes.
Length over couplings: 40710 mm.
Max. Speed: 130 km/h.

Z 3711   MON

Z 4100 CLASS   2-CAR UNITS (Bo–Bo–+2–2)

These units are the last examples of a large class originating on the PO-Midi lines and are still based in that area. Reduced now to two examples that are working out their time on staff trains around Toulouse.

ZBD+ZRBx (DMBSO–DTSO).

System: 1500 V dc.
Built: 1924–37.
Builder-Mech. Parts: Études.
Builder-Elec. Parts: Schneider-Jeumont.
Traction Motors: 4 x 140 kW.
Seats: 77S + 87S.
Weight: 65 + ? tonnes.
Length over couplings: 21150 + 21150 mm.
Max. Speed: 90 km/h.

Z 4185 ZR 14185   TOU |Z 4186 ZR 14186   TOU |

Z 5100 CLASS
2 & 3-CAR UNITS (Bo–Bo+2–2+2–2)

The American influence on the Z 3700 series seems to have found favour on the post war SNCF as stainless steel has been used quite a lot since. These 3-car units have this finish used to work suburban trains out of Paris Montparnasse and Lyon stations. Delivery of new stock to the Paris area has seen the class moving out to the provinces. Tours already has some and Lyon should get a batch soon. Z 5100F (f) are modified Z 5100 for working on the last remnant of the once extensive third rail network in Paris. Reduced to 2-car units and pantographs removed, they operate the service from Puteaux to Issy-Plaine. Despite operating on lower power they are still more powerful than the units they replaced. (Z 1500s from 1931).

ZBD+ZRB+ZRABx (DMBSO–TSO–DTCO). Non-gangwayed.

System: 1500 V dc.**Built:** 1954–57.
Builder-Mech. Parts: Carel & Fouché.
Builder-Elec. Parts: MTE.
Traction Motors: 4 x 225 kW.
Seats: 60S 1L + 86S 1L+ 24F 46S 1L.
Weight: 57 + 34 + 36 tonnes.
Length over couplings: 22850 + 22400 + 22850 mm.
Max. Speed: 120 km/h.

Only one example of the articulated stainless steel class Z 3700 still remains in traffic (Z 3711). No. Z 3713 is seen here at Montrouge whilst in use on the shuttle to Paris Montparnasse
[Brian Garvin

One of the two remaining Z 4100 class e.m.u.s No. Z 4186 at Les Aubrais, Orleans. [E. Dunkling

Z 5101	ZR 25101	ZR 15101	TSP	Z 5142	ZR 25142	ZR 15142	TSP
Z 5102	ZR 25102	ZR 15102	TSP	Z 5143	ZR 25143	ZR 15143	TSP
Z 5103	ZR 25103	ZR 15103	TSP	Z 5145	ZR 25145	ZR 15145	VSG
Z 5104	ZR 25104	ZR 15104	VSG	Z 5146	ZR 25146	ZR 15146	VSG
Z 5105	ZR 25105	ZR 15105	VSG	Z 5147	ZR 25147	ZR 15147	VSG
Z 5106	ZR 25106	ZR 15106	TSP	Z 5148	ZR 25148	ZR 15148	VSG
Z 5107	ZR 25107	ZR 15107	TSP	Z 5149	ZR 25149	ZR 15149	VSG
Z 5108	ZR 25108	ZR 15108	TSP	Z 5150	ZR 25150	ZR 15150	VSG
Z 5109	ZR 25109	ZR 15109	TSP	Z 5151	ZR 25151	ZR 15151	MON
Z 5110	ZR 25110	ZR 15110	TSP	Z 5152	ZR 25152	ZR 15152	VSG
Z 5111	ZR 25111	ZR 15111	TSP	Z 5153	ZR 25153	ZR 15153	VSG
Z 5112	ZR 25112	ZR 15112	TSP	Z 5154	ZR 25154	ZR 15154	VSG
Z 5113	ZR 25113	ZR 15113	TSP	Z 5155	ZR 25155	ZR 15155	VSG
Z 5114	ZR 25114	ZR 15114	VSG	Z 5156	ZR 25156	ZR 15156	VSG
Z 5115	ZR 25115	ZR 15115	VSG	Z 5157	ZR 25157	ZR 15157	VSG
Z 5116	ZR 25116	ZR 15116	VSG	Z 5158	ZR 25158	ZR 15158	MON
Z 5117	ZR 25117	ZR 15117	TSP	Z 5159	ZR 25159	ZR 15159	MON
Z 5118	ZR 25118	ZR 15118	TSP	Z 5160	ZR 25160	ZR 15160	MON
Z 5119	ZR 25119	ZR 15119	TSP	Z 5161	ZR 25161	ZR 15161	MON
Z 5120	ZR 25120	ZR 15120	VSG	Z 5162	ZR 25162	ZR 15162	MON
Z 5121	ZR 25121	ZR 15121	MON	Z 5163	ZR 25163	ZR 15163	MON
Z 5122	ZR 25122	ZR 15122	VSG	Z 5164	ZR 25164	ZR 15164	MON
Z 5123	ZR 25123	ZR 15123	TSP	Z 5165	ZR 25165	ZR 15165	MON
Z 5124	ZR 25124	ZR 15124	VSG	Z 5166	ZR 25166	ZR 15166	MON
Z 5125	ZR 25125	ZR 15125	VSG	Z 5167	ZR 25167	ZR 15167	MON
Z 5126	ZR 25126	ZR 15126	TSP	Z 5168	ZR 25168	ZR 15168	MON
Z 5127	ZR 25127	ZR 15127	VSG	Z 5169	ZR 25169	ZR 15169	MON
Z 5128	ZR 25128	ZR 15128	TSP	Z 5170	ZR 25170	ZR 15170	MON
Z 5129	ZR 25129	ZR 15129	TSP	Z 5171	ZR 25171	ZR 15171	MON
Z 5130	ZR 25130	ZR 15130	TSP	Z 5172	ZR 25172	ZR 15172	MON
Z 5131	ZR 25131	ZR 15131	TSP	Z 5173	ZR 25173	ZR 15173	MON
Z 5132	ZR 25132	ZR 15132	TSP	Z 5174	ZR 25174	ZR 15174	MON
Z 5133	ZR 25133	ZR 15133	VSG	Z 5175	ZR 25175	ZR 15175	MON
Z 5134	ZR 25134	ZR 15134	TSP	Z 5176	ZR 25176	ZR 15176	MON
Z 5135	ZR 25135	ZR 15135	TSP	Z 5177		ZR 15177	f PSL
Z 5136	ZR 25136	ZR 15136	VSG	Z 5178		ZR 15178	f PSL
Z 5137	ZR 25137	ZR 15137	TSP	Z 5179		ZR 15179	f PSL
Z 5138	ZR 25138	ZR 15138	TSP	Z 5180		ZR 15180	f PSL
Z 5139	ZR 25139	ZR 15139	TSP	Z 5181		ZR 15181	f PSL
Z 5140	ZR 25140	ZR 15140	TSP	Z 5182		ZR 15182	f PSL
Z 5141	ZR 25141	ZR 15141	TSP				

Spare trailers:

ZR 25144	MON	ZR 25179	MON	ZR 25182	MON	ZR 25184	MON	ZR 25186	MON
ZR 25177	MON	ZR 25180	MON	ZR 25183	MON	ZR 25185	MON	ZR 25187	MON
ZR 25178	MON	ZR 25181	MON						

Z 5300 CLASS 4-CAR UNITS (Bo–Bo+2–2+2–2+2–2)

With suburban traffic increasing these 4-car units were delivered and again features stainless steel bodywork. For years they have worked out of Paris Austerlitz and Lyon stations on suburban trains but the development of the Paris RER services and the introduction of double-deck e.m.u.s has seen more congregating on Paris Lyon services allowing Z 5100s to be released to other areas. There has also been a knock on effect to BB 8500 which have been transferred away from Villeneuve. In connection with RER duties many units are now being fitted with headcode panels.

ZBD+ZRB+ZRB+ZRABx (DMBSO–TSO (A)–TSO (B)–DTCO). (Non-gangwwayed to Z 5361).

System: 1500 V dc.
Built: 1965–75.
Builders: Carel & Fouché/MTE/Oerlikon.
Traction Motors: 4 x 245 kW.
Seats: 87S 1L + 112S + 106S 1L + 44F 40S.
Weight: 62 + 30 + 30 + 42 tonnes.

Z 5100 class No. Z 5182 at Paris Montparnasse on 12/04/83.   [E. Dunkling

Z 5300 class No. Z 5343 at Issy-Plaine, Paris on 12/04/83.   [E. Dunkling

Length over couplings: 25925 (25800*) + 25600 (25850*) + 25600 (25850*) + 25925 (25800*) mm.
Max. Speed: 120 km/h.

Z 5301*	ZR 25302*	ZR 25301*	ZR 15301*	VSG
Z 5302*	ZR 25304*	ZR 25303*	ZR 15302*	VSG
Z 5303*	ZR 25306*	ZR 25305*	ZR 15303*	VSG
Z 5304*	ZR 25308*	ZR 25307*	ZR 15304*	VSG
Z 5305*	ZR 25310*	ZR 25309*	ZR 15305*	VSG
Z 5306*	ZR 25312*	ZR 25311*	ZR 15306*	VSG
Z 5307*	ZR 25314*	ZR 25313*	ZR 15307*	VSG
Z 5308*	ZR 25316*	ZR 25315*	ZR 15308*	VSG
Z 5309*	ZR 25318*	ZR 25317*	ZR 15309*	VSG
Z 5310*	ZR 25320*	ZR 25319*	ZR 15310*	VSG
Z 5311*	ZR 25322*	ZR 25321*	ZR 15311*	VSG
Z 5312*	ZR 25324*	ZR 25323*	ZR 15312*	VSG
Z 5313*	ZR 25326*	ZR 25325*	ZR 15313*	VSG
Z 5314*	ZR 25328*	ZR 25327*	ZR 15314*	VSG
Z 5315*	ZR 25330*	ZR 25329*	ZR 15315*	VSG
Z 5316*	ZR 25332*	ZR 25591	ZR 15316	VSG
Z 5317*	ZR 25334*	ZR 25333*	ZR 15317*	VSG
Z 5318*	ZR 25336*	ZR 25335*	ZR 15318*	VSG
Z 5319*	ZR 25338*	ZR 25337*	ZR 15319*	VSG
Z 5320*	ZR 25340*	ZR 25339*	ZR 15320*	VSG
Z 5321*	ZR 25342*	ZR 25341*	ZR 15321*	VSG
Z 5322*	ZR 25344*	ZR 25343*	ZR 15322*	VSG
Z 5323*	ZR 25346*	ZR 25345*	ZR 15323*	VSG
Z 5324*	ZR 25348*	ZR 25347*	ZR 15324*	VSG
Z 5325*	ZR 25350*	ZR 25349*	ZR 15325*	VSG
Z 5326*	ZR 25352*	ZR 25351*	ZR 15326*	VSG
Z 5327*	ZR 25354*	ZR 25353*	ZR 15327*	VSG
Z 5328*	ZR 25356*	ZR 25355*	ZR 15328*	VSG
Z 5329*	ZR 25358*	ZR 25357*	ZR 15329*	VSG
Z 5330*	ZR 25360*	ZR 25359*	ZR 15330*	VSG
Z 5331*	ZR 25362*	ZR 25361*	ZR 15331*	VSG
Z 5332*	ZR 25364*	ZR 25363*	ZR 15332*	VSG
Z 5333*	ZR 25366*	ZR 25415*	ZR 15333*	VSG
Z 5334*	ZR 25368*	ZR 25367*	ZR 15334*	VSG
Z 5335*	ZR 25370*	ZR 25369*	ZR 15335*	VSG
Z 5336*	ZR 25372*	ZR 25371*	ZR 15336*	VSG
Z 5337*	ZR 25374*	ZR 25373*	ZR 15337*	VSG
Z 5338*	ZR 25376*	ZR 25375*	ZR 15338*	VSG
Z 5339*	ZR 25378*	ZR 25377*	ZR 15339	VSG
Z 5340*	ZR 25380*	ZR 25379*	ZR 15340*	VSG
Z 5341*	ZR 25382*	ZR 25381*	ZR 15341*	VSG
Z 5342*	ZR 25384*	ZR 25383*	ZR 15342*	VSG
Z 5343*	ZR 25386*	ZR 25385*	ZR 15343*	VSG
Z 5344*	ZR 25388*	ZR 25387*	ZR 15344*	VSG
Z 5345*	ZR 25390*	ZR 25389*	ZR 15345*	VSG
Z 5346*	ZR 25392*	ZR 25391*	ZR 15346*	VSG
Z 5347*	ZR 25394*	ZR 25393*	ZR 15347*	VSG
Z 5348*	ZR 25396*	ZR 25395*	ZR 15348*	VSG
Z 5349*	ZR 25398*	ZR 25397*	ZR 15349*	VSG
Z 5350*	ZR 25400*	ZR 25399*	ZR 15350*	VSG
Z 5351*	ZR 25402*	ZR 25401*	ZR 15351*	VSG
Z 5352*	ZR 25404*	ZR 25403*	ZR 15352*	VSG
Z 5353*	ZR 25406*	ZR 25405*	ZR 15353*	VSG
Z 5354*	ZR 25408*	ZR 25407*	ZR 15354*	PSO
Z 5355*	ZR 25410*	ZR 25409*	ZR 15355*	PSO
Z 5356*	ZR 25412*	ZR 25411*	ZR 15356*	PSO
Z 5357*	ZR 25414*	ZR 25413*	ZR 15357*	PSO
Z 5358*	ZR 25416*	ZR 25415*	ZR 15358*	PSO
Z 5359*	ZR 25592	ZR 25593	ZR 15359*	PSO
Z 5360*	ZR 25594	ZR 25595	ZR 15360*	PSO
Z 5361*	ZR 25596	ZR 25597	ZR 15361*	PSO

Z 5362	ZR 25424	ZR 25423	ZR 15362	PSO
Z 5363	ZR 25426	ZR 25425	ZR 15363	PSO
Z 5364	ZR 25428	ZR 25427	ZR 15364	PSO
Z 5365	ZR 25430	ZR 25429	ZR 15365	PSO
Z 5366	ZR 25432	ZR 25431	ZR 15366	PSO
Z 5367	ZR 25434	ZR 25433	ZR 15367	PSO
Z 5368	ZR 25436	ZR 25435	ZR 15368	PSO
Z 5369	ZR 25438	ZR 25437	ZR 15369	PSO
Z 5370	ZR 25440	ZR 25439	ZR 15370	PSO
Z 5371	ZR 25442	ZR 25441	ZR 15371	PSO
Z 5372	ZR 25444	ZR 25443	ZR 15372	PSO
Z 5373	ZR 25446	ZR 25445	ZR 15373	PSO
Z 5374	ZR 25448	ZR 25447	ZR 15374	PSO
Z 5375	ZR 25450	ZR 25449	ZR 15375	PSO
Z 5376	ZR 25452	ZR 25451	ZR 15376	PSO
Z 5377	ZR 25454	ZR 25453	ZR 15377	PSO
Z 5378	ZR 25456	ZR 25455	ZR 15378	PSO
Z 5379	ZR 25458	ZR 25457	ZR 15379	PSO
Z 5380	ZR 25460	ZR 25459	ZR 15380	PSO
Z 5381	ZR 25462	ZR 25461	ZR 15381	PSO
Z 5382	ZR 25464	ZR 25463	ZR 15382	PSO
Z 5383	ZR 25466	ZR 25465	ZR 15383	PSO
Z 5384	ZR 25468	ZR 25467	ZR 15384	PSO
Z 5385	ZR 25470	ZR 25469	ZR 15385	PSO
Z 5386	ZR 25472	ZR 25471	ZR 15386	PSO
Z 5387	ZR 25474	ZR 25473	ZR 15387	PSO
Z 5388	ZR 25476	ZR 25475	ZR 15388	PSO
Z 5389	ZR 25478	ZR 25477	ZR 15389	PSO
Z 5390	ZR 25480	ZR 25479	ZR 15390	PSO
Z 5391	ZR 25482	ZR 25481	ZR 15391	PSO
Z 5392	ZR 25484	ZR 25483	ZR 15392	PSO
Z 5393	ZR 25486	ZR 25485	ZR 15393	PSO
Z 5394	ZR 25488	ZR 25487	ZR 15394	PSO
Z 5395	ZR 25490	ZR 25489	ZR 15395	PSO
Z 5396	ZR 25492	ZR 25491	ZR 15396	PSO
Z 5397	ZR 25494	ZR 25493	ZR 15397	PSO
Z 5398	ZR 25496	ZR 25495	ZR 15398	PSO
Z 5399	ZR 25498	ZR 25497	ZR 15399	PSO
Z 5400	ZR 25500	ZR 25499	ZR 15400	PSO
Z 5401	ZR 25502	ZR 25501	ZR 15401	PSO
Z 5402	ZR 25504	ZR 25503	ZR 15402	PSO
Z 5403	ZR 25506	ZR 25505	ZR 15403	PSO
Z 5404	ZR 25508	ZR 25507	ZR 15404	PSO
Z 5405	ZR 25510	ZR 25509	ZR 15405	PSO
Z 5406	ZR 25512	ZR 25511	ZR 15406	PSO
Z 5407	ZR 25514	ZR 25513	ZR 15407	PSO
Z 5408	ZR 25516	ZR 25515	ZR 15408	PSO
Z 5409	ZR 25518	ZR 25517	ZR 15409	PSO
Z 5410	ZR 25520	ZR 25519	ZR 15410	PSO
Z 5411	ZR 25522	ZR 25521	ZR 15411	PSO
Z 5412	ZR 25416	ZR 25523	ZR 15412	PSO
Z 5413	ZR 25526	ZR 25525	ZR 15413	PSO
Z 5414	ZR 25528	ZR 25527	ZR 15414	PSO
Z 5415	ZR 25530	ZR 25529	ZR 15415	PSO
Z 5416	ZR 25532	ZR 25531	ZR 15416	PSO
Z 5417	ZR 25534	ZR 25533	ZR 15417	PSO
Z 5418	ZR 25536	ZR 25535	ZR 15418	PSO
Z 5419	ZR 25538	ZR 25537	ZR 15419	PSO
Z 5420	ZR 25540	ZR 25539	ZR 15420	PSO
Z 5421	ZR 25542	ZR 25541	ZR 15421	PSO
Z 5422	ZR 25544	ZR 25543	ZR 15422	PSO

Z 5423	ZR 25546	ZR 25545	ZR 15423	PSO		Z 5435	ZR 25570	ZR 25569	ZR 15435	PSO
Z 5424	ZR 25548	ZR 25547	ZR 15424	PSO		Z 5436	ZR 25572	ZR 25571	ZR 15436	PSO
Z 5425	ZR 25550	ZR 25549	ZR 15425	PSO		Z 5437	ZR 25574	ZR 25573	ZR 15437	PSO
Z 5426	ZR 25552	ZR 25551	ZR 15426	PSO		Z 5438	ZR 25576	ZR 25575	ZR 15438	PSO
Z 5427	ZR 25554	ZR 25553	ZR 15427	PSO		Z 5439	ZR 25578	ZR 25577	ZR 15439	PSO
Z 5428	ZR 25556	ZR 25555	ZR 15428	PSO		Z 5440	ZR 25580	ZR 25579	ZR 15440	PSO
Z 5429	ZR 25558	ZR 25557	ZR 15429	PSO		Z 5441	ZR 25582	ZR 25581	ZR 15441	PSO
Z 5430	ZR 25560	ZR 25559	ZR 15430	PSO		Z 5442	ZR 25584	ZR 25583	ZR 15442	PSO
Z 5431	ZR 25562	ZR 25561	ZR 15431	PSO		Z 5443	ZR 25586	ZR 25585	ZR 15443	PSO
Z 5432	ZR 25564	ZR 25563	ZR 15432	PSO		Z 5444	ZR 25588	ZR 25587	ZR 15444	PSO
Z 5433	ZR 25566	ZR 25565	ZR 15433	PSO		Z 5445	ZR 25590	ZR 25589	ZR 15445	PSO
Z 5434	ZR 25568	ZR 25567	ZR 15434	PSO						

Name: 5395 ISSY-LES-MOLINEAUX

Z 5600 CLASS   4 OR 5 CAR UNITS

These units followed Z 8100 in breaking away from the stainless steel bodywork. This class of double-deck e.m.u.s (Z2N) is operating suburban services out of Paris Lyon and Austerlitz stations. VSG units are made up into 5 car sets. These sets carry a plate on the side giving the set number (eg Z 01 being 5601/2) and is often also shown in the headcode panel on stabled units. The sets run as pairs of power cars with loose (or at any rate non-sequential) trailers in between. The trailers are common with the trailers of the new dual-voltage Z 8800 class.

ZB+ZRB(+ZRB)+ZRAB+ZB (DMSO–TSO–(+TSO)+TC+DMSO).

System: 1500 V dc.
Built: 1983–85.
Builder-Mech. Parts: ANF/CIMT.
Builder-Elec. Parts: Oerlikon/Alsthom.
Traction Motors: 4 x 350 kW per power car.
Max. Speed: 140 km/h.

Some units have TV sets in the cabs which display the view along the platform at certain stations. SNCF found it better to install receivers in the cabs rather than on the stations.

Power Car Sets. Seats 115S. 25100 mm long. 66 tonnes. Bo–Bo+Bo–Bo.

Z 5601	Z 5602	VSG		Z 5637	Z 5638	PSO		Z 5671	Z 5672	PSO
Z 5603	Z 5604	VSG		Z 5639	Z 5640	PSO		Z 5673	Z 5674	PSO
Z 5605	Z 5606	VSG		Z 5641	Z 5642	PSO		Z 5675	Z 5676	PSO
Z 5607	Z 5608	VSG		Z 5643	Z 5644	PSO		Z 5677	Z 5678	PSO
Z 5609	Z 5610	VSG		Z 5645	Z 5646	PSO		Z 5679	Z 5680	PSO
Z 5611	Z 5612	VSG		Z 5647	Z 5648	PSO		Z 5681	Z 5682	PSO
Z 5613	Z 5614	VSG		Z 5649	Z 5650	PSO		Z 5683	Z 5684	PSO
Z 5615	Z 5616	VSG		Z 5651	Z 5652	PSO		Z 5685	Z 5686	PSO
Z 5617	Z 5618	VSG		Z 5653	Z 5654	PSO		Z 5687	Z 5688	PSO
Z 5619	Z 5620	VSG		Z 5655	Z 5656	PSO		Z 5689	Z 5690	PSO
Z 5621	Z 5622	VSG		Z 5657	Z 5658	PSO		Z 5691	Z 5692	PSO
Z 5623	Z 5624	VSG		Z 5659	Z 5660	PSO		Z 5693	Z 5694	PSO
Z 5625	Z 5626	VSG		Z 5661	Z 5662	PSO		Z 5695	Z 5696	PSO
Z 5627	Z 5628	VSG		Z 5663	Z 5664	PSO		Z 5697	Z 5698	PSO
Z 5629	Z 5630	VSG		Z 5665	Z 5666	PSO		Z 5699	Z 5700	PSO
Z 5631	Z 5632	VSG		Z 5667	Z 5668	PSO		Z 5701	Z 5702	PSO
Z 5633	Z 5634	PSO		Z 5669	Z 5670	PSO		Z 5703	Z 5704	PSO
Z 5635	Z 5636	PSO								

Names:

Z 5633/4 ATHIS-MONS   Z 5697/8 BRÉTIGNY-SUR-ORGE Z 5699/5700 ÉTAMPES

Trailer Seconds. Seats 168S. 24280 mm long. 42 tonnes.

ZR 25601	ZR 25607	ZR 25613	ZR 25619	ZR 25625
ZR 25602	ZR 25608	ZR 25614	ZR 25620	ZR 25626
ZR 25603	ZR 25609	ZR 25615	ZR 25621	ZR 25627
ZR 25604	ZR 25610	ZR 25616	ZR 25622	ZR 25628
ZR 25605	ZR 25611	ZR 25617	ZR 25623	ZR 25629
ZR 25606	ZR 25612	ZR 25618	ZR 25624	ZR 25630

ZR 25631	ZR 25649	ZR 25667	ZR 25684	ZR 25701
ZR 25632	ZR 25650	ZR 25668	ZR 25685	ZR 25702
ZR 25633	ZR 25651	ZR 25669	ZR 25686	ZR 25703
ZR 25634	ZR 25652	ZR 25670	ZR 25687	ZR 25704
ZR 25635	ZR 25653	ZR 25671	ZR 25688	ZR 25705
ZR 25636	ZR 25654	ZR 25672	ZR 25689	ZR 25706
ZR 25637	ZR 25655	ZR 25673	ZR 25690	ZR 25707
ZR 25638	ZR 25656	ZR 25674	ZR 25691	ZR 25708
ZR 25639	ZR 25657	ZR 25675	ZR 25692	ZR 25709
ZR 25640	ZR 25658	ZR 25676	ZR 25693	ZR 25710
ZR 25641	ZR 25659	ZR 25677	ZR 25694	ZR 25711
ZR 25642	ZR 25660	ZR 25678	ZR 25695	ZR 25712
ZR 25643	ZR 25661	ZR 25679	ZR 25696	ZR 25713
ZR 25644	ZR 25662	ZR 25680	ZR 25697	ZR 25714
ZR 25645	ZR 25663	ZR 25681	ZR 25698	ZR 25715
ZR 25646	ZR 25664	ZR 25682	ZR 25699	ZR 25716
ZR 25647	ZR 25665	ZR 25683	ZR 25700	ZR 25717
ZR 25648	ZR 25666			

Trailer Composites. Seats 70F 82S. 24280 mm long. 42 tonnes.

XR 35601	XR 35621	XR 35641	XR 35661	XR 35681
XR 35602	XR 35622	XR 35642	XR 35662	XR 35682
XR 35603	XR 35623	XR 35643	XR 35663	XR 35683
XR 35604	XR 35624	XR 35644	XR 35664	XR 35684
XR 35605	XR 35625	XR 35645	XR 35665	XR 35685
XR 35606	XR 35626	XR 35646	XR 35666	XR 35686
XR 35607	XR 35627	XR 35647	XR 35667	XR 35687
XR 35608	XR 35628	XR 35648	XR 35668	XR 35688
XR 35609	XR 35629	XR 35649	XR 35669	XR 35689
XR 35610	XR 35630	XR 35650	XR 35670	XR 35690
XR 35611	XR 35631	XR 35651	XR 35671	XR 35691
XR 35612	XR 35632	XR 35652	XR 35672	XR 35692
XR 35613	XR 35633	XR 35653	XR 35673	XR 35693
XR 35614	XR 35634	XR 35654	XR 35674	XR 35694
XR 35615	XR 35635	XR 35655	XR 35675	XR 35695
XR 35616	XR 35636	XR 35656	XR 35676	XR 35696
XR 35617	XR 35637	XR 35657	XR 35677	XR 35697
XR 35618	XR 35638	XR 35658	XR 35678	XR 35698
XR 35619	XR 35639	XR 35659	XR 35679	XR 35699
XR 35620	XR 35640	XR 35660	XR 35680	XR 35700

Z 6000 & Z 6100 CLASSES 3 CAR UNITS (2–Bo+2–2+2–2)

The Z 6000 series were prototypes for the Z 6100s. Like the early dc units these are finished off in stainless steel. They operate suburban services out of Paris Nord as far north as Amiens. The last three digits of the running number also appear on cabsides and in cab windows as set numbers. Z 6124 is withdrawn whilst Z 6168/9 have been sold to Luxembourg where they operate as CFL 262/1 respectively.

ZBD+ZRB+ZRABx (BMBSO–TSO–DTCOL). (Non-gangwayed*).

System: 25 kV ac.
Built: 1960–61*/1965–71.
Builder-Mech. Parts: Carel & Fouché/Schneider/De Dietrich.
Builder-Elec. Parts: CEM/Siemens/Alsthom.
Traction Motors: 2 x 307 kW (2 x 345 kW*).
Seats: 86S 1L + 107S 1L + 36F 51S 1L.
Weight: 51 + 28 + 31 tonnes.
Length over couplings: 25500 + 23800 + 25150 mm.
Max. Speed: 120 km/h.

Z 6006*	ZR 26006	ZR 16006	PLC	Z 6101	ZR 26101	ZR 16101	PLC
Z 6007*	ZR 26007	ZR 16007	PLC	Z 6102	ZR 26102	ZR 16102	PLC
Z 6008*	ZR 26008	ZR 16008	PLC	Z 6103	ZR 26103	ZR 16103	PLC
Z 6009*	ZR 26009	ZR 16009	PLC	Z 6104	ZR 26104	ZR 16104	PLC

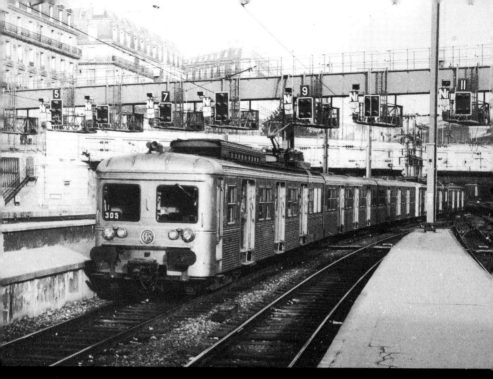

Z 6300 class No. Z 6305 at Paris St. Lazare on 24/02/85.   [E. Dunkling

Z 6400 class No. Z 6465/6, a high platform unit, departs from Puteaux with a Paris St. Lazare–St. Cloud stopping service.   [David Brown

Z 6105	ZR 26105	ZR 16105	PLC	Z 6145	ZR 26145	ZR 16145	PLC
Z 6106	ZR 26106	ZR 16106	PLC	Z 6146	ZR 26146	ZR 16146	PLC
Z 6107	ZR 26107	ZR 16107	PLC	Z 6147	ZR 26147	ZR 16147	PLC
Z 6108	ZR 26108	ZR 16108	PLC	Z 6148	ZR 26148	ZR 16148	PLC
Z 6109	ZR 26109	ZR 16109	PLC	Z 6149	ZR 26149	ZR 16149	PLC
Z 6110	ZR 26110	ZR 16110	PLC	Z 6150	ZR 26150	ZR 16150	PLC
Z 6111	ZR 26111	ZR 16111	PLC	Z 6151	ZR 26151	ZR 16151	PLC
Z 6112	ZR 26112	ZR 16112	PLC	Z 6152	ZR 26152	ZR 16152	PLC
Z 6113	ZR 26113	ZR 16113	PLC	Z 6153	ZR 26153	ZR 16153	PLC
Z 6114	ZR 26114	ZR 16114	PLC	Z 6154	ZR 26154	ZR 16154	PLC
Z 6115	ZR 26115	ZR 16115	PLC	Z 6155	ZR 26155	ZR 16155	PLC
Z 6116	ZR 26116	ZR 16116	PLC	Z 6156	ZR 26156	ZR 16156	PLC
Z 6117	ZR 26117	ZR 16117	PLC	Z 6157	ZR 26157	ZR 16157	PLC
Z 6118	ZR 26118	ZR 16118	PLC	Z 6158	ZR 26158	ZR 16158	PLC
Z 6119	ZR 26119	ZR 16119	PLC	Z 6159	ZR 26159	ZR 16159	PLC
Z 6120	ZR 26120	ZR 16120	PLC	Z 6160	ZR 26160	ZR 16160	PLC
Z 6121	ZR 26121	ZR 16121	PLC	Z 6161	ZR 26161	ZR 16161	PLC
Z 6122	ZR 26122	ZR 16122	PLC	Z 6162	ZR 26162	ZR 16162	PLC
Z 6123	ZR 26123	ZR 16123	PLC	Z 6163	ZR 26163	ZR 16163	PLC
Z 6125	ZR 26125	ZR 16125	PLC	Z 6164	ZR 26164	ZR 16164	PLC
Z 6126	ZR 26126	ZR 16126	PLC	Z 6165	ZR 26165	ZR 16165	PLC
Z 6127	ZR 26127	ZR 16127	PLC	Z 6166	ZR 26166	ZR 16166	PLC
Z 6128	ZR 26128	ZR 16128	PLC	Z 6167	ZR 26167	ZR 16167	PLC
Z 6129	ZR 26129	ZR 16129	PLC	Z 6170	ZR 26170	ZR 16170	PLC
Z 6130	ZR 26130	ZR 16130	PLC	Z 6171	ZR 26171	ZR 16171	PLC
Z 6131	ZR 26131	ZR 16131	PLC	Z 6172	ZR 26172	ZR 16172	PLC
Z 6132	ZR 26132	ZR 16132	PLC	Z 6173	ZR 26173	ZR 16173	PLC
Z 6133	ZR 26133	ZR 16133	PLC	Z 6174	ZR 26174	ZR 16174	PLC
Z 6134	ZR 26134	ZR 16134	PLC	Z 6175	ZR 26175	ZR 16175	PLC
Z 6135	ZR 26135	ZR 16135	PLC	Z 6176	ZR 26176	ZR 16176	PLC
Z 6136	ZR 26136	ZR 16136	PLC	Z 6177	ZR 26177	ZR 16177	PLC
Z 6137	ZR 26137	ZR 16137	PLC	Z 6178	ZR 26178	ZR 16178	PLC
Z 6138	ZR 26138	ZR 16138	PLC	Z 6179	ZR 26179	ZR 16179	PLC
Z 6139	ZR 26139	ZR 16139	PLC	Z 6180	ZR 26180	ZR 16180	PLC
Z 6140	ZR 26140	ZR 16140	PLC	Z 6181	ZR 26181	ZR 16181	PLC
Z 6141	ZR 26141	ZR 16141	PLC	Z 6182	ZR 26182	ZR 16182	PLC
Z 6142	ZR 26142	ZR 16142	PLC	Z 6183	ZR 26183	ZR 16183	PLC
Z 6143	ZR 26143	ZR 16143	PLC	Z 6184	ZR 26184	ZR 16184	PLC
Z 6144	ZR 26144	ZR 16144	PLC	Z 6185	ZR 26185	ZR 16185	PLC

Z 6300 CLASS   3 CAR UNITS (2–Bo+2–2+2–2)

These units operate services out of Paris St. Lazare. Based on Z 6100 they are in fact shorter as several St. Lazare routes have tight curves. These routes also have low platforms and the steps on the e.m.u.s are adjustable according to the type of platform.

ZBD+ZRAB+ZRBx (DMBSO–TCO–DTSO). Non-gangwayed.

System: 25 kV ac.
Built: 1967–70.
Builder-Mech. Parts: Carel & Fouché/Fives-Lille/De Dietrich.
Builder-Elec. Parts: CEM/Siemens/Alsthom.
Traction Motors: 2 x 307 kW.
Seats: 39S 1L + 40F 21S 1L + 67S 1L.
Weight: 52 + 26 + 28 tonnes.
Length over couplings: 20750 + 18825 + 20525 mm.
Max. Speed: 120 km/h.

Z 6301	ZR 26301	ZR 16301	PSL	Z 6308	ZR 26308	ZR 16308	PSL
Z 6302	ZR 26302	ZR 16302	PSL	Z 6309	ZR 26309	ZR 16309	PSL
Z 6303	ZR 26303	ZR 16303	PSL	Z 6310	ZR 26310	ZR 16310	PSL
Z 6304	ZR 26304	ZR 16304	PSL	Z 6311	ZR 26311	ZR 16311	PSL
Z 6305	ZR 26305	ZR 16305	PSL	Z 6312	ZR 26312	ZR 16312	PSL
Z 6306	ZR 26306	ZR 16306	PSL	Z 6313	ZR 26313	ZR 16313	PSL
Z 6307	ZR 26307	ZR 16307	PSL	Z 6314	ZR 26314	ZR 16314	PSL

Z 6315	ZR 26315	ZR 16315	PSL
Z 6316	ZR 26316	ZR 16316	PSL
Z 6317	ZR 26317	ZR 16317	PSL
Z 6318	ZR 26318	ZR 16318	PSL
Z 6319	ZR 26319	ZR 16319	PSL
Z 6320	ZR 26320	ZR 16320	PSL
Z 6321	ZR 26321	ZR 16321	PSL
Z 6322	ZR 26322	ZR 16322	PSL
Z 6323	ZR 26323	ZR 16323	PSL
Z 6324	ZR 26324	ZR 16324	PSL
Z 6325	ZR 26325	ZR 16325	PSL
Z 6326	ZR 26326	ZR 16326	PSL
Z 6327	ZR 26327	ZR 16327	PSL
Z 6328	ZR 26328	ZR 16328	PSL
Z 6329	ZR 26329	ZR 16329	PSL
Z 6330	ZR 26330	ZR 16330	PSL
Z 6331	ZR 26331	ZR 16331	PSL
Z 6332	ZR 26332	ZR 16332	PSL
Z 6333	ZR 26333	ZR 16333	PSL
Z 6334	ZR 26334	ZR 16334	PSL
Z 6335	ZR 26335	ZR 16335	PSL

Z 6400 CLASS 4 CAR UNITS (Bo–Bo+2–2+2–2+Bo–Bo)

This was the last type of e.m.u. to feature stainless steel bodywork. Introduced for services out of Paris St. Lazare some operated out of Paris Nord for a while. Like Z 6300s they have adjustable steps. The last three digits of the power car number appear in the cab widow.

ZAD+ZRB+ZRB+ZBD (DMBFO–TSO–TSO–DMBSO).

System: 25 kV ac.
Built: 1976–79.
Builder-Mech. Parts: Carel & Fouché.
Builder-Elec. Parts: Alsthom/Oerlikon.
Traction Motors: 4 x 295 kW per power car.
.Seats: 72F + 102S + 102S + 84S.
Weight: 64 + 32 + 32 + 63 tonnes.
Length over couplings: 22700 + 22390 + 22390 + 22700 mm.
Max. Speed: 120 km/h.

h Fixed steps for high platform use only.

Z 6401	ZR 26401	ZR 26402	Z 6402		PSL
Z 6403	ZR 26403	ZR 26404	Z 6404		PSL
Z 6405	ZR 26405	ZR 26406	Z 6406		PSL
Z 6407	ZR 26407	ZR 26408	Z 6408		PSL
Z 6409	ZR 26409	ZR 26410	Z 6410		PSL
Z 6411	ZR 26411	ZR 26412	Z 6412		PSL
Z 6413	ZR 26413	ZR 26414	Z 6414		PSL
Z 6415	ZR 26415	ZR 26416	Z 6416		PSL
Z 6417	ZR 26417	ZR 26418	Z 6418		PSL
Z 6419	ZR 26419	ZR 26420	Z 6420		PSL
Z 6421	ZR 26421	ZR 26422	Z 6422		PSL
Z 6423	ZR 26423	ZR 26424	Z 6424		PSL
Z 6425	ZR 26425	ZR 26426	Z 6426		PSL
Z 6427	ZR 26427	ZR 26428	Z 6428		PSL
Z 6429	ZR 26429	ZR 26430	Z 6430		PSL
Z 6431	ZR 26431	ZR 26432	Z 6432		PSL
Z 6433	ZR 26433	ZR 26434	Z 6434		PSL
Z 6435	ZR 26435	ZR 26436	Z 6436		PSL
Z 6437	ZR 26437	ZR 26438	Z 6438		PSL
Z 6439	ZR 26439	ZR 26440	Z 6440		PSL
Z 6441	ZR 26441	ZR 26442	Z 6442	h	PSL
Z 6443	ZR 26443	ZR 26444	Z 6444	h	PSL
Z 6445	ZR 26445	ZR 26446	Z 6446	h	PSL
Z 6447	ZR 26447	ZR 26448	Z 6448	h	PSL
Z 6449	ZR 26449	ZR 26450	Z 6450	h	PSL
Z 6451	ZR 26451	ZR 26452	Z 6452	h	PSL
Z 6453	ZR 26453	ZR 26454	Z 6454	h	PSL
Z 6455	ZR 26455	ZR 26456	Z 6456	h	PSL
Z 6457	ZR 26457	ZR 26458	Z 6458	h	PSL
Z 6459	ZR 26459	ZR 26460	Z 6460	h	PSL
Z 6461	ZR 26461	ZR 26462	Z 6462	h	PSL
Z 6463	ZR 26463	ZR 26464	Z 6464	h	PSL
Z 6465	ZR 26465	ZR 26466	Z 6466	h	PSL
Z 6467	ZR 26467	ZR 26468	Z 6468	h	PSL
Z 6469	ZR 26469	ZR 26470	Z 6470	h	PSL
Z 6471	ZR 26471	ZR 26472	Z 6472	h	PSL
Z 6473	ZR 26473	ZR 26474	Z 6474	h	PSL
Z 6475	ZR 26475	ZR 26476	Z 6476	h	PSL
Z 6477	ZR 26477	ZR 26478	Z 6478	h	PSL
Z 6479	ZR 26479	ZR 26480	Z 6480	h	PSL
Z 6481	ZR 26481	ZR 26482	Z 6482	h	PSL
Z 6483	ZR 26483	ZR 26484	Z 6484	h	PSL
Z 6485	ZR 26485	ZR 26486	Z 6486	h	PSL
Z 6487	ZR 26487	ZR 26488	Z 6488	h	PSL
Z 6489	ZR 26489	ZR 26490	Z 6490	h	PSL
Z 6491	ZR 26491	ZR 26492	Z 6492	h	PSL
Z 6493	ZR 26493	ZR 26494	Z 6494	h	PSL
Z 6495	ZR 26495	ZR 26496	Z 6496	h	PSL
Z 6497	ZR 26497	ZR 26498	Z 6498	h	PSL
Z 6499	ZR 26499	ZR 26500	Z 6500	h	PSL
Z 6501	ZR 26501	ZR 26502	Z 6502	h	PSL
Z 6503	ZR 26503	ZR 26504	Z 6504	h	PSL
Z 6505	ZR 26505	ZR 26506	Z 6506	h	PSL
Z 6507	ZR 26507	ZR 26508	Z 6508	h	PSL
Z 6509	ZR 26509	ZR 26510	Z 6510	h	PSL
Z 6511	ZR 26511	ZR 26512	Z 6512	h	PSL
Z 6513	ZR 26513	ZR 26514	Z 6514	h	PSL
Z 6515	ZR 26515	ZR 26516	Z 6516	h	PSL
Z 6517	ZR 26517	ZR 26518	Z 6518	h	PSL
Z 6519	ZR 26519	ZR 26520	Z 6520	h	PSL
Z 6521	ZR 26521	ZR 26522	Z 6522	h	PSL
Z 6523	ZR 26523	ZR 26524	Z 6524	h	PSL
Z 6525	ZR 26525	ZR 26526	Z 6526		PSL
Z 6527	ZR 26527	ZR 26528	Z 6528		PSL
Z 6529	ZR 26529	ZR 26530	Z 6530		PSL
Z 6531	ZR 26531	ZR 26532	Z 6532		PSL
Z 6533	ZR 26533	ZR 26534	Z 6534		PSL
Z 6535	ZR 26535	ZR 26536	Z 6536		PSL

Z 6537	ZR 26537	ZR 26538	Z 6538	PSL	Z 6545	ZR 26545	ZR 26546	Z 6546	PSL
Z 6539	ZR 26539	ZR 26540	Z 6540	PSL	Z 6547	ZR 26547	ZR 26548	Z 6548	PSL
Z 6541	ZR 26541	ZR 26542	Z 6542	PSL	Z 6549	ZR 26549	ZR 26550	Z 6550	PSL
Z 6543	ZR 26543	ZR 26544	Z 6544	PSL					

Names:

Z 6457/8	LOUVECIENNES		Z 6523/4	MARLY-LE-ROI
Z 6485/6	GARCHES		Z 6549/50	LA GARENNE-COLOMBES
Z 6505/6	VAUCRESSON			

Z 7100 CLASS 4 & 2-CAR UNITS (2–Bo+2–2+2–2+2–2)

This class carried on the diesel tradition of single power cars hauling loose trailers. They are now being refurbished and formed into fixed two or four car formations. Trailer cars are having 50 added to their numbers until refurbished, when they gain the number appropriate to the power car of the set which they happen to be in at the time (which may be different from their original number in the same series! The details shown below are for the refurbished condition, as the current situation of unrefurbished vehicles is chaotic.

ZABD+ZRAB+ZRB+ZRBDx (DMBCO–TCO–TSO–DTBSO).

System: 1500 V dc.
Built: 1960–62.
Builder-Mech. Parts: Decauville/De Dietrich.
Builder-Elec. Parts: Oerlikon.
Traction Motors: 2 x 470 kW.
Seats: 12F 46S 1L + 12F 62S 1L + 78S 1L + 65S 1L.
Weight: 56 + 26 + 26 + 27 tonnes.
Length over couplings: 26130 + 22680 + 22680 + 22680 mm.
Max. Speed: 130 km/h.

* Rheostatic braking.
r Refurbished.

Z 7101	Z 27201	Z 27101	Z 17101	r	VEN	Z 7118	Z 27218	Z 27118	Z 17118	r	VEN
Z 7102	Z 27202	Z 27102	Z 17102		VEN	Z 7119	Z 27219	Z 27119	Z 17119		VEN
Z 7103	Z 27203	Z 27103	Z 17103		VEN	Z 7120	Z 27220	Z 27120	Z 17120		VEN
Z 7104	Z 27204	Z 27104	Z 17104		VEN	Z 7121	*		Z 17121	r	AVI
Z 7105	Z 27205	Z 27105	Z 17105		VEN	Z 7122	*		Z 17122	r	AVI
Z 7106	Z 27206	Z 27106	Z 17106		VEN	Z 7123	*		Z 17123		AVI
Z 7107	Z 27207	Z 27107	Z 17107	r	VEN	Z 7124	*		Z 17124	r	AVI
Z 7108	Z 27208	Z 27108	Z 17108	r	VEN	Z 7125	*		Z 17125		AVI
Z 7109	Z 27209	Z 27109	Z 17109		VEN	Z 7126	*		Z 17126	r	AVI
Z 7110	Z 27210	Z 27110	Z 17110		VEN	Z 7127	*		Z 17127		AVI
Z 7111	Z 27211	Z 27111	Z 17111		VEN	Z 7128	*		Z 17128	r	AVI
Z 7112	Z 27212	Z 27112	Z 17112		VEN	Z 7129	*		Z 17129	r	AVI
Z 7113	Z 27213	Z 27113	Z 17113		VEN	Z 7130	*		Z 17130		AVI
Z 7114	Z 27214	Z 27114	Z 17114	r	VEN	Z 7131	*		Z 17131	r	AVI
Z 7116	Z 27216	Z 27116	Z 17116		VEN	Z 7132	*		Z 17132		AVI
Z 7117	Z 27217	Z 27117	Z 17117	r	VEN	Z 7133	*		Z 17133	r	AVI

Z 7300 CLASS   2–CAR UNITS (Bo–Bo+2–2)

The first of a new generation of e.m.u.s not intended for Paris suburban work and known as Z2 type. (Z1 being Z 7100). Those at Bordeaux have replaced old PO/Midi units on stopping services along the Paris–Bordeaux–Hendaye main line. Facing seats.

ZABD+ZRBx (DMBCO–DTSO).

System: 1500 V dc.
Built: 1980–85.
Builder: Alsthom/Francorail-MTE.
Traction Motors: 4 x 305 kW.
Seats: 24F 43S 1L + 84S 1L.
Weight: 64 + 40 tonnes.
Length over couplings: 25100 + 25100 mm.
Max. Speed: 160 km/h.

Z 7301	ZR 17301	BOR	Z 7327	ZR 17327	BOR	Z 7353	ZR 17353	TSP
Z 7302	ZR 17302	BOR	Z 7328	ZR 17328	BOR	Z 7354	ZR 17354	TSP
Z 7303	ZR 17303	BOR	Z 7329	ZR 17329	BOR	Z 7355	ZR 17355	TSP
Z 7304	ZR 17304	BOR	Z 7330	ZR 17330	BOR	Z 7356	ZR 17356	TSP
Z 7305	ZR 17305	BOR	Z 7331	ZR 17331	BOR	Z 7357	ZR 17357	MAR
Z 7306	ZR 17306	BOR	Z 7332	ZR 17332	BOR	Z 7358	ZR 17358	TSP
Z 7307	ZR 17307	BOR	Z 7333	ZR 17333	BOR	Z 7359	ZR 17359	TSP
Z 7308	ZR 17308	BOR	Z 7334	ZR 17334	BOR	Z 7360	ZR 17360	TSP
Z 7309	ZR 17309	BOR	Z 7335	ZR 17335	BOR	Z 7361	ZR 17361	TSP
Z 7310	ZR 17310	BOR	Z 7336	ZR 17336	BOR	Z 7362	ZR 17362	TSP
Z 7311	ZR 17311	BOR	Z 7337	ZR 17337	BOR	Z 7363	ZR 17363	TSP
Z 7312	ZR 17312	BOR	Z 7338	ZR 17338	BOR	Z 7364	ZR 17364	MAR
Z 7313	ZR 17313	BOR	Z 7339	ZR 17339	BOR	Z 7365	ZR 17365	MAR
Z 7314	ZR 17314	BOR	Z 7340	ZR 17340	BOR	Z 7366	ZR 17366	MAR
Z 7315	ZR 17315	BOR	Z 7341	ZR 17341	BOR	Z 7367	ZR 17367	MAR
Z 7316	ZR 17316	BOR	Z 7342	ZR 17342	BOR	Z 7368	ZR 17368	MAR
Z 7317	ZR 17317	BOR	Z 7343	ZR 17343	BOR	Z 7369	ZR 17369	MAR
Z 7318	ZR 17318	BOR	Z 7344	ZR 17344	BOR	Z 7370	ZR 17370	MAR
Z 7319	ZR 17319	BOR	Z 7345	ZR 17345	BOR	Z 7371	ZR 17371	MAR
Z 7320	ZR 17320	BOR	Z 7346	ZR 17346	BOR	Z 7372	ZR 17372	MAR
Z 7321	ZR 17321	BOR	Z 7347	ZR 17347	TSP	Z 7373	ZR 17373	TSP
Z 7322	ZR 17322	BOR	Z 7348	ZR 17348	TSP	Z 97301	ZR 917301	BOR
Z 7323	ZR 17323	BOR	Z 7349	ZR 17349	TSP	Z 97302	ZR 917302	BOR
Z 7324	ZR 17324	BOR	Z 7350	ZR 17350	TSP	Z 97303	ZR 917303	MAR
Z 7325	ZR 17325	BOR	Z 7351	ZR 17351	TSP	Z 97304	ZR 917304	MAR
Z 7326	ZR 17326	BOR	Z 7352	ZR 17352	TSP			

Names:

Z 7339	PESSAC	Z 97302	MIDI-PYRENÉES
Z 7346	MARMANDE	Z 97303	LANGUEDOC-ROUSILLON
Z 7370	MONTEUX	Z 97304	LANGUEDOC-ROUSILLON
Z 97301	MIDI-PYRENÉES		

Z 7500 CLASS   2-CAR UNITS (Bo–Bo+2–2)

This class is similar to Z 7300 but has more first class and unidirectional seating.

ZABD+ZRBx (DMBCO–DTSO).

System: 1500 V dc.
Built: 1982–83.
Builder: Alsthom/Francorail-MTE.
Traction Motors: 4 x 305 kW.
Seats: 32F 35S 1L + 84S 1L.
Weight: 64 + 40 tonnes.
Length over couplings: 25100 + 25100 mm.
Max. Speed: 160 km/h.

Z 7501	ZR 17501	MAR	Z 7506	ZR 17506	MAR	Z 7511	ZR 17511	MAR
Z 7502	ZR 17502	MAR	Z 7507	ZR 17507	MAR	Z 7512	ZR 17512	MAR
Z 7503	ZR 17503	MAR	Z 7508	ZR 17508	MAR	Z 7513	ZR 17513	MAR
Z 7504	ZR 17504	MAR	Z 7509	ZR 17509	MAR	Z 7514	ZR 17514	MAR
Z 7505	ZR 17505	MAR	Z 7510	ZR 17510	MAR	Z 7515	ZR 17515	MAR

Name: Z 7502 CHATEAUNEUF DU PAPE

Z 8100 CLASS 4-CAR UNITS (Bo–Bo+2–2+2–2+Bo–Bo)

This paris area suburban stock is known as MI 79 *(Matériel Interconnection 79)* stock and broke away from tradition by not using stainless steel bodywork. They are dual-voltage units for working over RER line B which incorporates SNCF lines to Roissy and Mitry Claye. The units are owned by SNCF or RATP and are shown as allocated to La Chapelle or RER respectively. All maintenance is carried out by RATP. The units carry cabside markings to show whether they are RATP or SNCF. The "first class seating" is identical to the second class! Later units of the series (from 8341) are built from 1985 and known as M184 stock. These are purely RATP and are not included in this book.

ZBD+ZRB+ZRAB+ZBD (DMSO-TSO-TCO-DMSO).

Systems: 1500 V dc & 25 kV ac.
Built: 1980–84.
Builder-Mech. Parts: Francorail-MTE.
Builder-Elec. Parts: Alsthom/Oerlikon.
Traction Motors: 4 x 310 kW per power car.
Seats: 72S + 84S + 32F 52S + 72S.
Weight: 56 + 48 + 48 + 56 tonnes.
Length over couplings: 26080 + 26000 + 26000 + 26080 mm.
Max. Speed: 140 km/h.

Z 8101	ZR 28101	ZR 28102	Z 8102	RER	Z 8207	ZR 28207	ZR 28208	Z 8208	PLC
Z 8103	ZR 28103	ZR 28104	Z 8104	PLC	Z 8209	ZR 28209	ZR 28210	Z 8210	RER
Z 8105	ZR 28105	ZR 28106	Z 8106	RER	Z 8211	ZR 28211	ZR 28212	Z 8212	RER
Z 8107	ZR 28107	ZR 28108	Z 8108	RER	Z 8213	ZR 28213	ZR 28214	Z 8214	PLC
Z 8109	ZR 28109	ZR 28110	Z 8110	RER	Z 8215	ZR 28215	ZR 28216	Z 8216	PLC
Z 8111	ZR 28111	ZR 28112	Z 8112	RER	Z 8217	ZR 28217	ZR 28218	Z 8218	RER
Z 8113	ZR 28113	ZR 28114	Z 8114	RER	Z 8219	ZR 28219	ZR 28220	Z 8220	RER
Z 8115	ZR 28115	ZR 28116	Z 8116	RER	Z 8221	ZR 28221	ZR 28222	Z 8222	PLC
Z 8117	ZR 28117	ZR 28118	Z 8118	RER	Z 8223	ZR 28223	ZR 28224	Z 8224	PLC
Z 8119	ZR 28119	ZR 28120	Z 8120	RER	Z 8225	ZR 28225	ZR 28226	Z 8226	RER
Z 8121	ZR 28121	ZR 28122	Z 8122	PLC	Z 8227	ZR 28227	ZR 28228	Z 8228	RER
Z 8123	ZR 28123	ZR 28124	Z 8124	RER	Z 8229	ZR 28229	ZR 28230	Z 8230	PLC
Z 8125	ZR 28125	ZR 28126	Z 8126	PLC	Z 8231	ZR 28231	ZR 28232	Z 8232	PLC
Z 8127	ZR 28127	ZR 28128	Z 8128	PLC	Z 8233	ZR 28233	ZR 28234	Z 8234	RER
Z 8129	ZR 28129	ZR 28130	Z 8130	RER	Z 8235	ZR 28235	ZR 28236	Z 8236	RER
Z 8131	ZR 28131	ZR 28132	Z 8132	PLC	Z 8237	ZR 28237	ZR 28238	Z 8238	PLC
Z 8133	ZR 28133	ZR 28134	Z 8134	PLC	Z 8239	ZR 28239	ZR 28240	Z 8240	PLC
Z 8135	ZR 28135	ZR 28136	Z 8136	PLC	Z 8241	ZR 28241	ZR 28242	Z 8242	RER
Z 8137	ZR 28137	ZR 28138	Z 8138	RER	Z 8243	ZR 28243	ZR 28244	Z 8244	PLC
Z 8139	ZR 28139	ZR 28140	Z 8140	PLC	Z 8245	ZR 28245	ZR 28246	Z 8246	PLC
Z 8141	ZR 28141	ZR 28142	Z 8142	PLC	Z 8247	ZR 28247	ZR 28248	Z 8248	PLC
Z 8143	ZR 28143	ZR 28144	Z 8144	PLC	Z 8249	ZR 28249	ZR 28250	Z 8250	PLC
Z 8145	ZR 28145	ZR 28146	Z 8146	RER	Z 8251	ZR 28251	ZR 28252	Z 8252	PLC
Z 8147	ZR 28147	ZR 28148	Z 8148	PLC	Z 8253	ZR 28253	ZR 28254	Z 8254	PLC
Z 8149	ZR 28149	ZR 28150	Z 8150	PLC	Z 8255	ZR 28255	ZR 28256	Z 8256	PLC
Z 8151	ZR 28151	ZR 28152	Z 8152	PLC	Z 8257	ZR 28257	ZR 28258	Z 8258	PLC
Z 8153	ZR 28153	ZR 28154	Z 8154	RER	Z 8259	ZR 28259	ZR 28260	Z 8260	PLC
Z 8155	ZR 28155	ZR 28156	Z 8156	PLC	Z 8261	ZR 28261	ZR 28262	Z 8262	PLC
Z 8157	ZR 28157	ZR 28158	Z 8158	PLC	Z 8263	ZR 28263	ZR 28264	Z 8264	PLC
Z 8159	ZR 28159	ZR 28160	Z 8160	PLC	Z 8265	ZR 28265	ZR 28266	Z 8266	RER
Z 8161	ZR 28161	ZR 28162	Z 8162	RER	Z 8267	ZR 28267	ZR 28268	Z 8268	RER
Z 8163	ZR 28163	ZR 28164	Z 8164	PLC	Z 8269	ZR 28269	ZR 28270	Z 8270	RER
Z 8165	ZR 28165	ZR 28166	Z 8166	PLC	Z 8271	ZR 28271	ZR 28272	Z 8272	RER
Z 8167	ZR 28167	ZR 28168	Z 8168	PLC	Z 8273	ZR 28273	ZR 28274	Z 8274	RER
Z 8169	ZR 28169	ZR 28170	Z 8170	RER	Z 8275	ZR 28275	ZR 28276	Z 8276	RER
Z 8171	ZR 28171	ZR 28172	Z 8172	PLC	Z 8277	ZR 28277	ZR 28278	Z 8278	RER
Z 8173	ZR 28173	ZR 28174	Z 8174	PLC	Z 8279	ZR 28279	ZR 28280	Z 8280	RER
Z 8175	ZR 28175	ZR 28176	Z 8176	PLC	Z 8281	ZR 28281	ZR 28282	Z 8282	RER
Z 8177	ZR 28177	ZR 28178	Z 8178	RER	Z 8283	ZR 28283	ZR 28284	Z 8284	RER
Z 8179	ZR 28179	ZR 28180	Z 8180	PLC	Z 8285	ZR 28285	ZR 28286	Z 8286	RER
Z 8181	ZR 28181	ZR 28182	Z 8182	PLC	Z 8287	ZR 28287	ZR 28288	Z 8288	RER
Z 8183	ZR 28183	ZR 28184	Z 8184	PLC	Z 8289	ZR 28289	ZR 28290	Z 8290	RER
Z 8185	ZR 28185	ZR 28186	Z 8186	PLC	Z 8291	ZR 28291	ZR 28292	Z 8292	RER
Z 8187	ZR 28187	ZR 28188	Z 8188	RER	Z 8293	ZR 28293	ZR 28294	Z 8294	RER
Z 8189	ZR 28189	ZR 28190	Z 8190	PLC	Z 8295	ZR 28295	ZR 28296	Z 8296	RER
Z 8191	ZR 28191	ZR 28192	Z 8192	PLC	Z 8297	ZR 28297	ZR 28298	Z 8298	RER
Z 8193	ZR 28193	ZR 28194	Z 8194	RER	Z 8299	ZR 28299	ZR 28300	Z 8300	RER
Z 8195	ZR 28195	ZR 28196	Z 8196	RER	Z 8301	ZR 28301	ZR 28302	Z 8302	RER
Z 8197	ZR 28197	ZR 28198	Z 8198	PLC	Z 8303	ZR 28303	ZR 28304	Z 8304	RER
Z 8199	ZR 28199	ZR 28200	Z 8200	PLC	Z 8305	ZR 28305	ZR 28306	Z 8306	RER
Z 8201	ZR 28201	ZR 28202	Z 8202	RER	Z 8307	ZR 28307	ZR 28308	Z 8308	RER
Z 8203	ZR 28203	ZR 28204	Z 8204	RER	Z 8309	ZR 28309	ZR 28310	Z 8310	RER
Z 8205	ZR 28205	ZR 28206	Z 8206	PLC	Z 8311	ZR 28311	ZR 28312	Z 8312	RER

Z 8313	ZR 28313	ZR 28314	Z 8314	RER	Z 8327	ZR 28327	ZR 28328	Z 8328	RER
Z 8315	ZR 28315	ZR 28316	Z 8316	RER	Z 8329	ZR 28329	ZR 28330	Z 8330	RER
Z 8317	ZR 28317	ZR 28318	Z 8318	RER	Z 8331	ZR 28331	ZR 28332	Z 8332	RER
Z 8319	ZR 28319	ZR 28320	Z 8320	RER	Z 8333	ZR 28333	ZR 28334	Z 8334	RER
Z 8321	ZR 28321	ZR 28322	Z 8322	RER	Z 8335	ZR 28335	ZR 28336	Z 8336	RER
Z 8323	ZR 28323	ZR 28324	Z 8324	RER	Z 8337	ZR 28337	ZR 28338	Z 8338	RER
Z 8325	ZR 28325	ZR 28326	Z 8326	RER	Z 8339	ZR 28339	ZR 28340	Z 8340	RER

Names:

Z 8257/8 RAISMES
Z 8262/2 MITRY-MORY

Z 8263/4 PERSAN

Z 8800 CLASS   4-CAR UNITS

These are a dual voltage version of Z 5600 and are allocated to Paris Sud Ouest. They will eventually be used on RER line C which will run out over SNCF lines in NW Paris. 10 units at a time are being based at La Chapelle for running under 25 kV catenary on trains out of Paris Nord. They return to Paris Sud Ouest for maintenance. The trailer cars are common with the Z 5600 class.

ZB+ZRB+ZRAB+ZB (DMSO–TSO–TCO–DMSO).

Systems: 1500 V dc & 25 kV ac.
Built: 1986 onwards.
Builder-Mech. Parts: ANF/CIMT.
Builder-Elec. Parts: Oerlikon/Alsthom.
Traction Motors: 4 x 350 kW per power car.
Max. Speed: 140 km/h.

Power Car Sets. Seats 107S. 25100 mm long. 69 tonnes. Bo–Bo+Bo–Bo.

Z 8801	Z 8802	PSO	Z 8833	Z 8834	PSO	Z 8865	Z 8866	PSO
Z 8803	Z 8804	PSO	Z 8835	Z 8836	PSO	Z 8867	Z 8868	PSO
Z 8805	Z 8806	PSO	Z 8837	Z 8838	PSO	Z 8869	Z 8870	PSO
Z 8807	Z 8808	PSO	Z 8839	Z 8840	PSO	Z 8871	Z 8872	PSO
Z 8809	Z 8810	PSO	Z 8841	Z 8842	PSO	Z 8873	Z 8874	PSO
Z 8811	Z 8812	PSO	Z 8843	Z 8844	PSO	Z 8875	Z 8876	PSO
Z 8813	Z 8814	PSO	Z 8845	Z 8846	PSO	Z 8877	Z 8878	PSO
Z 8815	Z 8816	PSO	Z 8847	Z 8848	PSO	Z 8879	Z 8880	PSO
Z 8817	Z 8818	PSO	Z 8849	Z 8850	PSO	Z 8881	Z 8882	PSO
Z 8819	Z 8820	PSO	Z 8851	Z 8852	PSO	Z 8883	Z 8884	PSO
Z 8821	Z 8822	PSO	Z 8853	Z 8854	PSO	Z 8885	Z 8886	PSO
Z 8823	Z 8824	PSO	Z 8855	Z 8856	PSO	Z 8887	Z 8888	PSO
Z 8825	Z 8826	PSO	Z 8857	Z 8858	PSO	Z 8889	Z 8890	PSO
Z 8827	Z 8828	PSO	Z 8859	Z 8860	PSO	Z 8891	Z 8892	PSO
Z 8829	Z 8830	PSO	Z 8861	Z 8862	PSO	Z 8893	Z 8894	PSO
Z 8831	Z 8832	PSO	Z 8863	Z 8864	PSO	Z 8895	Z 8896	PSO

Z 9500 CLASS   2-CAR UNITS (Bo–Bo+2–2)

This is a dual-voltage version version of Z 7300 and has unidirectional seating.

ZABD+ZRBx (DMBCO–RTDSO).

Systems: 1500 V dc & 25 kV ac.
Built: 1982–83.
Builders: Alsthom/Francorail-MTE.
Traction Motors: 4 x 305 kW.
Seats: 32F 35S 1L + 84S 1L.
Weight: 66 + 50 tonnes.
Length over couplings: 25100 + 25100 mm.
Max. Speed: 160 km/h.

Z 9501	ZR 19501	VEN	Z 9508	ZR 19508	VEN	Z 9515	ZR 19515	VEN
Z 9502	ZR 19502	VEN	Z 9509	ZR 19509	VEN	Z 9516	ZR 19516	VEN
Z 9503	ZR 19503	VEN	Z 9510	ZR 19510	VEN	Z 9517	ZR 19517	VEN
Z 9504	ZR 19504	VEN	Z 9511	ZR 19511	VEN	Z 9518	ZR 19518	VEN
Z 9505	ZR 19505	VEN	Z 9512	ZR 19512	VEN	Z 99501	ZR 919501	VEN
Z 9506	ZR 19506	VEN	Z 9513	ZR 19513	VEN	Z 99502	ZR 919502	VEN
Z 9507	ZR 19507	VEN	Z 9514	ZR 19514	VEN			

Names:

Z 9517   SAINT-PRIEST

Z 99501   EPR BOURGOGNE FRANCHE-COMPTE.

Z 9600 CLASS   2-CAR UNITS (Bo–Bo+2–2)

This is the dual-voltage version of Z 7300 and is used in recently electrified areas where the dc and ac systems meet.

ZABD+ZRBx (DMBCO–RDTSO).

Systems: 1500 V dc & 25 kV ac.
Built: 1984 onwards.
Builders: Alsthom/Francorail-MTE.
Traction Motors: 4 x 305 kW.
Seats: 24F 43S 1L + 84S 1L.
Weight: 66 + 50 tonnes.
Length over couplings: 25100 + 25100 mm.
Max. Speed: 160 km/h.

Z 9601	Z 19601	REN	Z 9613	Z 19613	REN	Z 9625	Z 19625	REN
Z 9602	Z 19602	REN	Z 9614	Z 19614	VEN	Z 9626	Z 19626	REN
Z 9603	Z 19603	REN	Z 9615	Z 19615	VEN	Z 9627	Z 19627	REN
Z 9604	Z 19604	VEN	Z 9616	Z 19616	VEN	Z 9628	Z 19628	REN
Z 9605	Z 19605	REN	Z 9617	Z 19617	VEN	Z 9629	Z 19629	REN
Z 9606	Z 19606	REN	Z 9618	Z 19618	VEN	Z 9630	Z 19630	
Z 9607	Z 19607	REN	Z 9619	Z 19619	VEN	Z 9631	Z 19631	
Z 9608	Z 19608	REN	Z 9620	Z 19620	VEN	Z 9632	Z 19632	
Z 9609	Z 19609	REN	Z 9621	Z 19621	REN	Z 9633	Z 19633	
Z 9610	Z 19610	REN	Z 9622	Z 19622	REN	Z 9634	Z 19634	
Z 9611	Z 19611	REN	Z 9623	Z 19623	VEN	Z 9635	Z 19635	
Z 9612	Z 19612	REN	Z 9624	Z 19624	REN	Z 9636	Z 19636	

Name:

Z 9624   LES PAYS DE LA LOIRE

Z 11500 CLASS   2-CAR UNITS (Bo–Bo+2–2)

To be introduced 1986/7. An ac only version of Z 7300 for use around Metz at first.

ZABD+ZRBx (DMBCO–DTSO).

System: 25 kV ac.
Built: 1986//.
Builders: Alsthom/Francorail-MTE.
Traction Motors: 4 x 305 kW.
Seats: 24F 43S 1L + 84S 1L.
Weight: +   tonnes.
Length over couplings: 25100 + 25100 mm.
Max. Speed: 160 km/h.

Z 11501	Z 111501	Z 11509	Z 111509	Z 11516	Z 111516
Z 11502	Z 111502	Z 11510	Z 111510	Z 11517	Z 111517
Z 11503	Z 111503	Z 11511	Z 111511	Z 11518	Z 111518
Z 11504	Z 111504	Z 11512	Z 111512	Z 11519	Z 111519
Z 11505	Z 111505	Z 11513	Z 111513	Z 11520	Z 111520
Z 11506	Z 111506	Z 11514	Z 111514	Z 11521	Z 111521
Z 11507	Z 111507	Z 11515	Z 111515	Z 11522	Z 111522
Z 11508	Z 111508				

TURBOTRAINS
T 1000 CLASS (ETG)   4-CAR UNITS

In 1967 SNCF converted d.m.u. X 4375, XR 8575 into an experimental gas turbine unit. X 4375 had a new cab provided but the diesel motor and transmission retained. The trailer car also had a new cab fitted but this received a gas turbine power unit and was renumbered to X 2061. After detailed testing it was decided to order a production series of 4 car sets. These became the ETGs where the T 1000 are the turbine cars and T 1500 the diesel cars. For many years the class was allocated to Venissieux shed at Lyon but recently they have moved to Lyon Vaise depot. The electrification of the Grenoble line has led to new duties being found for these sets including workings to Clermont Ferrand and Metz.

TB+TRA+TRB+TBD (DMSO–TFO–TSO–DMBSO).

Built: 1969–72.
Builder: ANF.
Engine: Turmo IIIF3 of 820 kW + Saurer SDHR of 320 kW.
Transmission: Hydraulic (Voith L 411 r) + mechanical.
Seats: 44S + 56F + 54S + 48S.
Total Weight: 42 + 28 + 33 + 44 tonnes.
Length over couplings 22840 + 20750 + 20750 + 22840 mm.
Max. Speed: 160 km/h.

T 1001	TR 21001	TR 51001	T 1501	LYV		T 1008	TR 21008	TR 51008	T 1508	LYV
T 1002	TR 21002	TR 51002	T 1502	LYV		T 1009	TR 21009	TR 51009	T 1509	LYV
T 1003	TR 21003	TR 51003	T 1503	LYV		T 1010	TR 21010	TR 51010	T 1510	LYV
T 1004	TR 21004	TR 51004	T 1504	LYV		T 1011	TR 21011	TR 51011	T 1511	LYV
T 1005	TR 21005	TR 51005	T 1505	LYV		T 1012	TR 21012	TR 51012	T 1512	LYV
T 1006	TR 21006	TR 51006	T 1506	LYV		T 1013	TR 21013	TR 51013	T 1513	LYV
T 1007	TR 21007	TR 51007	T 1507	LYV		T 1014	TR 21014	TR 51014	T 1514	LYV

CLASS T 2000 (RTG)   5-CAR UNITS

Pleased with the success of the ETGs SNCF went one better and built some 5 car sets with a gas turbine power car at each end. The odd numbered power cars have a slightly more powerful turbine and once on the move the lower powered one is usually shut down. Two units can run together but until recently were not multiple working fitted so that each set had to have its own driver. They kept in contact over an intercom. However the units are now being modified to permit multiple working. The Caen based units work many of the through trains from Paris St.Lazare to destinations off the electrified main line and also certain services out of Paris Nord including trains that connect with the hovercrafts from the Boulogne to Dover. Those at Vénissieux work mostly on the Strasbourg–Lyon–Bordeaux axis. The set formations vary between units allocated to Caen and Vénissieux.

TBD+TRB (TRAB*)+TRA+TRBr+TBD.
(DMBSO–TSO [TCO§]–TFO–TSORK [TSORB§]–DMBSO).

Built: 1972–76.
Builder: ANF/MTE.
Engine: Turmo XII of 1200 kW (uneven numbers), Turmo IIIF1 of 820 kW (even numbers).
Transmission: Hydraulic. Voith L 411 r U.
Seats: 48S 1L + 80S 2L (29F 40S 2L*) + 60F 2L + 48S 1L (44S 24 chairs 1L§) + 48S 1L.
Total Weight: 54 + 38 + 42 + 37 + 54 tonnes.
Length over couplings: 26230 + 25510 + 25510 + 25510 + 26230 mm.
Max. Speed: 160 km/h.

T 2001	TR 32001*	TR 22001	TR 52001§	T 2002	VEN	AIX-LES-BAINS
T 2003	TR 32002*	TR 22002	TR 52002§	T 2004	VEN	LYON
T 2005	TR 32003*	TR 22003	TR 52003§	T 2006	VEN	SAUMUR
T 2007	TR 32004*	TR 22004	TR 52004§	T 2008	VEN	VÉNISSIEUX
T 2009	TR 32005*	TR 22005	TR 52005§	T 2010	VEN	BOURGES
T 2011	TR 32006*	TR 22006	TR 52006§	T 2012	VEN	CLERMONT FERRAND
T 2013	TR 32007*	TR 22007	TR 52007§	T 2014	VEN	QUIMPER
T 2015	TR 32008*	TR 22008	TR 52008§	T 2016	VEN	LE VERDON
T 2021	TR 32011*	TR 22011	TR 52011§	T 2022	VEN	BESANÇON
T 2023	TR 32012*	TR 22012	TR 52012§	T 2024	VEN	GUÉRET

T 2025	TR 32013*	TR 22013	TR 52013§	T 2026 VEN	EYGURANDE-MERLINES
T 2027	TR 32014*	TR 22014	TR 52014§	T 2028 VEN	
T 2029	TR 32015*	TR 22015	TR 52015§	T 2030 VEN	MONTBÉLIARD
T 2031	TR 32016*	TR 22016	TR 52016§	T 2032 VEN	MONTLUÇON
T 2033	TR 32017*	TR 22017	TR 52017§	T 2034 VEN	NANTES
T 2036	TR 32018*	TR 22018	TR 52018	T 2035 CAN	PÉRIGUEUX
T 2038	TR 32019*	TR 22019	TR 52019	T 2037 CAN	ROYON
T 2040	TR 42020	TR 22020	TR 52020	T 2039 CAN	DINARD
T 2042	TR 42021	TR 22021	TR 52021	T 2041 CAN	CAEN
T 2044	TR 42022	TR 22022	TR 52022	T 2043 CAN	DINAN
T 2046	TR 42023	TR 22023	TR 52023	T 2045 CAN	
T 2048	TR 42024	TR 22024	TR 52024	T 2047 CAN	LAON
T 2050	TR 42025	TR 22025	TR 52025	T 2049 CAN	ANGERS
T 2052	TR 42026	TR 22026	TR 52026	T 2051 CAN	
T 2054	TR 42027	TR 22027	TR 52027	T 2053 CAN	BRIOUZE
T 2056	TR 42028	TR 22028	TR 52028	T 2055 CAN	
T 2058	TR 42029	TR 22029	TR 52029	T 2057 CAN	SANCY LES-CHEMINOTS
T 2060	TR 42030	TR 22030	TR 52030	T 2059 CAN	
T 2062	TR 42031	TR 22031	TR 52031	T 2061 CAN	CALAIS
T 2064	TR 42032	TR 22032	TR 52032	T 2063 CAN	BOULOGNE-SUR-MER
T 2066	TR 42033	TR 22033	TR 52033	T 2065 CAN	
T 2068	TR 42034	TR 22034	TR 52034	T 2067 CAN	
T 2070	TR 42035	TR 22035	TR 52035	T 2069 CAN	
T 2072	TR 42036	TR 22036	TR 52036	T 2071 CAN	BERNAY
T 2074	TR 42037	TR 22037	TR 52037	T 2073 CAN	TOURS
T 2076	TR 42038	TR 22038	TR 52038	T 2075 CAN	
T 2078	TR 42039	TR 22039	TR 52039	T 2077 CAN	
T 2080	TR 42040	TR 22040	TR 52040	T 2079 CAN	
T 2082	TR 42041	TR 22041	TR 52041	T 2081 CAN	

TRAINS À GRANDE VITESSE

23000 CLASS (TGV SUD EST) 10 CAR ARTICULATED UNITS (Bo–Bo+Bo–2–2–2–2–2–2–2–Bo+Bo–Bo)

The TGV is a modern day success story for SNCF. It is the fastest service train in the world. Each TGV set is in effect a 10–car e.m.u. with 1+ power cars at each end. Yes 1+! It is not always appreciated that each TGV Sud-Est set has 6 motor bogies. There are two under each outer power car and the bogie next to the power car on the adjoining vehicles is also powered. The power cars are numbered as dual-voltage locomotives but referred to as TGV 23001 etc or by their set numbers. Normally the sets keep in formation but obviously changes take place following the discovery of defects etc. Nos.23176/7 are presently running as TGV Atlantique prototypes 02301/2 together with the trailers from set 82. The names of the TGV sets are carried on the non-driving motor car (semi-motrice) (TGVZR).

Electro-pneumatic brakes. Rheostatic brakes. Multiple working. Disc brakes on trailers in addition to blocks. Radio fitted. Cab signalling.

TGV+TGVZRADr+TGVRAr+TGVRA+TGVRBr+3TGVRB+TGVZRB+TGV.
(DM–MBFORK–TFORK–TFO–TSORB–3TSO–MSO–DM).

* First class only sets:
TGV+TGVZRADr+TGVRAr+TGVRA+TGVRAr+2TGVRA+TGVRAr+TGVZRA+TGV.
(DM–MBFORK–TFORK–TFO–TFORB–2FO–TFORK–MFO–DM).

Systems: 1500 V dc/25 KV ac.
Built: 1978–86.
Builders: Alsthom/Francorail-MTE/De Dietrich.
Traction Motors: 12 x TAB676 per set of 525 kW each.
Seats: 0 + 35F 1L + [2 x 38F 1L] + 35S 1L + 60S 2L + 60S 1L + 60S 2L + 60S 1L + 0. (0 + 35F 1L + [2 x 38F 1L] + 24F 1L + [4 x 38F 1L] + 0*).
Weight: 65 + 43 + [6 x 28] + 44 + 65 tonnes.
Length over couplings: 22150 + 21845 + [6 x 18700] + 21845 + 22150 mm.
Max. Speed: 280 km/h.

Non-driving motors and trailer cars are numbered in sequence. The numbers are not shown individually, but the sequence is as follows:

Set nnn: 123nnn/223nnn/323nnn/423nnn/523nnn/623nnn/723nnn/823nnn.
The set numbers shown on the side of the sets apply only to the TGV Sud-Est. It appearsthat the numbers will be duplicated on the TGV=Atlantique sets.

SET 01	TGV 23001	TGV 23002	PSE	
SET 02	TGV 23003	TGV 23004	PSE	MARSEILLE
SET 03	TGV 23005	TGV 23006	PSE	BELFORT
SET 04	TGV 23007	TGV 23008	PSE	RAMBOUILLET
SET 05	TGV 23009	TGV 23010	PSE	RIS-ORANGIS
SET 06	TGV 23011	TGV 23012	PSE	FRASNE
SET 07	TGV 23013	TGV 23014	PSE	CONFLANS-SAINTE-HONORINE
SET 08	TGV 23015	TGV 23016	PSE	ROUEN
SET 09	TGV 23017	TGV 23018	PSE	VINCENNES
SET 10	TGV 23019	TGV 23020	PSE	HAYANGE
SET 11	TGV 23021	TGV 23022	PSE	NÎMES
SET 12	TGV 23023	TGV 23024	PSE	LE HAVRE
SET 13	TGV 23025	TGV 23026	PSE	ABLON-SUR-SEINE
SET 14	TGV 23027	TGV 23028	PSE	MONTPELLIER
SET 15	TGV 23029	TGV 23030	PSE	PAU
SET 16	TGV 23031	TGV 23032	PSE	LYON
SET 17	TGV 23033	TGV 23034	PSE	TERGNIER
SET 18	TGV 23035	TGV 23036	PSE	LE CREUSOT
SET 19	TGV 23037	TGV 23038	PSE	SAINT ARMAND-LES-EAUX
SET 20	TGV 23039	TGV 23040	PSE	COLMAR
SET 21	TGV 23041	TGV 23042	PSE	DIJON
SET 22	TGV 23043	TGV 23044	PSE	VALENCIENNES
SET 23	TGV 23045	TGV 23046	PSE	MONTBARD
SET 24	TGV 23047	TGV 23048	PSE	ALFORTVILLE
SET 25	TGV 23049	TGV 23050	PSE	BESANÇON
SET 26	TGV 23051	TGV 23052	PSE	SAINT ÉTIENNE
SET 27	TGV 23053	TGV 23054	PSE	MÂCON
SET 28	TGV 23055	TGV 23056	PSE	MONTÉLIMAR
SET 29	TGV 23057	TGV 23058	PSE	VILLENEUVE-SAINT-GEORGES
SET 30	TGV 23059	TGV 23060	PSE	LILLE
SET 31	TGV 23061	TGV 23062	PSE	COMBS-LA-VILLE
SET 32	TGV 23063	TGV 23064	PSE	MAISONS-ALFORT
SET 33	TGV 23065	TGV 23066	* PSE	FÉCAMP
SET 34	TGV 23067	TGV 23068	* PSE	DUNKERQUE
SET 35	TGV 23069	TGV 23070	* PSE	GRENOBLE
SET 36	TGV 23071	TGV 23072	* PSE	SEINE SAINT-DENIS
SET 37	TGV 23073	TGV 23074	* PSE	SAINT GERMAIN-EN-LAYE
SET 38	TGV 23075	TGV 23076	* PSE	
SET 39	TGV 23077	TGV 23078	PSE	EVIAN + THONON
SET 40	TGV 23079	TGV 23080	PSE	VERSAILLES
SET 41	TGV 23081	TGV 23082	PSE	VILLIERS-LE-BEL
SET 42	TGV 23083	TGV 23084	PSE	CHAMBÉRY
SET 43	TGV 23085	TGV 23086	PSE	AIX-LES-BAINS
SET 44	TGV 23087	TGV 23088	PSE	CLERMONT-FERRAND
SET 45	TGV 23089	TGV 23090	PSE	VALENCE
SET 46	TGV 23091	TGV 23092	PSE	CONTREXÉVILLE
SET 47	TGV 23093	TGV 23094	PSE	NANCY
SET 48	TGV 23095	TGV 23096	PSE	COMTÉ-DE-NICE
SET 49	TGV 23097	TGV 23098	PSE	RENNES
SET 50	TGV 23099	TGV 23100	PSE	BEAUVAIS
SET 51	TGV 23101	TGV 23102	PSE	GIVORS + GRIGNY-BADAN
SET 52	TGV 23103	TGV 23104	PSE	GENÈVE
SET 53	TGV 23105	TGV 23106	PSE	LE PUY-EN-VELAY
SET 54	TGV 23107	TGV 23108	PSE	CHAGNY
SET 55	TGV 23109	TGV 23110	PSE	DENAIN
SET 56	TGV 23111	TGV 23112	PSE	ANNECY
SET 57	TGV 23113	TGV 23114	PSE	BOURG-EN-BRESSE
SET 58	TGV 23115	TGV 23116	PSE	OULLINS

```
SET  59 TGV 23117    TGV 23118        PSE    HAUTMONT
SET  60 TGV 23119    TGV 23120        PSE    LANGEAC
SET  61 TGV 23121    TGV 23122        PSE    FONTAINEBLEAU
SET  62 TGV 23123    TGV 23124        PSE    TOULOUSE
SET  63 TGV 23125    TGV 23126        PSE    VILLEURBANNE
SET  64 TGV 23127    TGV 23128        PSE    DOLE
SET  65 TGV 23129    TGV 23130        PSE    SÈTE
SET  66 TGV 23131    TGV 23132        PSE    AVIGNON
SET  67 TGV 23133    TGV 23134        PSE    BELLEGARDE-SUR-VAISERINE
SET  68 TGV 23135    TGV 23136        PSE    MODANE
SET  69 TGV 23137    TGV 23138        PSE    VICHY
SET  70 TGV 23139    TGV 23140        PSE    MELUN
SET  71 TGV 23141    TGV 23142        PSE    BRUNOY
SET  72 TGV 23143    TGV 23144        PSE    CAHORS
SET  73 TGV 23145    TGV 23146        PSE    CHARENTON-LE-PONT
SET  74 TGV 23147    TGV 23148        PSE    ARBOIS-MOUCHARD-PORT LESNEY
SET  75 TGV 23149    TGV 23150        PSE
SET  76 TGV 23151    TGV 23152        PSE    PONTARLIER
SET  77 TGV 23153    TGV 23154        PSE    NUITS-SAINT-GEORGES
SET  78 TGV 23155    TGV 23156        PSE    CULOZ
SET  79 TGV 23157    TGV 23158        PSE    ANNEMASSE
SET  80 TGV 23159    TGV 23160        PSE    TOULON
SET  81 TGV 23161    TGV 23162        PSE    TONNERRE
SET  82 TGV 23163    TGV 23164        PSE    TRAPPES
SET  83 TGV 23165    TGV 23166        PSE    MOISSY CRAMAYEL
SET  84 TGV 23167    TGV 23168        PSE    DIEPPE
SET  85 TGV 23169    TGV 23170        PSE    BEAUNE
SET  86 TGV 23171    TGV 23172        PSE    MONTLUÇON
SET  87 TGV 23173    TGV 23174        PSE    MONTCHANIN
SET  88 TGV 23175    TGV 23176        PSE
SET  89 TGV 23177    TGV 23178        PSE
SET  90 TGV 23179    TGV 23180        PSE
SET  91 TGV 23181    TGV 23182        PSE
SET  92 TGV 23183    TGV 23184        PSE
SET  93 TGV 23185    TGV 23186        PSE
SET  94 TGV 23187    TGV 23188        PSE
SET  95 TGV 23189    TGV 23190        PSE
SET  96 TGV 23191    TGV 23192        PSE
SET  97 TGV 23193    TGV 23194        PSE
SET  98 TGV 23195    TGV 23196        PSE
SET  99 TGV 23197    TGV 23198        PSE
SET 100 TGV 23199    TGV 23200    *   PSE    SAINT GERVAIS-LES-BAINS
SET 101 TGV 23201    TGV 23202    *   PSE
SET 102 TGV 23203    TGV 23204    *   PSE
```

33000 CLASS (TGV SUD EST) 10-CAR ARTICULATED UNITS

TGV 33000 are similar to TGV 23000 but fitted for triple-voltage selection for working into Switzerland. Details as for 23001 except:
Systems: 1500 V dc/25 kV ac 50 Hz/15 kV ac 16⅔ Hz.

```
SET 110 TGV 33001    TGV 33002        PSE    PAYS DE VAUD
SET 111 TGV 33003    TGV 33004        PSE
SET 112 TGV 33005    TGV 33006        PSE    LAUSANNE
SET 113 TGV 33007    TGV 33008        PSE
SET 114 TGV 33009    TGV 33010        PSE
SET 115 TGV 33011    TGV 33012        PSE
SET 116 TGV 33013    TGV 33014        PSE
SET 117 TGV 33015    TGV 33016        PSE
```

923000 CLASS (TGV POSTAL) 12 CAR ARTICULATED UNITS

Formation as for 23000 series, but no windows or seats. Painted yellow. There are five half-sets. Non-driving motors and trailers are numbered as follows:

SET *n*: 91230*n*/92230*n*/93230*n*/94230*n*.

| SET P1 | 923001 | PSE | SET P3 | 923003 | PSE | SET P5 | 923005 | PSE |
| SET P2 | 923002 | PSE | SET P4 | 923004 | PSE | | | |

24000 CLASS (TGV ATLANTIQUE) 12 CAR ARTICULATED UNITS (Bo–Bo+2–2–2–2–2–2–2–2–2–2–2+Bo–Bo)

These sets will be even longer, even more powerful and even faster than the TGV Sud-Est sets and will be painted in a new blue and white livery. The sets will be even more luxurious than the TGV-PSE. Trailer 1 will have unidirectional seating with trailers 2 and three having facing seating including 6 semi-compartments with four seats in each. The bar coach will include a telephone, as will coach 6. Coaches 8 and 9 will include 4 family semi-compartments of 4 seats and coach 9 will also include facilities for nursing mothers. Coach 10 will have a special 17 seat childrens compartment at the end.

TGV+TGVRADr+TGVRAr+TGVRA+TGVRBr+6TGVRB+TGV.
(DM–MBFORK–TFORK–TFO–TSORB–6TSO–DM).

Systems: 1500 V dc/25 KV ac.
Built: 1988 onwards.
Builders: Alsthom/Francorail-MTE/De Dietrich.
Traction Motors: 8 x 1100 kW per set.
Seats: 0 + 44F 1L + [2 x 36F 1L] + Bar + 60S 2L + 60S 1L + 60S 2L + 60S 1L + 56S 1L + 77S 2L + 0.
(0 + 35F 1L + [2 x 38F 1L] + 24F 1L + [4 x 38F 1L] + 0*).
Weight:
Length over couplings:
Max. Speed: 300 km/h.

Trailer cars will be numbered in sequence. The numbers are not shown individually, but the sequence is as follows:

Set *nnn*: 241*nnn*/242*nnn*/243*nnn*/244*nnn*/245*nnn*/246*nnn*/247*nnn*/248*nnn*/249*nnn*/240*nnn*.

SET 01	TGV 24001 /24002	SET 33	TGV 24065 /24066	SET 65	TGV 24129 /24130
SET 02	TGV 24003 /24004	SET 34	TGV 24067 /24068	SET 66	TGV 24131 /24132
SET 03	TGV 24005 /24006	SET 35	TGV 24069 /24070	SET 67	TGV 24133 /24134
SET 04	TGV 24007 /24008	SET 36	TGV 24071 /24072	SET 68	TGV 24135 /24136
SET 05	TGV 24009 /24010	SET 37	TGV 24073 /24074	SET 69	TGV 24137 /24138
SET 06	TGV 24011 /24012	SET 38	TGV 24075 /24076	SET 70	TGV 24139 /24140
SET 07	TGV 24013 /24014	SET 39	TGV 24077 /24078	SET 71	TGV 24141 /24142
SET 08	TGV 24015 /24016	SET 40	TGV 24079 /24080	SET 72	TGV 24143 /24144
SET 09	TGV 24017 /24018	SET 41	TGV 24081 /24082	SET 73	TGV 24145 /24146
SET 10	TGV 24019 /24020	SET 42	TGV 24083 /24084	SET 74	TGV 24147 /24148
SET 11	TGV 24021 /24022	SET 43	TGV 24085 /24086	SET 75	TGV 24149 /24150
SET 12	TGV 24023 /24024	SET 44	TGV 24087 /24088	SET 76	TGV 24151 /24152
SET 13	TGV 24025 /24026	SET 45	TGV 24089 /24090	SET 77	TGV 24153 /24154
SET 14	TGV 24027 /24028	SET 46	TGV 24091 /24092	SET 78	TGV 24155 /24156
SET 15	TGV 24029 /24030	SET 47	TGV 24093 /24094	SET 79	TGV 24157 /24158
SET 16	TGV 24031 /24032	SET 48	TGV 24095 /24096	SET 80	TGV 24159 /24160
SET 17	TGV 24033 /24034	SET 49	TGV 24097 /24098	SET 81	TGV 24161 /24162
SET 18	TGV 24035 /24036	SET 50	TGV 24099 /24100	SET 82	TGV 24163 /24164
SET 19	TGV 24037 /24038	SET 51	TGV 24101 /24102	SET 83	TGV 24165 /24166
SET 20	TGV 24039 /24040	SET 52	TGV 24103 /24104	SET 84	TGV 24167 /24168
SET 21	TGV 24041 /24042	SET 53	TGV 24105 /24106	SET 85	TGV 24169 /24170
SET 22	TGV 24043 /24044	SET 54	TGV 24107 /24108	SET 86	TGV 24171 /24172
SET 23	TGV 24045 /24046	SET 55	TGV 24109 /24110	SET 87	TGV 24173 /24174
SET 24	TGV 24047 /24048	SET 56	TGV 24111 /24112	SET 88	TGV 24175 /24176
SET 25	TGV 24049 /24050	SET 57	TGV 24113 /24114	SET 89	TGV 24177 /24178
SET 26	TGV 24051 /24052	SET 58	TGV 24115 /24116	SET 90	TGV 24179 /24180
SET 27	TGV 24053 /24054	SET 59	TGV 24117 /24118	SET 91	TGV 24181 /24182
SET 28	TGV 24055 /24056	SET 60	TGV 24119 /24120	SET 92	TGV 24183 /24184
SET 29	TGV 24057 /24058	SET 61	TGV 24121 /24122	SET 93	TGV 24185 /24186
SET 30	TGV 24059 /24060	SET 62	TGV 24123 /24124	SET 94	TGV 24187 /24188
SET 31	TGV 24061 /24062	SET 63	TGV 24125 /24126	SET 95	TGV 24189 /24190
SET 32	TGV 24063 /24064	SET 64	TGV 24127 /24128		

SNCF NARROW GAUGE VEHICLES

There are three metre gauge lines in France operated by the SNCF, plus the Chemins de Fer du Corse (Corsica) which is now owned by the SNCF. These lines are described separately.

SNCF LIGNE DE CERDAGNE

This line opened 1910–29 was electrified from opening at 850 V dc third rail. Running from Villefranche-le-Conflent to La Tour-de-Carol it traverses mountain scenery with extremely sharp curves and steep gradients and several spectacular bridges. The line was under threat of closure for several years and freight traffic ceased in 1974. However efforts to promote the tourist potential of the line seem to have been successful. All the stock was refurbished in 1962–8 and painted in the then current red and yellow railcar livery. Commencing in 1983 the stock has been undergoing further refurbishment and painting in a mainly yellow livery. The depot is at Villefranche-le-Conflent, although stock is nominally alllocated to Béziers where overhauls are carried out.

Z 100 CLASS — SINGLE UNITS (Bo–Bo)

Formerly Midi E ABDe 2–9/11–3/15–8. Cars marked * were built as trailers, these were converted to motor cars in 1912–21. They were originally Midi ABDe 14/11–3/15–8 respectively. EABDe 5 replaced an accident victim. The internal layout of these cars differs from the others which were built as motor cars.

ZBD (DMBSO).

Built: 1908–09.
Builder-Mech. Parts: Carde & Cie/SACM.
Builder-Elec. Parts: Sprague–Thomson.
Traction Motors: 4 x 66 kW.
Seats: 40 S.
Length over couplings: 14904 (14384*) mm.

Weight: 32 (28*) tonnes.
Max. Speed: 55 km/ h.

Z 102	Z 105 *	Z 107	Z 109	Z 112 *	Z 115 *	Z 117*
Z 103	Z 106	Z 108	Z 111 *	Z 113 *	Z 116 *	Z 118*
Z 104						

Z 200 CLASS — SINGLE UNITS (Bo–Bo)

The last survivors of ten motored vans built for freight use. Originally Midi E.De 8–9, then SNCF Z 208–9, later Z 201–2. Now used on snowplough duties.

XD (DMLV).

Built: 1908–09.
Builder-Mech. Parts: Carde & Cie/SACM.
Builder-Elec. Parts: Sprague–Thomson.
Traction Motors: 4 x 66 kW.
Seats: None.
Length over couplings: 11284 mm.

Weight: 27 tonnes.
Max. Speed: 25 km/h.

Z 201	Z 202

ZR 20000 CLASS — TRAILER CARS (2–2)

Three types of trailer car are in use:
   The surviving original cars not converted to motors (ex Midi ABDe 1–4).
* Open-top cars, originally roofed (ex Midi Be 30–4).
† Cars second-hand from the CF Economiques du Nord in 1936.
Built: 1908–09, 1912*, 1910–12†.
Builders: Carde & Cie. (Decauville†).
Seats: 44S (59S*, 46S†).
Length over couplings: 14384 (10500*, 13370†) mm.

Weight: 14.5 (10*, 13†) tonnes.
Max. Speed: 55 km/h.

ZR 20001	ZR 20003	ZR 20023 *	ZR 20031 *	ZR 20033 *	ZR 20036 †	ZR 20038 †
ZR 20002	ZR 20004	ZR 20030 †	ZR 20032 *	ZR 20034 *	ZR 20037 †	ZR 20039 †

SNCF LIGNE DE SAVOIE

This line, opened in 1901, is one of the steepest adhesion railways in the world. Electrified from opening at 750 V dc third rail, it extends from St. Gervais les Bains to Vallorane, where a connection is made with the Swiss Martigny–Châtelard Railway. Some through operation exists between the two railways.

The original stock is unusual since all vehicles are powered and multiple working fitted (including wagons!). However freight operations ceased in 1970, the remaining wagons being in departmental use. Modern stock introduced in 1958 included trailer cars.

The depot is at St. Gervais-les-Bains.

Z 200 CLASS   SINGLE UNITS (Bo)

The surviving motored vans with one driving cab. Used at each end of formations of original stock. Z 205TGV 8 are in departmental use, and Z 209TGV 16 are in the historic train.

ZD (DMB).

Built: 1901–09.
Builder-Mech. Parts: Horme & Buire.
Builder-Elec. Parts:
Traction Motors: 2 x   kW.
Seats: None.
Length over couplings: 10150 mm.
Weight: 23 tonnes.
Max. Speed: 35 km/h.

| Z 205 | Z 208 | Z 209 | Z 216 |

Z 450 CLASS   ROTARY SNOWPLOUGH (Bo)

Built: 1901–09.
Builder-Mech. Parts: Horme & Buire.
Traction Motors: 2 x   kW.
Weight: 35 tonnes.
Length over couplings: 8700 mm.
Max. Speed: 20 km/h.

Z 450

Z 600 CLASS   SINGLE UNITS (Bo–Bo)

ZABD (DMBCO).

Built: 1958.
Builder-Mech. Parts: Decauville.
Builder-Elec. Parts: Oerlikon.
Traction Motors: 4 x   kW.
Seats: 8F 34S.
Length over couplings: 18200 mm.
Weight: 40 tonnes.
Max. Speed: 70 km/h.

| Z 601 | Z 603 | Z 604 | Z 605 | Z 606 | Z 607 | Z 608 |
| Z 602 | | | | | | |

Z 691 CLASS   ROTARY SNOWPLOUGH (1–Bo)

Built: 1958.
Builder-Mech. Parts: SNCF.
Weight: 33 tonnes.
Length over couplings: 9015 mm.
Max. Speed: 40 km/h.

Z 691

ZS 10000 CLASS   SINGLE UNITS (Bo)

The original powered intermediate cars, used in the historic train.

ZB (MSO). [ZAB (MCO*)]. **Built:** 1901–09.

Builder-Mech. Parts: Horme & Buire.
Seats: 38S (44S†, 16F 26S*).
Length over couplings: 10150 mm.

Weight: 20 tonnes.
Max. Speed: 35 km/h.

| ZS 10003 | ZS 10004 | ZS 10066 † | ZS 10118 * | ZS 10119 * | ZS 10129 * | ZS 10130 * |

ZS 10200 CLASS   SINGLE UNITS (Bo)

The original powered goods wagons. a Ballast wagon, 19 tonnes, b Bolster wagon, 19 tonnes, c Breakdown van, 21 tonnes, d Covered van, 22 tonnes, e Open wagon, 19 tonnes.

Built: 1901–09.
Builder-Mech. Parts: Horme & Buire.
Length over couplings: 8600 mm.   **Max. Speed:** 35 km/h.

| ZS 10204 a | ZS 10208 a | ZS 10212 b | ZS 10301 c | ZS 10316 d | ZS 10421 e | ZS 10429 e |
| ZS 10205 a | ZS 10211 b | ZS 10222 b | ZS 10308 d | ZS 10420 e | ZS 10423 e | |

ZS 10400 CLASS   SNOWPLOUGH (Bo)

Built: 1901–09.
Builder-Mech. Parts: Horme & Buire.
Weight: 20 tonnes.
Length over couplings: 6875 mm.   **Max. Speed:** 30 km/h.

ZS 10450

Z 20600 CLASS   TRAILER CARS (2–2)

Intermediate trailers for Z 601–8.

ZRAB (DTBCO).

Built: 1958.
Builder-Mech. Parts: Decauville.
Seats: 24F 35S.
Length over couplings: 18200 mm.

Weight: 20 tonnes.
Max. Speed: 70 km/h.

| ZR 20601 | ZR 20602 | ZR 20603 | ZR 20604 |

CHEMIN DE FER DU BLANC–ARGENT.

This line, owned by the SNCF is operated by the above company. Formerly running between the towns in its title, it now operates a passenger service only between Salbris to Luçay le Mâlé, the section onwards to Buzançais being freight only. The passenger stock has recently been modernised, but the future of the freight service is uncertain. The depot and workshops are located in Romorantin.

DIESEL LOCOMOTIVES   C

Built on the frames of 0–6–0T steam locos. T 11/12 came to the BA in 1952 from CFD Réseau de Yonne; rebuilt at Romorantin before entering service. T 13/14 were formerly steam locos 25TGV 28.

Built: 1940–41 (1953*).
Builder: CFD Neuillé Pont Pierre (Périguex Works*).
Engine: Willème 517F8 of 132 kW.
Transmission: Mechanical.
Train Heating: None   **Weight in Full Working Order:** 16 (17*) tonnes.
Maximum Tractive Effort: kN.   **Length over Buffers:** 6000 (8450*) mm.
Driving Wheel Dia.: 1050 mm.   **Max. Speed:** 30 km/h.

| T 11 | T 12 | T 13 * | T 14 * |

X 200 CLASS   SINGLE UNIT (1A–A1)

The last survivor of 6 cars (X 201–206) transferred from the Réseau Breton in 1968. Reserve car, still in red and cream livery.

XB (DMSO).

Built: 1948.
Builder: De Dion Bouton.
Engine: Willème 517F8 of 132 kW.
Transmission: Mechanical.
Seats: 51S 1L.
Length over couplings: 19120 mm.

Weight: 18 tonnes.
Max. Speed: 70 km/h.

X 205

X 210 CLASS   SINGLE UNITS (B–2)

X 211/2 came from the PO Corrèze in 1967. All four cars were refurbished in 1983–4 and fitted with new engines,when X 213/4 were renumbered from X 223/1 respectively. Brown & cream livery.

XB (DMSO).

Built: 1950–51.
Engine: Poyaud 6L520S1 of 185 kW.
Seats: 54S 1L.
Length over couplings: 18535 mm.

Builder: Verney.
Transmission: Mechanical.
Weight: 21 tonnes.
Max. Speed: 85 km/h.

X 211 | X 212 | X 213 | X 214

X 220 CLASS   SINGLE UNITS (B–2)

The last survivor in original condition of 4 cars (X 221–4) purchased new in 1950–1. Two others have been refurbished (see X 211–4). In resrve (red & cream livery).

XB (DMSO).

Built: 1951. **Builder:** Verney.
Engine: Willème 517F6 of 103 kW.
Seats: 53S 1L.
Length over couplings: 18535 mm.

Transmission: Mechanical.
Weight: 18 tonnes.
Max. Speed: 80 km/h.

X 224

X 240 CLASS   SINGLE UNITS (B–2)

Delivered as part of the modernisation programme for passenger stock. Brown & cream livery.

XBD (DMSO).

Built: 1951.
Builder: CFD Montmirail.
Engine: Poyaud 6L520CS2 of 175 kW.
Transmission: Hydraulic.
Seats: 54S 1L.
Length over couplings: mm.

Weight: 25 tonnes.
Max. Speed: 85 km/h.

X 241   ROMORANTIN LATHENAY | X 242   VALENÇAY

XR 700 CLASS   TRAILERS (2–2)

Delivered as part of the modernisation programme for passenger stock. Brown & cream livery. (* Ex PO Corrèze. 1967). All refurbished 1983–4.

XRB (DTSO).

Built: 1951.
Seats: 39S 1L.
Length over couplings: 12975 mm.

Builder: Verney.
Weight: 9.5 tonnes.
Max. Speed: 85 km/h.

XR 701 | XR 702 | XR 703

CHEMINS DE FER DE LA CORSE (CORSICA)

The SNCF took over operation of this system on 01/01/83 after the last of a series of concessionary companies gave up. The main line runs from Bastia to Ajaccio with a branch from Ponte Leccia to Calvi. The central section of the manin line is particularly scenic. The depot and workshops are located at Cassamozza, having been moved from Bastia in recent years.

XR 100 CLASS   TRAILERS (2–2)

Rebuilt: 1977 by Garnero. Ex Billard A210D.

R 104 | R 105

X 110 CLASS   SINGLE UNITS (B–2)

The only survivor of a batch of six (111–6), this car was modernised in 1966.

XB (DMSO).

Built: 1938.
Builder: Billard. Type A 150 D.
Engine: Willème 112 kW.
Transmission: Mechanical.
Seats: 30S 1L.   **Weight:**   tonnes.
Length over couplings: mm.   **Max. Speed:** 75 km/h.

113

X 200 CLASS   SINGLE UNITS (Bo–Bo)

Originally a batch of eight, certain cars have been modernised and multiple working fitted recently.

XB (DMSO).

Built: 1949–50.
Builder: Renault. Type ABH 8.
Engine: Two Renault 112 kW.
Transmission: Electric.
Seats: 42S 1L.   **Weight:**   tonnes.
Length over couplings: mm.   **Max. Speed:** 60 km/h.

201 |202 |203   (S)|204 |205   (S)|206 |207

X 210 CLASS   TRAILERS (2–2)

Ex Tarn 1966 (Seine et Marne 1966*). Rebodied except 212.

Built: 1938–49.
Builder: Billard. Type R 210.

210 |211 |212   * |7   (S)

X 240 CLASS   TRAILERS (2–2)

Billard type A 80 D. Ex PO Corrèze 1970.

Built: 1937.

242 |243

XR 500 CLASS   DRIVING TRAILERS (2–2)

Converted from Billard type A 150 D6. Ex tramways d'Ille et Villaine and Réseau Breton. Works with X 202 between Calvi and Ile Rousse.

Built: 1947.

526

X 2000 CLASS

SINGLE UNITS (Bo–Bo)

Originally numbered X 1201–5.

XB (DMSO).

Built: 1975–76.
Builder: CFD Montmirail.
Engine: Two 123 kW.
Transmission: Mechanical.
Seats: 42S 1L.
Length over couplings:　　mm.

Weight:　tonnes.
Max. Speed:　km/h.

X 2001　｜X 2002　｜X 2003　｜X 2004　｜X 2005

X 5000 CLASS

SINGLE UNITS (Bo–Bo)

A longer and more powerful version of X 2000.

XB (DMSO).

Built: 1982–3.
Builder: CFD Montmirail.
Engine: Two 179 kW.
Transmission: Mechanical.
Seats: 42S 1L.
Length over couplings:　　mm.

Weight:　tonnes.
Max. Speed:　km/h.

X 5001　｜X 5002

DIESEL　　　　　　　　　LOCOMOTIVES

The Corsican system boasts a somewhat heterogeneous collection of diesel locomotives:

No.	Type	Builder	Date	Rating		Notes
1	C dm	CFD Montmirail	1948	150	kW	ex CFD du Tarn 1967
2	C dm	VFD Vizille	1951	150	kW	ex VFD 1967
3	C–1 dm	SE Cosne	1948	150	kW	ex SE Seine & Marne 1967
114	B–2 dm	Bastia Works	1938	112	kW	rebuilt from railcar 1955
401	Bo–Bo de	Brissonneau & Lotz	1951	450	kW	
403	B dm	Bastia Works	1956	157	kW	built on power bogie of railcar 103
404	BB dh	CFD Montmirail	1963	310	kW	ex CF de la Provence 1974
405	BB dh	CFD Montmirail	1966	310	kW	
413	Bo–Bo de	Brissonneau & Lotz	1951	450	kW	ex CF de la Provence 1963

PRIVATE RAILWAYS

The following gives details of French private railways (other than preserved lines) which operate passenger services. All are metre gauge.

CHEMINS DE FER DE LA PROVENCE

This is the only non-SNCF adhesion non-preserved passenger railway left in France. It runs from Nice Gare du Sud to Digne, a distance of 151 km, and is the last remnant of the Chemins de Fer du Sud whose network included lines from Nice to Vence, Grasse, Draguignan & Meyrargues and from Saint Raphael to Toulon via St. Tropez.

Depots are at Nice and Digne, with steam locos based at Puget-Théniers. There is a works at Lingostière (L).

The railcar stock is at present being renumbered in the X 300/XR 1300 series.

DIESEL LOCOMOTIVES

No.	Type	Builder	Date	Rating		Notes
51	D dm	CFD Montmirail	1934	150	kW	
62	BB de	Brissonneau & Lotz	1951	450	kW	
BB 401	BB dm	CFD Montmirail	1948	310	kW	ex PO Corrèze in 1971.

BB 402BB dm	CFD Montmirail	1938	310 kW	Under repair at Lingostière.
E 327*4–6–0T	Fives-Lille	1909		ex Réseau Breton
E 211†2–4–6–0T	Henschel	1923		ex CP (Portugal)

* Preserved by FACS (Fédération des Amis des Chemins de Fer Secondaires).
† Preserved by the Group d'Étude des Chemins de Fer de la Provence.

X 200 CLASS — SINGLE UNITS (B–2)

The only survivor of this class. Now in departmental service.

XB (DMSO).

Built: 1937.
Builder: Billard. Type A 150 D.
Engine: 172 kW.
Transmission: Mechanical.

212

X 300 CLASS — SINGLE UNITS (Bo–Bo)

XB (DMSO).

Built: 1972/77*.
Builder: CFD Montmirail.
Engine: Two x 123 kW.
Transmission: Mechanical.
Seats: 48S 1L   **Weight:**   tonnes.

* Series 1 with flat ends. † Series 2 with angled ends.

X 301 (SY 01)	X 303 (SY 03)	X 305 (SY 05) *	X 306 (SY 06) *
X 302 (SY 02)	X 304 (SY 04)		

X 320 CLASS — SINGLE UNITS (Bo–Bo)

The survivors of twelve cars (ZZ 1–12) built 1935–45. ZZ 21/2 were formerly ZZ 1/2.
§ Under conversion to driving trailer. Will presumably never carry X 328.

XB (DMSO).

Built: 1935–36.
Builder: Renault. Type ABH 1 (ABH 5*).
Engine: Two Renault 123 kW.
Transmission: Electric.
Seats: 44S 1L (56S 1L†)   **Weight:**   tonnes.

X 320 (ZZ 10) *	X 322 (ZZ 22) Digne	X 326 (ZZ 6) †	X 328 (ZZ 8) *§
X 321 (ZZ 21) L(U)	X 323 (ZZ 3) L(Ü)		

X 350 CLASS — 2-CAR UNIT (Bo–Bo+2–2)

A new two-car unit built for the "Alpazur" service.

XBD+Bx (DMBSO–DTSO).

Built: 1984.
Builder: Soulé/Garnéro.
Engine: Two Renault 123 kW.
Transmission: Electric.
Seats: 56S 1L + 65S 1L   **Weight:**   tonnes.

X 351 XR 1351

XR 1330 CLASS — TRAILERS (2–2)

Built: 1937–58.
Builder: Billard. Type R 210.
Seats: 32S 1L   **Weight:**   tonnes.

* Rebodied by Garnéro.
s In departmental use.
p In parcels service.
t ex CF du Tarn 1964.
v ex Vivarais 1969.

XR 1331(RL 1) *	XR 1333(RL 3) st	XR 1335(RL 5) *	XR 1337(RL 7) sp
XR 1332(RL 2) (U)	XR 1334(RL 4) *t	XR 1336(RL 6) *v	

XR 1340 CLASS   HAULED STOCK (2–2)

Built: 19
Builder: Garnéro.
Seats: 52S 1L   **Weight:**   tonnes.

XR 1341(AT 1)	XR 1342(AT 2)	XR 1343(AT 3)	XR 1344(AT 4)

CFD Montmirail diesel No.BB 401 of the Chemins de Fer de la Provence stands at Nice Gare du Sud on 03/10/86.   [Peter Fox

CHEMIN DE FER DE LA RHUNE

This rack line is the last remnant of the once extensive Voies Ferées Départementales du Midi metre gauge system. Running from St. Ignace to La Rhune, it has been isolated from other railways since the closure of the line to St. Ignce in 1936. The line climbs into the Pyrénées giving views of the Basque Coast. Electrified since opening in 1924 at 3000 V ac three-phase, the original locos are still in use together with others from the similar closed line at Luchon. The line can be reached by bus from St. Jean du Luz.

4 WHEEL RACK LOCOS)

Built: 1912–15.
Builder-Mech. Parts: SLM.   **Weight:** 12 tonnes.
Builder-Elec. Parts: Brown Boveri.   **Length over Buffers:** 5050 mm.
One hour Rating: 240 kW.   **Max. Speed:** 8.5 km/h.

* ex Luchon–Superbagnères line in 1966.

1	2	3 *	4 *	5 *

CHEMIN DE FER DE CHAMONIX AU MONTENVERS

This rack line, opened 1908–09 climbs into amazing mountain and glacier scenery. The 5 km line was electrified in 1954 at 11 kV ac 50 Hz. However diesel traction is used for works trains and in emergency and also for extra trains at peak periods.

DIESEL LOCOS

1–B

These locos work with articulated coaches 61–63.

Built: 1967/72*.
Engine: Poyaud A12-150 Se of 485 kW or 520 kW*.
Transmission: Hydraulic.
Builder: SLM.   **Weight:** 23.3 tonnes.
Driving Wheel Dia: 790 mm.   **Length over Buffers:** 7500 mm.
Max. Speed: 21 km/h.

31 | 32   * | 33   *

ELECTRIC RAILCARS

Bo–Bo

These railcars have driving cabs at the lower end only. They normally work coupled to trailers 51–56.

Built: 1954/60*/79†.
Builder-Mech. Parts: SLM.   **Weight:** 29.5 tonnes.
Builder-Elec. Parts: Oerlikon.   **Length over Buffers:** 15370 (15940*†) mm.
One hour Rating: 475 kW.   **Max. Speed:** 20 km/h.
Seats: 84S (80S*†).

41 | 42 | 43 | 44 | 45   * | 46   †

TRAMWAY DU MONT BLANC

This rack line in the Savoy Alps was opened in 1909–14 between St. Gervais les Bains and Glacier Bionnassay, but never achieved its intended terminus closer to Mont Blanc. The 12 km line was electrified in 1957 at 11 kV ac 50 Hz. The depot is located at St. Gervais.

Bo–Bo RACK RAILCARS

These cars have driving cabs at the lower end only. They normally work with a trailer coupled at the upper end.

Built: 1956.
Builder-Mech. Parts: SLM/Decauville.**Weight:** 12 tonnes.
Builder-Elec. Parts: Oerlikon.**Length over Couplings:** 15370 mm.
One hour Rating: 475 kW.**Max. Speed:** 20 km/h.

1 | 2 | 3

PRESERVED LOCOMOTIVES & MULTIPLE UNITS

Number	Type	Built	Status	Location
5 "SEZANNE"	2–2–2	1847	M	NRM Mulhouse (CF Montereau–Troyes)
6 "L'AIGLE"	2–2–2	1846	M	NRM Mulhouse (CF Avignon–Marseille)
33 "ST.PIERRE"	2–2–2	1843	M	NRM Mulhouse (CF Paris–Rouen)
80 "LE CONTINENT"	4–2–0	1852	M	NRM Mulhouse (CF Paris–Strasbourg)
NORD 701	4–2–2–0	1885	M	NRM Mulhouse
ÉTAT 2029"PARTHENAY"	2–4–0	1882	MS	Aulnoye (NRM) SNCF 120A36
PO 340 "FORQUENOT"	2–4–2	1882	M	NRM Mulhouse SNCF 121A340
PLM C 145	4–4–0	1902	M	NRM Mulhouse SNCF 220A85
NORD 2.670	4–4–2	1903	M	NRM Mulhouse SNCF 221A30
PLM 1423	0–6–0	1854	M	NRM Mulhouse SNCF 030A1
NORD 3486	0–6–0	1890	MS	Hausbergen (NRM)
030C815	0–6–0	1878	MS	Aulnoye (NRM)
030C841	0–6–0	1883	M	Delson,Canada
030TA628	0–6–0T	1874	MS	Aulnoye (NRM)
030TB2	0–6–0T	1870	P	NRM Mulhouse
030TB130	0–6–0T	1900	MA	Neuf Brisach CFTR
030TB134	0–6–0T	1900	MR	Neuf Brisach CFTR
030TU13	0–6–0T	1943	P	Caen (USA Tank)

030TU22	0–6–0T	1943	M	Longueville (USA Tank)
MIDI 312 "L'ADOUR"	0–6+4T	1856	M	NRM Mulhouse
130B348	2–6–0	1862	MA	Longueville
130B439	2–6–0	1882	P	Capdenac
130B476	2–6–0	1883	M	NRM Mulhouse
EST 32.031	2–6–2T	1925	M	NRM Mulhouse SNCF 131TB31
MIDI 1314	4–6–0	1902	M	NRM Mulhouse SNCF 230B614
230B114	4–6–0	1908	M	NRM Mulhouse
230C531	4–6–0	1905	MS	Hausbergen (NRM)
230D9	4–6–0	1908	M	NRM Mulhouse
230D116	4–6–0	1911	MA	Nene Valley Railway, Wansford, GB.
230G352	4–6–0	1922	MR	Gray
230G353	4–6–0	1922	TA	SNCF Noisy Le Sec
PO 4546	4–6–2	1908	M	NRM Mulhouse SNCF 231A546
NORD 3.1192	4–6–2	1936	M	NRM Mulhouse SNCF 231E22
231C78	4–6–2	1930	MS	Hausbergen (NRM)
231E41	4–6–2	1937	P	St.Pierre des Corps
231G558	4–6–2	1921	A	Sotteville
231H8	4–6–2	1912	MS	Aulnoye (NRM)
231K8	4–6–2	1912	MR	Le Landy
231K22	4–6–2	1914	M	Carnforth, GB
231K82	4–6–2	1920	MS	St.Étienne
NORD 3.1102	4–6–4	1911	M	NRM Mulhouse
232U1	4–6–4	1949	M	NRM Mulhouse
PLM 4A51	0–8–0	1878	M	Miramas SNCF 040A51
PLM 4B9	0–8–0	1892	M	Carnoules SNCF 040B9
NORD 4853	0–8–0T	1880	M	Longueville
040TA137	0–8–0T	1922	MA	Mortagne
040TA141	0–8–0T	1923	P	Montigny lès Metz
140A259	2–8–0	1928	MS	Hausbergen (NRM)
140A908	2–8–0	1892	MS	Aulnoye (NRM)
140C22	2–8–0	1916	P	Vierzon-Chaillot. (No tender)
140C27	2–8–0	1916	MA	Belfort
140C38	2–8–0	1919	P	Caen
140C231	2–8–0	1916	MA	Longueville
140C287	2–8–0	1917	MR	Pontcharra
140C313	2–8–0	1917	P	Rheims
140C314	2–8–0	1917	MR	Gray
140C344	2–8–0	1917	M	NRM Mulhouse
141C100	2–8–2	1922	MA	Connerré
141F282	2–8–2	1925	M	NRM Mulhouse
141R73	2–8–2	1945	M	Bressingham, GB.
141R420	2–8–2	1946	MA	Clermont Ferrand
141R568	2–8–2	1945	MR	Pontcharra
141R840	2–8–2	1946	MR	Cosne
141R1108	2–8–2	1946	M	Nice St.Roch
141R1126	2–8–2	1947	P	Narbonne
141R1187	2–8–2	1947	M	NRM Mulhouse
141R1199	2–8–2	1947	M	Vitré
141R1207	2–8–2	1947	MA	Montargis
141R1244	2–8–2	1947	MA	Rapperswil CH
141R1298	2–8–2	1947	M	Miramas
141R1332	2–8–2	1947	P	Jarnac
PO 5452	2–8–2T	1922	M	NRM Mulhouse SNCF 141TA452
141TB407	2–8–2T	1913	M	Longueville
141TB424	2–8–2T	1913	M	NRM Mulhouse
141TC19	2–8–2T	1922	M	Chinon
141TC51	2–8–2T	1935	M	NRM Mulhouse
141TD740	2–8–2T	1931	MA	La Buisson
241A1	4–8–2	1925	M	NRM Mulhouse
241A65	4–8–2	1931	M	Samstagern Switzerland
241P9	4–8–2	1947	M	Guîtres
241P16	4–8–2	1947	M	NRM Mulhouse
241P17	4–8–2	1947	P	Le Creusot

241P30	4–8–2	1949	P	Vallorbe
150A065	2–10–0	1912	MS	Hausbergen (NRM)
150P13	2–10–2	1940	M	NRM Mulhouse
BB 36	Bo Boe	1924	MS	NRM
BB 102	BoBoe	1925	MS	Brive (NRM)
BB 915	BoBoe	1936	T	Reserved
BB 1282	BoBoe	1900	M	NRM Mulhouse
BB 1436	BoBoe	1927	MS	Brive (NRM)
BB 1501	BoBoe	1922	MS	Narbonne (NRM)
BB 1632	BoBoe	1925	MS	Narbonne (NRM)
2CC2 3402	2CoCo2e	1929	MS	Clermont Ferrand (NRM)
1ABBA1 3603	1ABoBoA1e	1927	M	NRM Mulhouse
BB 4175	BoBoe	1932	MS	NRM
BB 4177	BoBoe	1932	M	Miramas
2D2 5516	2Do2e	1934	MR	Vitry (NRM)
2D2 5525	2Do2e	1935	MA	Montrouge
CC 7107	CoCoe	1953	T	Reserved for NRM
BB 9004	BoBoe	1954	M	NRM Mulhouse
2D2 9135	2Do2e	1951	T	Reserved for NRM
CC 14018	CoCoe	1959	M	NRM Mulhouse
CC 20001	CoCoe	1958	MS	Clermont Ferrand (NRM)
BB 60032	BoBode	1938	M	NRM Mulhouse
C 61046	Cde	1953	MS	Le Havre
C 61107	Cde	1951	MS	Le Havre
A1AA1A 62029	A1AA1Ade	1946	MA	Neuf Brisach
A1AA1A 62036	A1AA1Ade	1947	MA	Chinon
CC 65012	CoCode	1956	A	Reserved for NRM
CC 65501	CoCode	1955	T	Reserved for NRM
BB 71017	BBdh	1965	MA	Saujon
X 3601	B–2dm	1948	MA	Chinon
X 3623	B–2dm	1949	MA	St.Quentin
XBDPi 3710	1AA1dm	1949	MA	Sentheim
XBD 3810	B–2dm	1950	MA	Sabres
XBD 3858	B–2dm		MA	Neuf Brisach
XBD 3890	B–2dm	1950	MA	Rennes
XBD 3926	B–2dm		MA	Saujon
XBD 3937	B–2dm		MP	Rambouillet (clubroom).
XBD 3953	B–2dm		MA	Conneré
XBD 3971	B–2dm		M	Miramas
XBD 3976	B–2dm	1959	MA	Guitres
XBD 3989	B–2dm		MP	Annonay
XBD 3998	B–2dm		MA	CFV3V Mariembourg, Belgium
XBD 4025	B–2dm	1960	MA	Besancon
XBD 4028	B–2dm	1961	MA	Narbonne
XBD 4039	B–2dm	1961	MA	Besançon
XBD 4046	B–2dm	1961	M	Denain
XBD 4051	B–2dm	1961	MA	Besançon
X 4203	Bo–2de	1959	MS	NRM
X 4204	Bo–2de	1959	MA	Belfort
X 4206	Bo–2de	1959	MA	CF Anduze–St. Jean du Gard
X 4208	Bo–2de	1959	MA	AGRIVAP (Ambert)
X 5506	1A–2dm	1950	MA	Chinon
XBD 5815	1A–2dm	1953	MA	Pontcharra
XBD 5822	1A–2dm	1953	MA	Sabres
XBD 5830	1A–2dm	1954	MA	St.Quentin
XBD 5845	1A–2dm	1954	MA	Miramas
XBD 5852	1A–2dm	1954	MA	Sentheim
ZABEyf 23001			MS	NRM Mulhouse
PO ZZEty 23859	B–2dm	1934	M	NRM Mulhouse
Etat ZZB2Ef 23901		1921	M	NRM Mulhouse
Etat ZZy 24091	B–2dm	1937	M	NRM Mulhouse
Etat ZZy 24408		1935	M	NRM Mulhouse
XDi 42502	1AA1dm	1937	MS	Hausbergen NRM
XADi 42627	1AA1dm	1937	MS	Hausbergen NRM

XABDf 52103	BoBode	1945	MS	Aulnoye NRM
Est ZZAB5C Ety 54005		1936	MS	NRM
PLM LZZBE 39	Bdm	1928	MA	La Barque
Y 2402	Bdm	1962	MA	Neuf Brisach
YBD 12004	Bdm	1932	MA	Sabres
YBE 15053	Bdm	1936	MA	Pontcharra
Y 51125	Bdhm	1954	MA	Sabres
Z 209	Bo	1901	T	Reserved for NRM
Z 1208	A1A A1A	1914	MS	La Folie NRM
Z 1567	BoBo	1930	MS	Le Mans NRM
Z 1572	BoBo	1930	MS	PSL for St. Mande Museum
Z 3714	BoBoBo	1938	MS	Le Mans NRM
Z 4001	Bo–2	1904	MS	Brive NRM
Z 4156	BoBo		MS	NRM
Z 4909	BoBo	1913	MS	Brive NRM
Z 4313	BoBo	1927	MS	NRM

Errata: Please note that the prototype gas turbine TGV No. TGV-01 has been accidentally missed out. The caption on page 64 top should read *CFD* Montmirail.

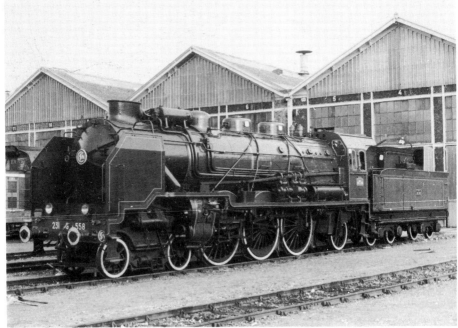

Above: Preserved pacific No. 231G558 stands at Sotteville Depot on 10/04/83. This loco has now been restored to main-line running order. [Brian Garvin.

Front cover photograph: BB 15000 class No. BB 15022 PANTIN approaches Mulhouse with a Basel–Strasbourg train on 30/09/86. [Peter Fox

Back cover photograph: BB 300 class No. BB 319 shunts stock at Paris Austerlitz on 07/06/86. [Peter Fox

Further copies of this publication may be obtained from our Mail order department, 15 Abbeydale Park Rise, Sheffield, S17 3PB, England price £5.25 including postage (GB), £5.60 (Europe). Please send for full list.